Coach Education

Preparation for a Profession

Coach Education

Preparation for a Profession

Proceedings of the
VIII Commonwealth and International
Conference on Sport, Physical Education,
Dance, Recreation and Health

Conference '86 Glasgow
18–23 July

PATRON

H.R.H. THE PRINCESS ANNE

LONDON   NEW YORK
E. & F.N. SPON

First published in 1986 by E. & F.N. Spon Ltd
11 New Fetter Lane, London EC4P 4EE
Published in the USA by E. & F.N. Spon
29 West 35th Street, New York NY 10001

© 1986 This collection: The Management Committee,
VIII Commonwealth and International
Conference on Sport, Physical Education,
Dance, Recreation and Health

Printed in Great Britain
at the University Press, Cambridge

ISBN 0 419 13960 5

British Library Cataloguing in Publication Data

Commonwealth and International Conference on Sport,
Physical Education, Dance, Recreation and Health *(8th: 1986:
Glasgow)*
Coach education: preparation for a profession.
1. Coaching (Athletics)
I. Title
796'.07'7   GV711
ISBN 0 419 13960 5

Contents

SECTION III STRUCTURE AND CONTENT

SECTION IV PROFESSIONAL DEVELOPMENT

SECTION V WORKSHOPS AND SUPPORTING PAPERS

Preface

The Conference Management Committee wish to express their sincere appreciation to H.R.H. The Princess Anne, Mrs Mark Phillips, a sportswoman of international renown, for her kindness in agreeing to become Patron to the VIII Commonwealth and International Conference.

Conference '86 has been a combined undertaking and credit for its success must be shared among the Conference Organising Committees, Professional Associations, The Scottish Sports Council, The Scottish Health Education Group, Glasgow District Council and Strathclyde Regional Council. The Conference has also benefitted from generous financial support provided by the Bank of Scotland and Guinness PLC.

The Management Committee has taken responsibility for all major decisions and guided the Conference administration from its inception. Membership of the Management Committee was as follows: Mr Telfer Blacklock (Scottish Education Department), Mr Derek Casey (Scottish Sports Council), Mr Graeme Donald (Adviser Borders Region), Mr Ben Fryer (Scottish Education Department), Mr Stanley Mitchell (Scottish Health Education Group), Mr Robin Smeaton (Coach to Scottish Squash Rackets Association), Mr David Wilkie (Jordanhill College of Education). The Management Committee also enjoyed the support of His Excellency Mr George Mamba (High Commissioner for Swaziland) and His Excellency Mr Ben Kipkulei (High Commissioner for Kenya).

The Programme Committee has worked with unswerving application and enthusiasm to create an interesting and attractive programme. The seven volumes of Conference Proceedings, published and available to delegates on the opening day of the Conference, are a fitting testimony to their skill and commitment.

The Programme Committee was formed with representatives drawn from the following associations: The Scottish Council for Physical Education, The British Society for Sports History, The International Association for the History of Sport and Physical Education (HISPA), The Scottish Sports Council and the Association of Scottish National Coaches, The British Association of Sports Sciences, The Scottish Council for Dance and the British Association for Sport and Medicine. The Programme Committee included the following members: Mr Graeme Donald, Mrs Sheena Good, Dr J.A. Mangan, Mr Roy Small, Dr Thomas Reilly, Dr James Watkins, Ms Peggy Woodeson, Mr Edwin Liddell, Mr Brian Porteous, Mr Robin Smeaton, Dr James Moncur and Dr James MacGregor.

The Finance and General Purposes Committee, a Subcommittee formed from the Management Committee controlled all financial matters and undertook responsibility for general administration. This Committee made a significant contribution to the success of the

Conference. Members of this Committee were as follows: Mr Ian Craik, Mr Derek Casey and Mr David Wilkie.

The co-operation and support of Jordanhill College of Education has been greatly appreciated. The Principal, Dr T.R. Bone, kindly made all the facilities and resources of the College available to the Conference.

Special mention must be made of the invaluable contribution made by the Conference Secretary, Ms Alison Maxwell, her assistant Ms Marie McCunn, Mrs Anne McLaren and Mrs Helen Smith for additional administrative support.

We are grateful to the speakers and participants for allowing us to publish their papers and hope that the Conference Proceedings will provide a valuable source of information and reference.

Bernard Wright
Director, Conference '86

Introduction

Sports coaching has entered a period of increased recognition, development and provision. Consequently the education and training of sports coaching is receiving more critical attention than previously. Conference '86 recognised and welcomed this heightened interest in sports coaching; hence the bold step of approving a Conference Theme devoted exclusively to coach education.

The Coach Education Theme Committee agreed to the preparation of a discussion paper to realise the following objectives:

1 to stimulate the submission of papers for the Coach Education Theme,
2 to provide a focus for submissions,
3 to establish a framework for the Conference.

Mr John Lyle's paper "Coach education: preparation for a profession" achieved those aims and the Committee is extremely grateful to him for his contribution. The Committee's thanks are also extended to the many people who submitted papers.

To complement the responses to the discussion paper the Committee invited several keynote addresses. The major issues covered include:

1 evaluations by Australia, Canada and the UK of their respective coach education programmes,
2 the nature of coaching; training of coaches – structure and content; professional development,
3 the political dimension.

The Committee is grateful to the keynote speakers for their major contribution to the Conference.

Special thanks are also extended to Mr Tom McNab who agreed to the difficult tasks of setting the scene for the five days of disscussion, and of summarising his impressions of the Conference.

The ultimate success of most conferences is determined by the quality of delegates' responses to the papers presented. The Committee therefore welcomed the opportunity given to delegates by the pre-Conference publication of the proceedings to consider critically each paper in advance of its presentation. This volume is intended for such preparatory reading and as a record of the Conference papers.

Finally, thanks are due to the Scottish Sports Council and the Association of Scottish National Coaches who were jointly responsible for the Coach Education Theme, and particularly to the Committee members: Mr Gordon Forster, Mr Brian Porteous, Mr Robin Smeaton, Dr Ian Thomson, and Mr Richard Yule.

K.D.A. Johnston
Chairman, Coach Education Theme Committee

PARADIGM PAPER

COACH EDUCATION - PREPARATION FOR A PROFESSION

- JOHN LYLE

This paper will present a number of issues concerning
the training and education of coaches, with specific
reference to the United Kingdom. These issues will
include the nature of coaching; current structures for
the training of coaches; the relationship of sports
policy to coaching provision; and coaching as a
profession.

In dealing with these issues I have drawn upon my
personal experience as a national volleyball team
coach and as the Course Director for a one-year
full-time Diploma in Sports Coaching which is the only
one of its kind in Britain. The presentation is
intended to stimulate responses from delegates to
Conference 86 and is deliberately controversial. The
format is not that of a paper for an academic journal,
annotated with reference to research findings.

Inevitably, the paper merely identifies the issues and
poses many more questions than it answers. The style
of the paper has, therefore, restricted discussion and
curtailed explanations of my personal views on the
issues.

THE NATURE OF COACHING

(a) Characteristics of the coaching process

Perhaps the first step is to try to define the
boundaries of what is called sports coaching. The
assumption of a universal interpretation of the term,
whether in theory or in practice, would be misguided,
and yet, is easily recognised. There is
unquestionably a need to establish the unity of
purpose which describes the essence of all coaching
and is the basis for professional development. This
is a demanding task for the theorist and the educator

since the diversity of approach and circumstance which characterises coaching must be reconciled with a sufficiently circumscribed description of that which gives coaching its uniqueness.

Normally, the question of demarcation involves definitions. This is a far from pedantic exercise, since the terminology used to describe sports practitioners presents a confusing array of titles. However, definitions have a limited value and it is more enlightening to identify the characteristics which are universal to coaching. To do so is to challenge the boundary which often distinguishes prescriptive assertions about the manner in which coaching tasks should be approached from the essential defining characteristics themselves.

Coaching exhibits the following features:

1   It is a process, that is, a serial operation which takes place over an extended period of time.

2   The athlete(s) or team form a stable grouping which demonstrates a degree of commitment resulting in regular and significant involvement.

3   A maximal development of sporting potential is achieved through a competitive outlet.

4   The relationship between coach and athlete(s) is an empathetic one extending beyond the instrumental operation of the process.

5   The coach is the person who directs the process undertakes an element of leadership.

6   Enacting the process requires a systematic, progressive and planned programme of preparation and competition.

To present a definition is merely to articulate these characteristics in an integrated statement.

This concept of coaching is controversial since it may be considered a rather narrow interpretation excluding many groups of sports leaders to whom the term 'coach' might normally be applied. Quite clearly, the concept is more appropriate to competitive forms of organised sporting activity involving highly committed and motivated athletes. This does not deny, however, the need for appropriately trained and sympathetic leaders in all levels of sport. For example, much of the Northern American literature and the coach education programme which has responded to it, assumes an involvement with young sports people to whom the coaching process as I have defined it above, does not, and should not apply.

There are implications here for the deployment of resources and the training of all sports practitioners. The structures employed must reflect practice and policy. Should all practitioners be thought of as part of one hierarchy or should the avenues of training be distinct? Furthermore, should Governing Bodies continue to be responsible for the training of each category? Nonetheless, developmental sports levels and recreational forms of sport in all countries have quite distinctive objectives and values, and coaching behaviour and practice must recognise this.

Much of the terminological confusion and with it a loss of conceptual clarity is caused by focusing upon the coach and not the process. The coaching process is created, not by the qualities or characteristics of the coach, but by the needs of the athletes concerned and the circumstances within which the relationship will take place. To reexamine the roles of other sports practitioners from this perspective would resolve this confusion.

Figure 1 provides an example of a simple taxonomy of sport practitioners based on a profile of the athletes with whom they work and the levels of competition appropriate to it. It would be naive to suggest that such terminology is not important. Bound up in the use of terminology are questions of status, individual esteem and resource deployment. More significantly, coach education and professional development are dependent upon a lack of confusion in defining the scope and the boundaries of the occupation.

(b)   Professional Practice

It is also important to separate issues concerning the coaching process from those arising from the occupational circumstances in which the coach operates. The latter might be termed professional practice, and concerns all matters which do not directly impinge upon the coach - athlete relationship. These responsibilities are usefully divided into those arising from the coach's occupational duties, such as administration or managing assistants, and those arising from personal development e.g. courses, conferences, travel, reading. Professional practice, more specifically those responsiblities derived from the coach's employment circumstances and the skill necessary to implement these, is a more prominent concern for full-time professional coaches. Those coaches operating in a voluntary, part-time capacity are perforce less concerned. Nonetheless, the impact on the athletes of continued professional development in this sense is undervalued in practice, and, more importantly, under-represented in coach education for positions of greater responsibility.

(c)   Coaching Theory

Developments in coach education have lacked an underpinning conceptual base which would establish the unity of purpose and would provide a rationale for the selection of appropriate skills and knowledge. This lack of attention to coaching theory may be explained by:

   (i)   The practical nature of many of the tasks
          involved in coaching and the reluctance of
          many of those concerned for engaging in
          theoretical concerns.

   (ii)   The obviously eclectic and often disparate
          nature of the disciplines and knowledge bases
          relevant to the coaching process.

   (iii) The unsystematic and rather piecemeal
          occupational development which has not fostered
          a significant level of enquiry into either
          explanations of structure or the basis for
          career enhancement.

   (iv)   A tendency amongst coaches to promote the art
          rather than the science of the process and a
          sense of coaching
          and to mystify the process, all of which has
          bedevilled communication.

(v)   The lack of commitment by Universities and
        other institutions to fundamental research in
        this topic.

(vi)   The lack of cross-cultural exchange about
        coaching practices, career patterns and
        coaching philosophies.

(vii)   The historically low status of the coach within
        British sport and the (arguably) consequent
        lack of attention to theory by administrators
        and Governing Bodies.

(viii) The concentration of highly specific sports
        research on performance.

(d)   Models of the Coaching Process

Models of the coaching process have received little
attention in Britain. As a result explanations of the
constituent parts of the process and analyses of its
operation in practice are not available for the
simulation of coaching behaviour in training courses
appropriate to various stages of sports development.

This vacuum has largely been filled by a reliance on
the Eastern European performance model. This is
solidly based on training theory with its attendent
science based disciplines and modest input of
'didactics'. Such a model is suited to physical
capacity sports such as swimming and athletics but its
assumptions about the role of the coach, the support
matrix available to coaches within the Eastern 'bloc'
and its lack of attention to interpersonal concerns
have resulted in its falling somewhat short of
providing the necessary answers.

On a recent study tour of institutions in Western
Europe concerned with coach education, I specifically
enquired about the model of the coching process which
provided the rationale for course design. In no case
was the model able to be articulated beyond a reference
to an assumed performance model with modified
methodological or interpersonal inputs.

The North American literature on coaching is more
relevant to the British situation. This theory of
coaching, which is mainly concerned with children and
youth sports, emphasises the human aspects involved and

the interpersonal skills required. Nevertheless
conceptual clarity has been made more difficult by the
broad range of leadership roles encompassed in the
literature. Assumptions about the particular
occupational circumstances have reduced the
applicability of the model to other situations.

For the reasons adduced above, models of the coaching
process either do not exist or have been taken for
granted, and few
attempts at verification have been made in Britain.
Where models have been adopted, the emphasis on
performance variables at the expense of coach behaviour
and professional practice elements has limited their
value.

(e)   The Knowledge base for Coaching

Sports coaches are eclectic both by design and
expediency. However, there is a growing consensus on
the more obvious kinds of knowledge required for sports
coaching. Sports psychology and exercise physiology
are examples of specialised applications of established
disciplines. Perhaps less obvious are the principles
of good practice which form the foundation for
organisation, practice management, contest management,
planning and the teaching of strategy.

As yet there is little evidence of the emergence of
pedagogy which is of central concern in the training of
teachers. Training theory and periodisation have,
however, attained something of a conceptual agreement
via the work of coaches in other countries. Whether
the identification of these kinds of knowledge is the
result of systematic observation, derivation from a
model of the coaching process or based solely on custom
is less clear.

A taxonomy is required which recognises the relative
contribution of established disciplines such as
physics, psychology and physiology, the principles
which underpin motor skill acquisition, learning theory
and training theory and the principles of sound
practice already identified. Coach education must
strike a balance between these types of knowledge and
the purely technical requirements of particular sports.
It is undeniable that an intimate knowledge of one's
sport is indispensable.

Although coaches express their knowledge in, for
example, training schedules, interpersonal situations,
design of drills, strategy selections and in all forms
of feedback, it might be argued that not all coaches
need work from first principles. Training sessions
might, therefore, be chosen in recipe fashion. Even
so, appropriate choices depend upon informed
judgements. It is this application of knowledge which
is given least attention in coach education.

(f)   Coaching Skills

The skills of coaching are also problematical.
Communication is the basis of coaching behaviour and
therefore of distinguishing between coaching styles.
The development of appropriate interpersonal skills
appears largely to be a matter of personal disposition
and experience and owes little to coach training
programmes. With the exception of specific sports
demonstration skills, behaviour modification has yet to
make an impact on coach education. Research on coaches
has concentrated upon personal qualities, particularly
in psychometric terms, and has contributed little, if
anything, to identifying the skills required for
successful transactions between coaches and athletes.

A second set of skills involves the selection,
analysis, translation and presentation of data in such
activities as planning and devising training schedules.
Some further consideration is required on the relative
importance of these skills to different levels of
coaching but they are undoubtedly prerequisites for
full-time coaches.

(g)   The Role of the Coach

The literature dealing with the role of the coach is as
imprecise as other aspects of coaching theory. Role
theory is well established in social science literature
but its application to sports coaching has been limited
to distinguishing between the coach as teacher, trainer
or counsellor.

There is a need to distinguish between role used as a
generalised statement about the part played by the
coach, and the more precise application of the term to
indicate expectation about the sort of behaviour

required of the incumbent by others in his role set. In the latter sense the role of the coach prescribes the limits of acceptable behaviour, and particular individuals may experience conflict in attempting to meet those demands. Role is intimately tied to status and prestige.

The boundaries of the coaching role are very loose with considerable room for manoeuvre for individual coaches. For this reason, a tight definition is not useful. The main function in the role of a coach is to assist athletes or teams to improve their performance in sport. To achieve this, the coach mediates between the athletes and their objectives. In doing so, the coach assumes a leadership role in directing a programme designed to effect a correspondence between these objectives and eventual achievements.

Role problems experienced by coaches of young people can generally be solved by an open, consistent approach to interpersonal behaviour. A sharper focus is required on the matter of role conflict arising from the management of coaching support personnel; and on the variety of role interpretations imposed by individuals and groups in top-level sport. A similarly productive area, particularly for a developing occupation, is the stress brought about by the uncertainty of expectation within an organisation between coaching process responsiblities and professional practice duties.

(h)   Coaching Philosophies

Acceptance of the notion of 'coaching philosophy' creates opportunities for individual interpretations of the coaching role. These individual approaches however display sufficient common features to allow for generalisation. There are two principal philosophies: the one espousing a largely humanistic approach embodying a central concern for the personal growth and development of the individual through sport and the other a performance based philosophy which overtly values competitive success. Although such a distinction is too broad to be useful in practice, professional development is unlikely to benefit from any perceived disparity between official and unofficial philosophies. Any such disparity, particularly between that demonstrated in practice by coaches and that transmitted in coach education courses and through the

literature, should perhaps be viewed as a dynamic in
which the forces operating have yet to be clearly
articulated.

Every coach has a philosophy which has been developed
through time and experience. It is a reflection of
some of the deeper values which shape attitudes to
life, morals, the rights of individuals and the place
of sport in society. A coach translates these values
and beliefs into a reasonably coherent set of
principles covering the implementation of the coaching
process and what should be emphasised within it. His
philosophy will be reflected in his behaviour towards
the athlete, in communication styles, in ethical
behaviour and in attitudes to objectives reflecting
competitive success.

Such an approach will be fairly constant, and, although
articulated in conceptual terms, is an everpresent
behavioural influence. It cannot be said that any one
philosopy is better than another on the basis of
coaching success as measured by athlete performance.

However, coaching philosophies can be evaluated and
must be examined in terms of expectation and reality.
In particular the relationship between professional
position and acceptable and appropriate philosopy must
be recognised. Quite correctly, the application of
appropriate ethical standards is a significant issue in
professional development.

(i)   Coach Evaluation

Any discussion about the nature of coaching must
include assessment of coaches' effectiveness. Attempts
at measuring success in coaching has foundered where
the public and the media have equated success in
athlete performance with successful coaches. It would
be more appropriate to suggest that this is only one
form of success, albeit one which is characteristic of
top-level sport and likely to be a demand placed on
coaches at all levels. There are other measures,
however. The coach's personal qualities, manner of
working,
knowledge and experience, influence on individuals'
personal development, influence on club and sport
development and ability to achieve appropriate
objectives may all offer alternative yardsticks.

Nevertheless, an intrinsic feature of coaching is the improvement of competitive performance and this must inevitably be a central consideration in coach evaluation. In the public and highly visible profile of the occupation of coaching, results are the most obvious focus and these are likely to be emphasised by athletes and the coach's peers alike. The alternative criteria suggested are probably seen as means to the end of competitive success.

This has significant implications for professional development. The conclusion to be drawn from the assessment criterion is that coaching is an insecure, short-term, high-pressure occupation on a payment-by-results system of rewards. Such a situation is hardly likely to be attractive to prospective coaches. Although a coach may achieve a broad range of successes, the occupational circumstances surrounding representative and professional coaches are likely to demand a measure of success which is tenable in the public domain.

In the United Kingdom, one of the relatively few groups of professional coaches are those employed by the governing bodies and designated National Coaches. Few of these individuals are employed on short term contracts linked to the results of national representatives. Is the absence of this form of evaluation a confirmation that the term is a misnomer and that developmental and administrative duties are paramount?

(j)   The Art and Science of Coaching

Debate about coaching as an art or science owes more to the political philosophies of individual coaches than to a useful extension into practice. Any rational analysis would lead to the conclusion that coaching is neither but must aspire to both. Coaches may be regarded as technocrats in some sports: a reflection of a rational age and a move towards exact measurement and decisions based upon objectivity. Sports performance is not an exact science, however, and the individuality of the coach, decisions based upon experience, and the vagaries of the psychological aspects of performance all suggest a process which owes much to the human factor. The question itself is flawed. In this context art and science are not at opposite ends of a continuum. Undoubtedly, too mechanistic an approach reduces the process beyond that which can reasonably be termed sport. However, the informed application of the physical and behavioural sciences to elements of the coaching process are normally far removed from this. The proponents of coaching as an art form maintain an esoteric tradition which may owe more to politics than practice.

TRAINING OF COACHES - STRUCTURE AND CONTENT

(a) Centralised and Decentralised Provision

A major issue in the provision for coach education is the question of centralised versus decentralised provision and control. Until the mid-1970's state-financed and controlled systems of coach education existed only in totalitarian societies such as East Germany. Since then there has been a trend for Western democracies to adopt this system, via at-arms-length from government agencies. These attempts either precede or lead to full-scale Government intervention in the structure of sport which inevitably threatens the authority and status of governing bodies of sport. Canada, Australia and New Zealand have, to varying degrees, all experimented with this centralised approach.

Britain appears to be moving much more cautiously in this direction in that the National Coaching Foundation is financed by the UK Sports Council, itself an at-arms-length agency. However, there has as yet been no attempt to accompany this with any form of pressure on grant aid, or to link it to wider issues of governing body control.

One benefit of centralised control is that coaching can be developed as a part of an integrated sports policy embracing all aspects of participation and provision. Developments in coaching are not isolated alterations to previous structures but a vital part of a planned national approach to sport. This is evident in resource allocation, research, publications, scholarships and support services.

The position in Great Britain has been characterised by a completely decentralised arrangement in which largely autonomous governing bodies have operated independently

in offering courses to prospective coaches. These
courses have lacked any form of consensus in
presentation, structure, content or assessment.
Historically, the CCPR, the Sports Council and the
National Coaches Association have exerted little, if
any, control or influence and there is no system of
equivalence or national recognition. Great Britain is
on the threshold of change in provision for coach
education and this review is therefore, timely. The
intercession of the National Coaching Foundation,
however, would seem to rely upon a system of voluntary
coordination.

Lessons may be learned from countries which have
implemented centralised structures: in particular,
Canada and, thereafter, Australia have such a system.
The essential feature of the Canadian scheme is the
national certification programme and accreditation
scheme in which control is exercised over the levels,
presentation and content of courses. Levels of
achievement are recognised to have national standing.
The value of common elements of coaching theory is
recognised and required and duplication of provision by
governing bodies is obviated by the organisation of
concurrent coaching theory courses. Although the
Canadian scheme is perhaps best known for its
formalised organisation and presentation of coach
training courses, this initiative is only one part of a
much larger process of planned change.

(b)   Accredition of Coaches

The arguments in favour of an accreditation scheme and
the centralised control which this implies embrace
improvements in coach competence, status and
professional integrity. Nonetheless, concern has been
expressed about the problems of attracting candidates
to theoretical courses, establishing the need for
qualification, the gap between official philosophy and
practice, the organisational difficulties for smaller
sports, and ensuring that the programme operates
through to the production of the top coaches in a
sport. These problems may be the result of the
diminishing of voluntary effort which has followed the
introduction of the scheme. They may be endemic to
sports coaching given an embryonic professional
development.

The concept of accreditation itself depends upon a conviction that a multi-tiered hierarchy appropriately reflects the professional development of coaches. The concept of coaching outlined earlier in the paper would suggest that the training of coaches and other sport practitioners may benefit from a separate approach. It is clearly inappropriate for governing bodies to be given the task of training the full range of practitioners from sports leaders to elite coaches. Proposed changes in coach education must be careful not to strive from a unidimensional training structure which relfects efficiency rather than the reality of sports practice.

Sports structures in general and coach education in particular reflect the values of the society in which they operate. In this context, significant change must be achieved against the influence of vested interest, apathy and ignorance. A presumption of political will to undertake a revision of such magnitude and its consequences in resource terms and to implement via control for the centre, might be misplaced.

(c)   Coach Education Programmes

The substance and structures of formal training must reflect the objectives of the coach educaiton programme as a whole. Is it intended to generate the top tier of coaches? If so, is it successful or are avenues other than the hierarchical programme, more appropriate. Canada is in the process of designing and implementing a Master Coach level which would operate in a 4 + 1 fashion, beyond the 4 stage certification process. The Diploma in Sports Coaching in Dunfermline College of Physical Education in Edinburgh is intended to operate in a similar manner and at a similar level. The absence of an accreditation system in the UK however, has made it very difficult to make assumptions, across sports, about previous training.

There are a number of issues arising from the substance of coach education itself. No specific sport would demonstrate the gamut of problems discussed here but the generality of the arguments is descriptive of coach education in toto. The difficulties alluded to earlier in achieving an underpinning conceptual base for coach education permeate the system: content is dictated by custom and with few exceptions is very much sports

specific. Many courses with a coach training label
consist entirely of technical and tactical information
applicable only to that sport. This may be appropriate
on occasions but highlights the dearth of training in
communication, observation, analysis and other
professional practice skills. A body of knowledge is
presented but only in the more sophisticated sports
does its application receive any formal attention.
Behaviour modification is still an underdeveloped
aspect of coach training.

The addition of common coaching theory courses to
qualification requirements warrants further attention.
These courses may discourage potential recruits and the
focus on theoretical issues often provokes a defensive
reaction from those whose expertise grew out of
practical coaching. Perhaps a re- examination of the
implications for the individual in time and finance,
and the applied and specific sports related nature of
the course material would result in a more appropriate
implementation of such courses to the benefit of coach
education.

Education implies more than formal training programmes.
Coach education programmes ought, therefore, to imply
conferences, seminars, literature and exhibitions in
addition to training courses, and, at a personal level,
the variety and richness of exposure of individual
coaches to the sport and to other coaches. Coach
educators should consider the extent of the integration
to the practice of coaching and the requirements of
different levels of coach within their coach education
programme. When a certification programme is in
operation, is the certificate simply a recognition of
proven ability, or is it a license to operate at a
certain level? This has implications for assessment
policies and the notion of in- service or continuing
education.

(d)   Certification and Regulation

An emphasis on the structure and substance of coach
education will tend to mask the individual coach's
perspective. However,
an appreciation of the incentives to engage in the
formal education process is vital for developmental
planning at governing body level. What conditions can
be created under which coaches will wish to invest
their time and effort in pursuing a formal training

programme? One answer would be a licensing system enforced by legislation in which certification would become mandatory for participation as a coach in a sport. Such a proposal is certainly controversial. However, the procedure has already been adopted by teachers, doctors etc., and may have long-term benefits for occupational development.

The appropriateness of such a course of action, far less its practicality, can be called into question in a situation where voluntary participation is the norm. Nonetheless, adoption of this practice can have considerable implications for professional enhancement. A total acceptance of the value of formal education will be difficult to achieve until unqualified coaches are superceded by certificated coaches. It may be that incentives need to be re-evaluated in the context of the motives of individual coaches. Appealing to practitioners to attend courses as a form of personal development is unlikely to yield the results made possible by a judicious exercise of compulsory regulation.

(e) <u>Coach Education and Sports Development</u>

It is important for coach educators to be aware of the relationship between coaching and a sport's developmental level. This must be taken into account in the sophistication of the provision.

The measure of generality which exists between sports should not disguise the need to tailor the content of coach education courses to specific coaching practice. This is particularly relevant in striking the difficult balance between improving knowledge and skills, sports appear to progress in a cyclical fashion along a number of indices reflecting growth, complexity and sophistication, and exhibit discernible regularities in the transition. At a given point in this development the incentives presented by the competition structure result in a related level of athlete commitment. This and the depth and complexity of knowledge available will constrain coaching practice and determine the nature and number of career opportunities available. The nature of the sport itself will influence the relative significance of each of the constituent parts of the coaching process. In summary, the education process must be sensitive to the application of knowledge which the intensity of the coaching process makes possible and desirable.

COACHING PROVISION AND SPORT POLICY

National Policy is reflected in the structure of sport although this may owe more to tradition and to political interpretations of the place of sport in society. These general trends and the policies of Governing Bodies result in a number of avenues of transmission for sport which clearly influence professional development. Mere descriptions and comparison alone is inadequate although this is a first stage to assessing the implications of each pattern and evaluating the appropriateness of an amended distribution. The very minimum is to understand the way in which the schools, voluntary associations and professional sports pattern of Great Britain constrains the development of coaching in a manner which the High School/university pattern of North America or the state controlled pattern of Eastern Europe may not. Career development requires continuing demand for coaches which is inherent within the structure, and which is reinforced by policy.

(a) Elite Sport

Sports policy at national level has operated in two directions. Firstly, a concern for standards of performance relative to other countries and International prestige has resulted in the funding of elite levels of performance. This has largely been implemented via the governing bodies of sport and ought to have had a positive effect on the development of coaching. There have been shortcomings, however. Developmental issues in the education and training of the top tier of coaches have been ignored; the contribution of coaching relative to facility expenditure, equipment and event support has been undervalued; and efforts have been focused on the provision of the lower tiers of coaching services. Undoubtedly, this policy has had some success in performance terms, the criterion used by policy makers to determine coaches' success, but this focus is rather narrow and with little 'rebound' effect, and professional enhancement has been limited.

Local government has made little impact on elite or competitive sport. This statement is perhaps too all-embracing: the grants to top-level performers and the example of swimming provision at this level suggest that opportunities do exist. The career pattern which has emerged for swimming coaches has been dependent upon a job description which encompasses both instruction and coaching. Debate about the essence of coaching may need to be tempered somewhat to take advantage of possible initiatives. In any case, the lack of interest in sports policy shown by coaches and a collective apathy towards the regulation and licencing of coaches restricts career opportunities.

(b)   Sport for All

A second group of policies have embraced the notion of increased participation. Often targeting special groups, these 'sport for all' policies have been enacted at the recreation end of the continuum. Implementation has been via local government agencies; and until recently, have been accompanied by little specialist training. Once again, financial subsidy has been concentrated mainly upon facilities and promotion. These local authority efforts are analogous to the work of the governing bodies of sport in increasing the numbers of participants, often through local or regional initiatives. Given the absence of conditions characteristic of a rigorous definition of the coaching process, there appears to have been little scope for professional development. However, this would be to misjudge the situation.

(c)   Legislation and Training

Sports coaching has much to learn from the way in which regulation, licencing and association have followed from Government Reports and/or legislation in Education, Social Work, and Community Education. When legislation has led to specialist training, the benefits have been obvious. The career opportunities which have arisen in these areas are examples of emerging occupations assisted by legislation and recommendations. Similarly, legislation to reorganise local government throughout Britain has led to the formation of very large departments of leisure and recreation, and a new professional Association has introduced a system of professional examinations for

recreation management. Nevertheless, even in these
recreation related areas, the practical and conceptual
problems of occupational boundaries, philosophy etc are
scarcely better developed than in sports coaching.

(d) Coach Education in Higher Education

The extent to which coach education and training can be
pursued beyond Governing Body award level is a
reflection both of deep- seated values about sport and
of more exigent concerns about the supply of qualified
coaches. The pivotal concentration of sports coaching
in central institutions or Universities in both Eastern
Europe or North America follows from, in the former
case, the state regulations of supply and demand within
a society cogniscent of the value of physical culture.
In the latter, the Universities' dominant position in
competitive sports, and in particular spectator sports,
has spawned a matrix of education, research and
competition which is self- perpetuating. In contrast,
the conservative nature of Higher Education in Britain
has been far less favourable for acceptance of
non-traditional subjects. The spread of non-
vocational Sports Studies degrees in Higher Education
has reflected institutional survival rather than
demand, and University sport is not an important medium
of elite level competition. Some Universities have
taken initiatives in sports scholarships, have active
research programmes and play a significant role as
resource centres for coaches and coach education.

The scale of vocational training for all social
services is controlled by the Government on the basis
of demographic statistics, forecasts of birth rates and
perceived social problems. Thus the supply of new
teachers of physical education relates directly to the
number of pupils in secondary schools. With the
current economic situation involving relatively high
unemployment and in the face of threats to the social
order in inner city areas, available resources are
being ploughed into schemes which compensate these
problems. This is not a climate for high investment in
sports coaching, even when it can be shown that there
is a demand for trained full-time coaches.
Consequently, Government is unlikely to finance new
courses in Colleges and Universities or provide student
grants. Indeed successive British Governments have
been party to closures and mergers of most of the

specialist institutions which might have been expected
to play leading roles in coach development. Fresh
plans for cuts in Higher Education announced in summer
of 1985 pose major threats to existing courses and are
not conducive to innovative measures in coach
education. It would appear that the trend in Higher
Education is leading to centres of academic excellence,
with second and even third tier institutions taking up
the demand for lower level teaching. Sports coaching
must find an outlet in this evolving system because
professional development is singularly dependent on
institutional support, offering eventual parity with
traditional professions in terms of training and
qualifications. Currently there is no indication that
the Government will introduce legislation to foster the
creation of courses for sports coaching in Higher
Education.

(e) Professional Associations

An alternative to Government legislation is pressure
from professional Associations. The recently formed
Institute of Leisure and Amenity Management has a
membership of 4,000 full- time professional workers and
it can negotiate with Colleges and Universities to run
self-financing courses. There is an insufficient
number of full-time sports coaches to form a powerful
Association. As a final solution it is necessary to
turn attention to the National Coaching Foundation. It
was established in 1983 by the UK Sports Council. It
seeks to operate with the voluntary co-operation of
governing bodies of sport and local authorities.

(f) National Coaching Foundation

The establishing of the National Coaching Foundation
sprang from the notion that the availability of a range
of resources is a necessary part of successful
coaching. Dealing with problems of provision, access,
duplication and relationships between groups of sports
practitioners, especially sports scientists and
coaches, is a vital first step to the production of
better standards of performance. obviously, planned
provision is preferable to the co-ordination of
haphazard development. A more readily available
support structure may have a direct influence on the
efficient and effective practice of coaches and is,
therefore, supportive of professional development. The

emphasis on performance related knowledge and services to athletes is one example of the way in which the influence on professional enhancement of coaches has been less direct.

(g) Policy Making

Involvement in policy making has not been a high priority for sports coaches. There is a difficult balance to be struck between complaining about imposition by others and collective concern for practice rather than policy. Nonetheless, coaches can be criticised for being reactive, for accepting a passive role. Relationships with voluntary employers have undoubtedly affected professional status but within these limitations, coaches have rarely taken an aggressive attitude to ensuring that information is available to the policy maker, to influencing decisions on, for example, competition formats, which are of direct relevance to coaching practice, or even to matters affecting professional development. It would seem at least possible that decisions on matters related to coaching and coaches are often taken in the vacuum created by the profession's somewhat limited interest in its affairs.

(h) Conclusion

Some forty years after the appointment of the first full-time National Coach by a governing body of sport, sports coaching can still be described as an emerging occupation. It has been shown that coaching has not found a recognised place in courses in Higher Education. There are too few full-time coaches to form a powerful Association which might lobby for recognition. No British Government has shown an inclination to place sports coaching on an equal footing with teaching or the other social services professions. The National Coaching Foundation may fill this gap but this will largely be dependent on the creation of a labour market. This possibility will be considered in the final section of this paper.

PROFESSIONAL DEVELOPMENT OF COACHES

(a) Professionalisation of the Coaching Occupation

Emerging occupation or aspiring profession: the more
appropriate question may not be whether such ambitions
are likely or feasible under given conditions but
whether either description is valid. Occupational
structures are important for providing the basis from
which career patterns will emerge. In Great Britain,
the relatively small cadre of coaches who earn their
living solely from coaching are vastly outnumbered by
the overwhelming majority of part-time, usually
voluntary, coaches. The form of professionalism most
appropriate to such an irregular and, as yet, slowly
changing prospect is far from clear. Even less clear
is whether a collective unity of purpose and
willingness to engage in the process would signify a
desire for professional enhancement. This may be partly
the result of uncrystalised occupational structures
but, in addition, coaches have demonstrated an
inclination towards achieved rather than ascribed
status.

Professionalisation implies a degree of acceptance,
recognition and status. The corollary of such
recognition is a functional autonomy in which the
profession obtains control of entry to the profession
and of the organisation of much of its activity. The
main benefit accruing from professionalisation is a
more widely perceived estimation of status and prestige
accorded to the occupation.

One method of estimating professional development is to
examine a number of attributes displayed by an
occupational grouping. Entry requirements, that is,
educational demands, length of training, qualification;
recognition of the uniqueness and exclusivity of the
individual's skills; the self-regulation of a code of
conduct with appropriate discipline, are indicators of
professional status. In the contemporary workplace,
technological advances and specialisation have created
a situation in which skills are highly specific.
Attention has therefore been focussed on the codes of
practice of occupational groups, their organisation and
regulation and the circumstances of their training.

(b) Contemporary Evaluation of Professional
Development

Sports coaching does not measure up to the requirements
described above. Training is unregulated, of minimum

duration in many instances and unqualified persons can become recognised as 'top coaches'. The status of sports coaches will continue to be severely restricted if unqualified coaches are recruited to influential positions within Governing Bodies. The certification and accreditation programmes from overseas have had an aim of raising the status of sport coaches. They have failed to do so because no occupation entry control has been exercised, particularly in elite-level or professional sport. Sports coaches have not been organised in such a fashion as to make possible the self-regulation of conduct. Furthermore, the reluctance of a great many coaches to engage in a discussion about ethics is perhaps an indication of their desire to sidestep the issues involved.

The concerns expressed earlier in the paper over the lack of conceptual clarity can be translated into a degree of public uncertainty about the role of the coach. There is a concomitant problem in identifying the knowledge and skills unique to coaching. It seems likely that a definition of the coach as a technocrat has lessened the approbation which might have followed wider recognition of the coach's interpersonal skills.

The use of the term profession may be less descriptive of an ascribed status than of a spirit of unity and purpose which pervades an occupational grouping, and distinguishes it from others. Such a development is not unrelated to a betterment of member interests and an establishment of occupational mystique. Sports coaches should, therefore, reinforce the boundaries of the profession which characterises the ocupation as different to others. There is a difficult equation, therefore, between the art or mystique of coaching and the knowledge and skills which are sufficiently distinctive and transferable as to demand training. The professional recognition sought in this way seems hardly attainable without a degree of entry control and regulation of qualifying courses.

(c) Career Patterns

The absence of a systematic career structure has militated against the investigation of aspects of occupational development in a British context. For example, recruitment into coaching has not been sufficiently related to a hierarchy of coaching positions. Custom seems to indicate that top-level coaches, in the main, have shortened pathways into such positions and that this transition reflects performer experience or master/apprentice experience rather than certification. Coaching structure may, therefore, operate within broad horizontal bands. In a similar fashion, the question of upward mobility would bear investigation in the light of coaching effectiveness issues. The career structure now evident in swimming may demonstrate how mobility within the labour market is dependent upon movements into a number of core positions with a consequent ripple effect.

(d)   The Female Coach

The coaching profession is heavily male-dominated. Inasmuch as sport reproduces the social relationships in society in general, the issue of women in sport has received considerable attention. Nonetheless, the number of female coaches i sport is illustrative of then problem and in top-level sport it is particularly acute. There may be a number of contributory factors. The smaller numbers of women involved in sport and their earlier retirement from sport, often due to domestic pressures, do not explain the disproportionate figures although it helps to perpetuate the male stereotype of the coach and the absence of suitable role models for young girls. The conscious or unconscious discrimination of male administrators is undoubtedly a factor as is the generally 'higher' standard of performance of males in sports participated in by both sexes. It seems likely that these factors combine with a residue of the unfemininity issue to produce a psychological barrier t women coaches. The o motivation, incentive and confidenc to enter the e coaching profession is constrained not onl by the y attitudes of male coaches but also by the expectations of athletes. Although the knowledge and skills required of the coach suggest no obstacles to women coaches, the recruitment avenues for top level coaches, dependent as they are on lengthy experience, may erode the already small numbers who surmount the attitudinal barrier.

(e)   Professional Associations

One significant feature of the established professions is the power and influence of their professional associations. The inception of these associations affords an opportunity to an emerging occupation to protect its specialised skills, control entry to the profession and establish codes of ethical behaviour. There was and is a relationship between the power and influence of the associations and the status of the profession. Such an association does not exist for sports coaches at the present time although at this stage of development this is perhaps not surprising. Nonetheless, the functions required of an association have been shown to benefit professional development. The experiences of the British Association of Swimming Coaches, one of the few of its kind, are shaped by the constraints operating on coaching as a whole: mutual benefit is yet to take over from self-interested protectionism and the association's influence stops short of regulation.

The British Association of National Coaches is the only body to aspire to an aim of the development of the profession. Although the membership has been recently extended, however, the focus of the Association has been fairly restricted. Despite its broad aim, the Association has focussed much more on service provision and dissemination of knowledge. There has been no attempt to establish codes of behaviour or to regulate entry to the profession. Provision is being made for a profession which does not, as yet, exist.

The interests of the profession will be best served by a strong association: one which critically examines its boundaries, standards, education and training and, in particular, codes of behaviour, and which works to regulation through recommendation. The influence of such an association would be lessened by an overemphasis on external relationships and the mistaken assumption of introverted isolation for positive professional protection.

CONCLUSION

The dynamics of historical development and the structur of sports provision have evolved a labour market for e sports coaches which is relatively small. Despite the attention being given to sports coaching at the present time, the prospects of occupational growth are illusory rather than real. The emphasis placed on competitive success, standards of performance and International prestige has resulted in a demand for material resource, technology and performance related sports science. As a consequence there has been less reflection on conceptual issues of boundary and philosophy, and an undervaluing of the vocational and educational responsibilities of the coach.

Coach education is ill-prepared for professional development. Governing Body award schemes are generally inadequate in these terms and the reliance of coaches on experience and imitation lends support to those who, for whatever reason, mistrust coach educators and who reinforce the disincentives to engage in formal processes. Higher Education must accept some responsibility for failing to adequately service coach education. The situation in Britain has been confused by the coordinating and funding bodies who have espoused the tradition of decentralisation but attempted to indirectly regulate and control. This has been insufficient to influence coaching developments and little practical direction has been made available to Governing Bodies.

Lessons may be learned from other countries where the political and structural environment is quite different. These lessons must be shaped into a British response. Sports coaching will not become an established profession, but the work of sports coaches can be professionalised and the occupation established and valued. It seems inevitable that some form of regulation will be necessary for this, and coaches must recognise that change is always political. Entrenched positions should not be allowed to prevent a move towards a collective unity.

Coach education must underly professional development. Inevitably a 'chicken and egg' discussion will arise. Regulation of activity, initially of Governing Body appointees, representative group coaches and local government officials will affect control and status and will be reflected in the career patterns available. The incentives created should influence the demand for coach education in its many forms, from Governing Body awards, through apprentice schemes to Higher Education. The circular pattern created is the basis for future development. The initial problem is to correctly judge the appropriate thrust into the circle. Coach education underpins professional development and ought, therefore, to be a priority.

Section I

Where Are We Now?

THE EDUCATION OF SPORTS COACHES AND SPORTS ADMINISTRATORS IN
AUSTRALIA.

F.S. PYKE   Centre for Sports Studies,
                Canberra College of Advanced Education
L.R. WOODMAN   Australian Coaching Council,
                Australian Sports Commission

Abstract
It is the purpose of this paper to describe the sports coach and
administrator education programmes that presently exist in
Australia, to suggest ways in which they can be improved and to
indcate the vocational opportunities being afforded their graduates.

The national coaching accreditation programme is presently available at several different levels, ranging from the introductory to
the advanced. An administrator education programme is now being
developed in some areas along similar lines. These programmes are
mostly engaged in by members of the public who are working in sport
on a voluntary basis and who have no tertiary qualifications in
related subject areas.

There are a limited number of tertiary level courses, offered at
both associate diploma and undergraduate degree level, which permit
some specialisation in sports coaching and adminstration. The
Centre for Sports Studies at the Canberra College of Advanced
Education is one of these, being developed at the same time as the
Australian Institute of Sport to provide career training in sport
for some of the athletes attending the institute.

There are also a variety of short course packages aimed at
improving expertise in selected subject areas such as sports marketing, athlete assessment, talent identification, and sports and the
law.

Each of these programmes has certainly contributed to improving
the professional confidence and competence of its participants and
has subsequently elevated their status and acceptability in the
community. However, in order to optimise the impact of the programmes, greater attention must be given to planning and course
content, establishing quality controls, improving the communication
skills of the presenters and offering a learning environment which
is appropriate to the level of participants involved and to their
ultimate vocational responsibility.

1.   Introduction

There are increasing numbers of peole becoming involved as participants and spectators in Australian sport. This is making it more

and more difficult for volunteer and part-time personnel to cope
with the work load and responsibilities. It is also no longer
entirely appropriate for our sports coaches and adminstrators to
simply emerge from the ranks of players without any formal training
in these specialised fields. This situation has led to the development of several different forms of coach and administrator education
aimed at improving the expertise of the individuals involved.
However the introduction and acceptance of these programmes has not
been without its problems.

It is the purpose of this paper to describe the education programmes available to sports coaches and administrators in Australia,
to suggest areas in which problems have occurred and provide some
strategies for their solution in the future.

2. Coach Education Programmes

2.1 Existing Programmes
2.1.1 National Coaching Accreditation Scheme
Courses at three different levels are provided under this scheme.
Level 1 is an introductory course lasting a minimum of 14 hours.
One third of the course is devoted to general theory, the remainder
being sports specific theory and practical work. More than 80% of
the 35,000 accredited coaches in Australia are at level 1.

Level 2 is an intermediate course lasting a minimum of 60 hours,
one half of which includes general principles, the other half sports
specific theory and practice. About 15 percent of accredited
coaches are at level 2.

Level 3 involves advanced sports specific work in the theory and
practice of coaching and lasts for a minimum of 100 hours. Less
than 5 percent of accredited Australian coaches are at level 3.

The content of these courses is the responsibility of each sport
but is expected to meet the guidelines established by the Australian
Coaching Council. The courses are funded by the Commonwealth and
State governments, assisted in several sports by the Rothman's
National Sport Foundation. They are mostly taken by memebers of the
public who are working in sport on a voluntary basis and have no
tertiary qualifications in a related subject area.

It is recommended that participants in each of these courses only
be given credit when they have completed certain periods of practical coaching experience. This ranges from 1 season at level one
to three seasons at level 3.

There are two other "levels" of coach education in Australia
which are not presently part of the accreditation scheme, but which
are being utilised by some sports. Pre-level 1 courses (level 0),
of 4 hours minimum duration, have been developed to provide some
degree of organisational and management skill training, mainly for
junior coaches. These courses are valuable for individuals who do
not have the time and inclination to attend a full level 1 course
and are also a more appropriate starting point for coaches involved
in sports which have up-graded their level 1 courses.

Post-level 3 courses (level 4) are also available in some sports but, again, are not part of the accreditation scheme. These courses are usually offered to coaches who have given lengthy service to the sport and/or have attained a high level of academic achievement in tertiary level sports science courses. These qualifications are subject to wide interpretation by the few sports involved with this level of coach education.

2.1.2. Tertiary Level Courses

There are a number of human movement/physical education/exercise science/sports science courses taught at both degree and associate diploma level in tertiary institutions throughout Australia. These all generally provide a satisfactory background in the exercise sciences but are not specifically geared towards the preparation of coaches. In 1981, to coincide with the establishment of the Australian Institute of Sport (AIS) in Canberra, a 3 year under-graduate sports coaching degree course funded by the Commonwealth Government commenced at the Canberra College of Advanced Education. The objective of the course was to provide career training in sport both for athletes attending the Institute and for others involved in sports not represented there. The course involves the completion of the following 18 semester units.

Year 1
- Behavioural Science
- Concepts on Biology
    or
  Chemistry
- Functional Anatomy
- History of Sport in Society
- Introduction to Exercise Science
- Physiology and Anatomy

Year 2
- Acquisition of Sports Skill
- Behavioural Science
- Biomechanical Analysis of Sport
- Measurement and Statistics for Sport
- Psychology of Sport
- Social Analysis of Sport
- Sports Physiology

Year 3
- Human Nutrition
- Special Sports Studies Project A
- Special Sports Studies Project B
- Special Topics in Sports Medicine
- Sports Skill Analysis
- Theory and Practice of Coaching

A further 6 semester units are also taken in an elective study area; popular choices being biology, mathematics, sports adminis-

tration and sports journalism. The proximity of the AIS makes it
possible to involve many of its high performance coaches in the
programme. Students undertake coaching practice and are strongly
encouraged to become involved in coaching in the community throughout the duration of the course. Graduates of the course have
obtained employment as coaches (figure skating, skiing, gymnastics,
swimming) coaching development officers (Australian Football,
Soccer), fitness coordinators (National Heart Foundation, private
enterprise, State Government departments for sport and recreation,
State health authority, National hotel chain, YMCA), laboratory
assistant (Australian Institute of Sport) and sports teachers
(private schools). It remains to be seen whether the sports
community will continue to encourage the work of professional
coaches or whether they will be forced to seek employment in the
areas of health, fitness and recreation.

2.1.3. Continuing Education Courses
Short courses which attend to particular areas of interest or
difficulty are often conducted by State and/or Commonwealth
Govekrnment agencies. These courses provide useful updates for
accredited coaches. Examples of recently conducted courses include
talent identification, youth sport guidelines, co-educational sport,
nutrition, fitness testing, and methods of sports skill analysis.

2.2 Programme Difficulties
2.2.1. Course Planning
It is important that accreditation courses contain the right blend
of theory and practice. On many occasions the sports science
content has tended to become excessive and time has not always been
given to the practical needs of coaches. Coaches are practical
people. Their stage is the gymnasium, pool, track and field.
Whenever possible theory should be taught in these more active
environments rather than while seated behind a desk.
   Tertiary coach education programmes, in particular, run the risk
of being shackled by academic requirements. However, there are
signs that tertiary institutions are becoming more sympathetic to
vocational needs. Associate diploma courses, whose predominant
clientele are mature age students already engaged in part-time
coaching in the community, are particularly amenable to this
approach. Level 2 courses are now becoming acceptable study modules
for a tertiary-level qualification in the sport area. By the same
token, graduates of these tertiary courses usually receive credit
for the general principles component of level 2 coaching courses.
   It should be clearly understood by coach educators that coaching
cannot be learned merely from reading books. The "paper coach"
syndrome has come under a lot of criticism which can best be met by
giving credit for practical experience and imparting knowledge of
the theory of coaching in real-life sporting environments. The key
word is integration - of theory and practice. Time in courses must
be devoted to practical hands-on coaching experiences, integrated
with underlying theory. Coaching practice, work experience and
apprenticeship or internship schemes must be an integral part of the

courses.

Both practising coaches and sports scientists with some experience in the particular sport should have some input into the course
planning process. Knowledge should not merely cascade downwards
from the scientist to the coach to the athlete. Each should be
given the opportunity to learn from each other. It is therefore
important that workshop environments be provided in which coaches
and scientists can interact. Coaches have trialled their methods in
the field and, on consultation with their athletes, have developed a
feel for what is right and what is wrong. On the other hand, the
scientists may be able to provide the rationale behind the success
or failure of a particular training technique. In this cooperative
way the pool of knowledge increases.

2.2.2. Quality Control

Standards of course content, presentation and assessment still vary
widely, not only between sports but also within sports. While
sports should be encouraged to establish their own individuality and
standards, it is useful to establish general guidelines against
which they can work. It is the responsibility of national coaching
directors to conduct coach education programmes in accordance with
national coaching accreditation scheme guidelines. These directors
are required to design and conduct courses, to develop manuals,
handbooks and other resources and to regularly evaluate the impact
of their programmes.

Over the past few years the standard of coach education
programmes has improved greatly, but there is still concern with
certain aspects of the situation. In particular, sports should not
be prepared to turn their programmes over to government agencies or
tertiary institutions without having some say in the planning of
course content. Sports should be in charge of their own destiny,
but some need more guidance than others.

2.2.3 Course Lecturers

The communication skills of lecturers in accreditation scheme
courses has often left a lot to be desired. Their language has
often been too technical and rather than simplifying complex
scientific information, they have tended to complicate it. Course
lecturer programmes aimed at developing communication skills and
presenting a simplified and concise information package should be
considered. However, coaches also must be encouraged to play their
part in the communication process and put some effort into learning
terminology and concepts which have now become an integral part of
their sport.

2.2.4 Resource Material

Specific course manuals have not been developed by all sports.
While the general coaching manuals (levels 1 and 2) offer useful
information for all course participants, it is still necessary to
highlight the material that is most relevant for a particular
sport. This should be a high priority in coach education development. As well as being a valuable supplement to formally attended

coaching courses the manuals (perhaps also accompanied by workbooks) can also form the curriculum for correspondence courses. In a country as large as Australia there are many geographically isolated communities that could be reached with correspondence courses. This has become one of the latest initiatives of the Australian Coaching Council.

Video films also have the potential to reach the broader population of coaches. The widespread availability of video cassette recorders make them a viable proposition for spreading the coaching word. More sophisticated interactive video systems employ a computer to allow the use to interact with a video programme. Coaches can then work through an educational programme at a rate prescribed by their ability to answer questions posed at various stages throughout. This is a coach education tool of the future.

2.2.5 Acceptance of Accredited Coaches

One of the greatest difficulties with the coaching accreditation scheme is the lack of acceptance of these qualifications by many of the sports. This is particularly the case with the older and often more traditional sports. Advertisements for coaches and their ultimate appointment to a position usually take no account of formal qualifications. The procedure of appointing ex-players, with no formal preparation as coaches, seriously undermines the entire process of accreditation.

Administration must become prepared to go beyond competitive record and club affiliation in selecting coaches. In this respect they should be enlightened as to the benefits of coach education programmes. This involves establishing a better understanding and stronger union between administrators and coaches. If performance standards within the sport are to be elevated, each cannot work effectively in isolation It is therefore strongly recommended that sports develop a management plan that integrates the process of coaching accreditation into their development structure.

Even broader than this is the general community attitude towards coaching. Other than in sports such as swimming, skiing, tennis and golf - the social and life-time sports - there is a general reluctance to seek and pay for competent coaching in many other sports such as the football codes, hockey, volleyball, basketball and netball. This attitude restricts the employment opportunities of trained coaches and lessens the weight of their qualifications. A public education programme aimed at elevating the status of the coaching profession is required.

3. Administrator Education Programs

3.1 Existing Programs
3.1.1 Administrator Accreditation

An accreditation programme for administrators does not currently exist in Australia. However, some State Government departments responsible for sport have developed short courses for administrators which have been arbitrarily graded as level one and two.

These usually last between 10 and 15 hours and 30 hours, respectively.

3.1.2 Tertiary-Level Courses

Many of the top sports administrators in the country have completed tertiary courses in economics, commerce or business and combined this training with a background of experience in the administration of sporting clubs and associations. It has only been in the last five years that tertiary institutions have developed more specialised courses in sports administration, but there are very few of these available. The most prominent is that offered by the Canberra College of Advanced Education.

The 18 required semester-units of this three year undergraduate degree course are as follows:

Year 1
- Accounting
- Basic Information Systems
     or
  Computers and Computing
- Behavioural Science
- Concepts and Elements of Law
- History of Sport in Society
- Introduction to Exercise Science

Year 2
- Administration and Management in Sport
- Measurement and Statistics for Sport
- Organisational Communication
- Organisation and Policy in Sport
- Public Relations
- Social Analysis of Sport

Year 3
- Special Sports Studies Project A
- Special Sports Studies Project B
- Special Topics in Sports Administration
- Sports and the Law
- Sports Marketing
- Sports Skill Analysis

As in the Sports Coaching Course offered by the same institution, 6 elective units in a specific subject area must also be completed. Popular choices include economics, law, politics, sports coaching and sports journalism. A Master's degree programme, involving a substantial thesis component, is planned to commence in 1987. Graduates of the undergraduate course have obtained employment as executive directors (women's soccer, ice sports, paraplegics, touch), development officers (rugby league, soccer, skiing, government departments), recreation officers (hospitals) and facility managers. Sports administration seems to be a burgeoning area of employment.

3.1.3 Continuing Education Courses

As in the coaching area, a number of short courses have been
developed at the State level which attempt to improve the expertise
of administrators in certain subjects. Recent offerings include
sports and the law, sports marketing, seeking sports sponsorships
and sports club management.

3.2 Programme Difficulties

Similar difficulties exist in both administrator and coach education
programmes with respect to course planning, ensuring quality
control, training course lecturers and providing resource materials.

3.2.1 Course Planning

Practicing sports administrators should be involved in the planning
of courses as they bring to the drawing board an understanding of
the knowledges and skills that are essential for survival in the
sports marketplace. Some of these individuals can also play an
invaluable role as course lecturers.

Courses should include a practical component working with a
sports club or association. This serves the additional purpose of
providing some voluntary and part-time assistance to an organisation. The Canberra College of Advanced Education has developed a
work experience scheme which has forged strong connections with the
sports industry and, in many cases has paved the way for the future
employment of graduates within it. Representatives from the
industry have also been engaged by the college as part-time lecturers. Hence the industry becomes aware of the nature and quality of
the professional preparation process and the institution becomes
aware of the roles and responsibilities of its products within the
industry. A valuable symbiotic relationship has therefore been
established.

3.2.2 Quality Control

The Australian Society of Sports Administrators has been formed
recently. One of its functions is to establish guidelines for the
content, presentation and assessment of administrator education
programmes. It would then be left to the executive-director of the
sport to coordinate and regulate the programme within that sport.
At the moment the courses being offered by the government
departments responsible for sport in the States vary widely in
content and quality and should be subjected to review.

3.2.3 Course Lecturers

As with coach education programmes it is recommended that training
courses be provided to assist lecturers with identifying the most
efficient means of communicating information in short courses
presented outside tertiary institutions. In the short history of
these courses particular problems have been experienced with the law
and accounting components.

3.2.4 Resource Material

There remains a great deal of work to be done in developing books and manuals for sports administration courses. While overseas publications are available, there is a dearth of literature available that is suitable for the situation existing in Australia. Urgent attention should be given to this problem.

3.2.5 Acceptance of Professionally Trained Administrators

One of the greatest problems has occurred as a result of misunderstandings regarding the tasks and responsibilities of the full-time administrator and the volunteer office-bearers or board members. While the professional administrator is expected to have the initiative and foresight to chart a path for the sport, while still running an efficient office, many board members feel that they must "hold the reins". While some sports have hit upon the right formula, others have spent considerable time in the process of cycling executive-directors, or presidents, or both. This is unproductive and self-defeating.

Increased participation rates have made it more than a kitchen table operation to organise and manage the vast array of junior and senior sports competitions currently being conducted throughout the country. As a result, professional sports administrators have become an acceptable community commodity.

4. Conclusion

There are a number of sports coach education programmes available in Australia. These include those conducted under the coaching accreditation scheme, in tertiary institutions and as continuing education courses. Most of these programmes have been operating for a number of years but still require fine-tuning in terms of planning and control, and improvement of the learning environment. Particular attention needs to be given to establishing the place of accredited coaches in the sports community.

Sports administrator education programmes are a more recent development and have not, as yet, been placed under an accreditation scheme. However, they do exist in tertiary institutions and are offered as short courses on a somewhat ad hoc basis by State government departments responsible for the development of sport. Urgent attention is required in terms of course planning, establishing quality control and developing resources which will assist with the learning process. An increasing interest in participation in sport within the community makes it essential that administrators acquire the skills and knowledges necessary to cope with work demands.

References

Club Administration Manual (1984). Vicsport, Melbourne, Australia.
Corcoran, P., (1984). A Review of the National Coaching Accreditation Scheme. Sports Coach 8, 1, 43-44.
Pyke, F.S. (1984). Some Considerations in the Education of Sports Coaches. New Zealand J. AHPER 17, 3, 3-5.

<u>Review of the National Coaching Accreditation Scheme</u> (1985). Report
to the Sport and Recreation Ministers' Council, Commonwealth of
Australia, Canberra, Australia.

Woodman, L., (1983). The National Coaching Accreditation Scheme in
1983/84. <u>Sports Coach</u> 7, 3, 2-4.

THE CANADIAN APPROACH TO THE TRAINING OF COACHES: MATCHING THE
PARADIGM

GEOFF R. GOWAN, Ph.D. and WILLIAM G. THOMSON, M.A.
Coaching Association of Canada

Abstract
This paper describes the evolution of the training of Canadian
coaches. Information is presented in three sections covering past,
present and future.
Section 1 describes and discusses the development of the program from
1974-1984 and identifies key items related to the first decade
including the creation of the Coaching Association of Canada, the
formation of the National Coaching Certification Council, the numbers
and nature of courses taught and the parallel development of high
level supplementary courses. Some of the problems and the
approaches to their solutions are also discussed.
Section 2 describes the present status of the program, including the
shift in emphasis to higher levels of coaching development, the
development of a credit system, the training of higher level coaches,
and research on coaching effectiveness and performance analysis.
Section 3 identifies future tasks including long-term planning, use
of high technology in alternative delivery, coaching support and
incentives and the work needed to establish a coaching profession.
Key words: Coaching, Education, Organization, Structure, Profession,
Rewards.

Section 1

1.1 Seventeen years ago, February 1969, the findings of a task force
on sports for Canadians were submitted to the Minister, Department of
National Health & Welfare. The terms of reference were specifically
spelled out.
1. To report on prevailing concepts and definitions of both amateur
   and professional sport in Canada and the effect of professional
   sport on amateur sport;
2. To assess the role of the federal government in relation to non-
   governmental, national and international organizations and
   agencies in promoting and developing Canadian participation in
   sport; and
3. To explore ways in which the government could improve further, the
   extent and quality of Canadian participation in both sport at home
   and abroad.

In their covering letter to the Minister the three members of the task force concluded by stating:

"Canadian sport has reached a crossroad in its development. We hope our recommendations will do much for a restructuring of sports activity and administration in Canada; and in terms of momentum and direction that sport will set on a new, broad path for the future." On page 61 of the "Report of the task force on sport for Canadians", under the heading Coaching in Canada, the opening paragraph states: "One of the attributes of a profession is a system of recognized qualifications and a consequent certification. In this sense there is no coaching profession in Canada. No formal qualifications are needed, no certification is available."

Following a generally bleak description of the past coaching situation in Canada and comparatively glowing reports of the U.S. high school and college system and state subsidized Eastern and Western European practices the point was made that progress in the coaching field was essential as a means of competing on equal terms with other countries. The relationship between Canada's more successful sports internationally, swimming, skiing and figure skating, and the presence of coaches in those sports who make a living from their work was noted.

The text continued:

"Our backwardness in coaching dictates a long-range plan and short-term but thoroughly applied expedients. Most of the coaching in Canada will continue for a long time to be voluntary. Therefore the immediate emphasis should be put on providing leadership and assistance to our voluntary coaches."

Five recommendations were made at the conclusion of the coaching section:

We recommend that the government provide grants to employ professional coaches in a broad variety of sports. We further recommend that:

a) the government provide assistance to organize and develop a national coaches association;

b) a system be developed to identify outstanding young athletes through the national coaches association;

c) the government provide grants to establish a series of travelling clinics involving outstanding coaches and athletes;

d) the government institute a series of exchanges between Canada and other nations whereby our coaches could travel abroad to study the latest techniques and could bring foreign coaches here to inform and inspire our coaches and athletes.

The task force report was submitted to the Honourable John Munro, Minister, Department of National Health and Welfare, in 1969. In 1971 the Coaching Association of Canada was formed. Early in its existence a major aim of the association was identified.

Aim: to increase coaching effectiveness across all sports.

Twelve objectives were identified as important means of achieving the aim. The most significant of these in relation to the task force report was:

Establish a national coaching certification plan.

However, the overall task of improving the Canadian coaching situation and establishing the Coaching Association of Canada as a service organization and catalyst was sufficiently comprehensive to require a multi-faceted approach. Therefore in late 1971 and early 1972 eleven additional objectives were identified.

- Establish other programs related to the technical development of coaches.
- Develop an audio-visual resource centre.
- Develop a sports information resource centre (SIRC) of international scope.
- Produce a technical bulletin on coaching (quarterly).
- Produce an information tabloid newsletter (monthly).
- Produce a catalogue listing of publications, audio-visual material and coaching aids available for purchase and provide for their collection and sale.
- Establish and develop technical directors' seminars.
- Develop a liaison with universities.
- Act as consultant to national sport governing bodies in staging clinics, training camps, etc.
- Act as consultant to Game Plan.
- Lecture and act as advisory to any agency in the sport milieu.

Units of work leading to the achievement of the twelve objectives were listed and the work commenced in late 1972.

The original objectives have been modified over time, some no longer exist, new objectives have been identified and have been accompanied by new programs.

Because the development of a national coaching certification plan represented the highest priority of the CAC, this brief historical description will focus primarily on this objective.

As a first step, national sport governing bodies were contacted and presented with basic information about the proposed plan. Response was positive. Meetings were arranged at which further concepts were introduced and information was collected on the status of coaching in each sport governing body.

Coaching Theory Courses

While CAC was working primarily with NSGBs on the development of technical or sport specific coaching courses, the province of Ontario, on behalf of the other provinces and the territories, was developing the coaching theory courses. These courses can best be described as being basic to the broader education of the coach. Topics such as leadership and communication, growth and development, psychology of sport and exercise physiology, are covered in increasing depth from lower to higher levels. This broad base of coaching knowledge may be looked upon as the foundation stones upon which the sport specific pillars and roof of the coaching structure may be built.

The development of this double thrust of sport specific courses and general coaching principles courses at several levels represents the implementation of a task force report suggestion which stated:

"It is essential that emphasis in coaching clinics and courses be put on the techniques of coaching itself. Most coaching aids available in Canada deal with the mechanics of the activity concerned and give little on the art of coaching, as exemplified in such subjects as presentation techniques, laws of learning, psychology of athletes,

types of learners, problem-solving and organization of time. Good
coaching comes from an understanding of these subjects. There are
few more complicated and difficult forms of teaching than coaching.
The best coaches are ones who have an understanding of the imponder-
ables as well as the techniques of their specialty."

Problems:
In the early years of the Canadian coaching plan there were some
teething troubles. Communication of information in a country as vast
as Canada is always a problem. There was a lack of understanding
about the main aims of the theory program and this was compounded by
an initial implementation approach which was too rigid. Courses were
developed by discipline specialists with limited coaching experience
and with little or no input from sports bodies. As a consequence of
this unilateral approach, the plan, which required courses of sixteen
hours, forty hours and sixty hours for the three levels of theory,
was not well received by many coaches and several sport governing
bodies. In particular, the jump from 16 hours at level one to 40
hours at level two presented a considerable barrier to many potential
participants.
Sport specific programs also have varied in their content quality and
course duration. This variance has not always been an accurate
representation of their unique differences and needs. In the early
days it reflected differences in the level of sophistication and
available expertise. A strong attempt has been made, however, to
maintain minimum standards of course quality across sports.

1.2 National Coaching Certification Council
The formation of the National Coaching Certification Council in
January 1977 resulted in several important improvements in the overall coaching development scene. The composition of the Council is
significant. Council members comprise representatives of the
Coaching Association of Canada, Sport Canada, the Provincial Governments and the national sport governing bodies. This representation
includes all the key agencies involved in the program: developers,
funders, implementors and users. Thus the program belongs to everyone and the resultant commitment is high.
The major task of the Council during the first one and one-half years
of its existence was the evaluation and subsequent revision of the
coaching theory program. Full use was made of the available
expertise in sports bodies, universities, colleges, research
institutes, and the like, in order to ensure comprehensive and
quality advice and support for coaching development. Levels 1 and 2
were revised, course conductors were trained and coaching courses are
now held regularly across the country. Level 3, a brand-new course,
was completed in August 1981. Course conductors were trained and
courses are now being taught.

1.3 The Coaching Model
The Canadian model consists of five levels. For the training of a
competent coach, completion of both theory and technical components
of the model are essential. Progress from level to level also
requires active coaching involvement in order to implement the know-

ledge gained in the coaching courses and to gain coaching experience before proceeding to the next level.

When the coach has progressed to level 4 there would seem to be less value in a separate theory course. Instead, the concentration of the contributing disciplines needs to be more specifically related to the sport. Instruction focusses more on the exercise physiology of swimming, biomechanics of diving, or psychology of wrestling. Certainly there will be a need to examine the potential benefits of grouping coaches from sports having similar major characteristics. Such grouping encourages exchange of information by coaches and permits more economical delivery of important information. The complexity of the level 4 and 5 program will often require prolonged course work taught by subject specialists. Additionally, many courses will have residential requirements and will be staged nationally. An increasing number of level 4 coaches and almost all level 5 coaches will be working full-time as sport professionals. In the foreseeable future numbers will remain relatively small as a result of the difficulties of job placements in many Canadian sports. The task of designing and implementing level 4 courses is only now being approached by most NSGBs. Varied approaches will be utilized in the preparation of these high-level semi-professional and professional coaches. Certainly the universities, with their excellent resources, will be called upon to play an increasing role in this complex task.

In August 1981, the National Coaching Certification Council approved a "Guide to the Development and Implementation of Levels 4 and 5 of the National Coaching Certification Programs". This guide will be followed by those sports which are beginning work on their highest two levels.

Fig. 1 The Canadian Coaching Model

1 THEORY	2 TECHNICAL	PRACTICAL COACHING
2 THEORY	2 TECHNICAL	PRACTICAL COACHING
3 THEORY	3 TECHNICAL	PRACTICAL COACHING
4 THEORY AND TECHNICAL		PRACTICAL COACHING
5 THEORY AND TECHNICAL		PRACTICAL COACHING

The Theory or Principles of Coaching Package.

The development of the theory courses as a major segment of the Canadian program is, as mentioned earlier, in keeping with a task force report suggestion which made a plea for greater emphasis in coaching courses on the techniques of coaching per se and upon the importance of knowing more about the participants being coached.

Remarkably, the principles of coaching had not received much attention in earlier coaching clinics. Coaching principles may be considered as simply the basic aspects common to the job of coaching
athletes in any sport. As a consequence, theory courses can be
offered to all coaches, who are thus presented with additional
opportunities, both formally and informally, to share their own
methods and experiences with each other.

Theory Level 1.
The primary target group at this level can be generally described as
follows:
- volunteer coach working with novice athletes
- lightest time commitment
- likely coaching life 1-3 years
- little background in theory topics
The course involves 14 hours of instruction.

Course Topics.

Role of the Coach		2.5 hours
Sport Psychology		2.0 hours
How the Body Works and Grows		2.0 hours
Skill Analysis		1.0 hours
Sport Safety		2.0 hours
Teaching Skills		2.0 hours
Practice Planning		2.0 hours
Administration		0.5 hours
	Total	14.0 hours

Theory Level 2.
The primary target group for this level comprises:
- volunteer coaches
- more involved and committed than Level 1 coach
- generally working with young athletes
Level 2 is a 21-hour course.

Course Topics.

Role of the Coach		2.0 hours
Group Goal Setting		2.0 hours
Training Methods		3.0 hours
Nutrition		1.0 hours
Sport Psychology "A" Motivation		2.0 hours
Sport Psychology "B" Competitive Anxiety		2.0 hours
Care of Sports Injuries		2.0 hours
Teaching ADvanced Skills		2.0 hours
Skill Analysis		2.0 hours
Seasonal Planning		2.0 hours
Administration		1.0 hours
	Total	21.0 hours

Theory Level 3.
The primary target group will have the following characteristics:
- highest level volunteer coach
- spend considerable time coaching
- generally coach higher level athletes
- have a much longer coaching life than coaches in the lower two

levels
- are sound planners, good motivators and possess a high level of technical expertise
- possess the skills to co-ordinate resources (assistant coaches, trainers, etc.) to offer a more specialized approach to the development of athletes.

Level 3 is a 30-hour course.

Course Topics.

Selecting Sport Specific Training Programs	2.5 hours
Evaluating Aerobic Fitness)	4.0 hours
Evaluating Anaerobic Fitness)	
Organizing an Aerobic Training Program)	4.0 hours
Organizing an Anaerobic Training Program)	
Examination: 30 minutes	
Selecting a Strength Training Program	2.5 hours
Selecting a Flexibility Training Program)	3.0 hours
Advising on a Nutritional Program)	
Detecting and Correcting Errors in Skill	
Technique)	4.0 hours
Organizing Year-Round Training Programs)	
Examination: 30 minutes	
Identifying General Strategies for Mental	
Preparation in Sport	4.5 hours
Developing Pre-Competition Strategies)	2.5 hours
Developing Competition Strategies)	
Problem Solving - A: Athletes	
B: Coaches	1.5 hours
Motivating Athletes for the Long Term	1.5 hours
Examination: 30-45 minutes	
Total	30.0 hours

1.4 Implementation

The responsibility for running the coaching theory courses at all three levels rests with the provinces and territories. Courses are offered in various formats as follows:
- to coaches representing a wife variety of sports
- to coaches of a single sport
- to coaches of a single sport and integrated with a sport technical (sport specific) coaching course at equivalent level (e.g. theory level 1 and gymnastics level 1).

Course venues vary and include community centres, high schools, continuing education colleges and universities. In fact, any venue which has adequate classroom space, capable of providing audio-visual facilities, is acceptable.

Technical Programs.

For the development of sport specific or technical coaching programs, each involved NSGB receives annual grants and varying degrees of assistance. In particular, an eight-module curriculum design series has been developed for use by sport bodies in the preparation of coaching courses.

Each sport is eligible for annual financial and consultative assistance. With this assistance sports are able to produce coaching and course conductor manuals; develop A-V instructional programs; hold certification committee meetings; provide honoraria to writers; and conduct pilot course testing. Generally, increased financial assistance is available for the development of Levels 4 and 5. Because of the important role played by course conductors (those who teach the coaches) additional money is available for the training of these persons.

The provinces are responsible for the implementation of Levels 1-3 programs. The financing naturally varies somewhat from province to province. At Levels 4 and 5 implementation responsibilities are national. A sport which has completed all aspects of development of its Level 4 program is eligible for up to $20,000 annually for implementation costs.

Status of the Program, January 1986.
At the beginning of 1986, 54 sports have completed Level 1, 53 have finished Level 2 and 25 have Level 3. Two sports have fully approved Level 4 programs and 17 are piloting or developing programs. Soccer is piloting a program at Level 5.

Curriculum Design.
The development and implementation of a coaching program is not easy, quick or inexpensive. One major difficulty is the lack of curriculum design experience by members of coaching certification working committees charged with the responsibility of developing the technical or sport specific segments of the national model. While there is usually an abundance of sport technical knowledge, there is frequently a paucity of curriculum design experience. Further, for those committee members with comprehensive formal education, there are frequent difficulties when a practical training approach is introduced as opposed to the general, subject matter approach which is characteristic of much of our education system.

As a solution to this problem area, a modular educational package "The Curriculum Design Series" was produced for use by persons involved in the development of coaching programs.

The main purpose of this package is to produce curriculum design development and implementation capabilities in key national sport governing body technical staff and their volunteer working committees. The goal is to make them self-sufficient.

The information contained in this package also assists the CAC technical staff in their consulting roles with working committees. It is additionally an excellent resource for the development of other sport programs, including officials training.

Nine modules cover the following topics:
1. Analyzing tasks
2. Determining course content
3. Objectives
4. Testing
5. Instructional methods
6. Media
7. Developing instructional material
8. Validation and evaluation
9. Overview

Weekend training workshops were organized for NSGB personnel in order
that they could become fully familiar with the process of the
curriculum design. Feedback from participants indicated that the
workshops were extremely useful. The curriculum design process is now
an integral part of the total certification program development.
That which has been described above primarily concentrates on the
history and present status of the Canadian coaching plan. Some few
pages of description actually represent a decade of planning, development and implementation.

1.5 Problems and Solutions.
In attempting to implement a national program in a country as vast as
Canada; in an environment of fluctuating federal provincial relations;
where there are vast provincial differences and ever present
rivalries; and with the requirement to meet the needs of the anglo-
phone and francophone coaching populations there are sure to be some
problems. The fact that the program is now effectively national and
that it is working as well as it is, is a major triumph. The
composition of the National Coaching Certification Council has played
a significant part in this achievement, as noted earlier.
Communication continues to be a problem. The promotion of the program is certainly not as successful as desirable.
The CAC provides advice and material assistance in the form of
posters for national and provincial sports bodies and provincial
government coaching co-ordinators. Media kits, including audio
tapes and newspaper advertising copy, for use via public service
advertising are widely distributed.
Most provinces rely on the materials produced by CAC and with an
annual budget of approximately $30,000 coverage is inadequate.
A greater effort by all partners will improve this unsatisfactory
state. There is need for an increased financial support for a
promotion campaign. Since so much time is spent viewing television,
an awareness program will likely yield best results by tapping this
medium.
The Theory component of the program continues to be less well
supported by coaches than the technical courses. Hindsight suggests
that the original title of Theory was a major mistake, implying a
lack of relevance and applicability of the material to the everyday
coaching needs.
In some cases the inability of theory course conductors to provide
sufficiently varied and clear examples of the application of general
sports science principles and information to specific sport situations has caused frustration to trainee coaches. This is particularly true when coaches representing a wide variety of sports are
attending together.
The data collected from several evaluations of the theory program in
particular indicates that, once a coach has taken a theory course,
the level of satisfaction is generally high and the experience is
considered to be valuable. A very recent major study on the program
is providing some interesting and useful data which will provide
direction to the revision of the theory program which is presently
occurring.
A name change to Coaching Science or something which is perceived as

being more applicable and immediately useful than Theory will also be carefully examined.

The encouragement to fully integrate the "coaching science" modules into the technical (sport specific) courses may also provide a solution.

A major evaluation of the National Coaching Certification Program is currently underway and it is anticipated that many of the findings will be of value in providing solutions to problems that have been encountered.

Course Conductor training is crucial to program success. A well-trained, knowledgeable, committed course conductor plays a key role in the effective implementation of the program. He is the trans-mittor of the coaching message, and his skill in teaching the coaches is very important, particularly for those coaches who do not have a background in teaching or instructing.

While increasing emphasis has been placed upon course conductor training, including additional financial support and the production of a training and developmental handbook for course conductors, there continues to be a need for better training and evaluation of these key players.

Commitment to the program by the major partners is varied and fluctuating. There are reasons for this, the more valid ones being financial and resource limitations by NSGBs, PSGBs and provinces. The result is that there is a wide variance across sports in relation to the number of levels which have been developed and implemented and the number of coaches who are fully certified and the number who have taken only a technical or a theory course. There is also considerable variance regarding the degree of insistence on coaches being certified before being selected to certain coaching positions. There are increasing signs that both NSGBs and provinces are requiring certification of their coaches prior to appointment to coaching positions at national, provincial, and club level, but this is by no means common. The legislation model versus the intrinsic motivation approach is filled with a mix of philosophy, emotion, and some insecurity and the whole area of coaching support, reward and award, is only now beginning to receive the attention it warrants. That some clear leadership be demonstrated at national sport body level seems clear. If a start is made by requiring appropriate coaching certification of those coaches receiving financial support, the example is likely to be followed. The athletes deserve to have well-prepared coaches.

The Practical component of the program, that is the application of knowledge and skill obtained via the theory and technical courses, has been a problem. Two major reasons are lack of understanding by many sports concerning ways in which actual coaching of athletes can be verified and secondly, evaluation methods which are valuable as feedback to the practising coach and which can be effectively administered. The problem is much more difficult for the more popular sports with large numbers of coaches, particularly at lower levels.

This problem is being attacked by requiring sports to pay increased attention to this component of the program and by providing funding to assist sports in the development of evaluation instruments which,

48

for the coaches at Levels 1 and 2, will permit at least self-evaluation instruments to be used. In the case of Level 3 coaches, a practical coaching assessment is necessary and all coaches must complete this assessment which will be based on the coaching tasks of Levels 1 to 3. Since numbers are relatively small at Level 3, the more stringent evaluation of practical coaching is manageable and financially possible. In addition, the successful achievement of an acceptable level is a pre-requisite for entry into a Level 4 course.

1.6 Parallel Development of Supplementary Courses, Information and Experiences.
In addition to the formal NCCP coaching courses at progressive levels the Coaching Association of Canada provides coaching-related information on a wide range of topics, via several publications, from the Sport Information Resource Centre (SIRC) and from CAC Coaching Scholarship and Apprenticeship programs, the National Coaches' Seminar, the COA/CAC Seminars and local coaching conferences.

Coaching Review is Canada's national coaching magazine. This bi-monthly publication was designed to inform and educate coaches. Started in 1977, Coaching Review reaches coaches across Canada and around the world. It provides practical coaching information applicable to coaches in many sports. Although the material caters mainly for the practising coach, it does offer a section aimed at improving the coach's coaching science knowledge. It is also closely tied to the National Coaching Certification Program.
La Revue de l'entraîneur is the French counterpart of Coaching Review. As such it is the national coaching magazine for French-speaking coaches. The objectives of La Revue de l'entraîneur are similar to Coaching Review. Produced and written in Montreal its writers include coaches, researchers and journalists who have been closely involved with sport in the past 10 years.

The Science Periodical on Research and Technology in Sport (S.P.O.R.T.S.)
S.P.O.R.T.S. is a monthly periodical distributed to key agents in the sport and sport science community. CAC consultant staff are responsible for topic selection, recruitment of writers and final production. S.P.O.R.T.S. is designed to meet the needs of upper-level coaches.

The Sport Information Resource Centre (SIRC) contains a wealth of coaching-related information.
For more thorough dissemination of information which is identified, acquired and analyzed, SIRC's internationally-recognized SPORT database of over 178,000 document citations is now accessible worldwide on four separate computer systems: BRS, CAN/OLE, DIMDI and SDC.
A coach equipped with microcomputer can have a world of information right at his fingertips. Another new innovation allows the coach to receive automatically every month a listing of the most recent documentation in his subject area.
SIRC once more has taken the lead with its publication of the monthly SportSearch, consisting of the table of contents pages of over 240 sports journals in all areas - exercise physiology, sport psychology,

sport techniques, sports sciences, coaching and much more. Many
universities subscribe to this monthly service, allowing students,
faculty and coaches across the country access to a valuable resource
of information.
The eight-volume Sport Bibliography, the most exhaustive bibliography
on sport ever compiled and published, has been kept current with the
addition of three more volumes now in print. Annual volumes are
planned.
SIRC's international exchanges mean that other countries contribute
data for SIRC's database. So far six countries contribute their
data: they are Australia, Brazil, West Germany, Israel, the Nether-
lands and Switzerland.

The COA/CAC Seminar Series.
In conjunction with the Canadian Olympic Association, a series of
sport science seminars has been implemented in major centres across
the country for coaches of elite athletes.
These weekend seminars concentrate on selected areas such as strength
training, long-term planning and periodization and development of
endurance, and are designed to allow one day of presentation of
material followed by an opportunity on the second day for private
consultation with the presenter related to the application of new
knowledge to a specific sport area.

Consultation Service.
A follow-up to this initial opportunity as described above is the
provision of additional consultation, on a regular basis, with any
sport scientist whom the coach wishes to contract for a prescribed
learning program over a number of months. In this way a gradually
increasing network of consultants in various disciplines is being
established. This enables questions raised as a result of seminar
involvement to be discussed at some length over time. This over-
comes the frustration often experienced at courses when time per se
does not permit full coverage of a topic.
Funding is available to coaches of potential Olympic athletes who
wish to access follow-up consultation.

The annual National Coaches' Seminar involves approximately 175
coaches and technical directors. Topics covered are designed to be
appropriate for the needs of high-level athletes and coaches. The
three and one-half days' seminar in 1980, the first of the quadrennial
centred on the theme "Planning Elite Athlete Performance". The 1981
seminar represented the second phase of the quadrennial and its theme
was "From Planning to Implementation: Evaluation and Control of Elite
Athlete Performance". As well as the information received and shared
by the delegates at the seminar, proceedings, primarily in the form of
sports articles, are produced and disseminated to a key client group.
The 1982 seminar, phase three, was titled, "Preparation for
Competition: Psychological Aspects". In October 1983, the final
phase of the quadrennial series, the theme was "Final Preparation for
Major Games".
In May 1983, the first seminar was staged for coaches of Winter
Olympic sports. The topic was "Final Preparations for Sarajevo".
For the 1984 seminar, the first of the present quadrennial, a decision

was made to offer more topic choices to coaches and to provide
greater opportunity for in-depth study. This was in response to
evaluation data which showed a desire for this approach. During the
present quadrennial series plenary sessions are kept to a minimum
and each delegate is allowed to opt for two major topics. A sample
of the topics offered in the 1985 seminar follows:

Topic 1A Advanced Planning and Periodization (speed and power sports)
Topic 1B Advanced Planning and Periodization (endurance sports)
Topic 2A Impact of Sophrology (Mental Training) in High Performance
Topic 2B Impact de la sophrologie (entraînement mental) dans les
         performances de haut niveau
Topic 3A Coach Effectiveness Training
Topic 3B Motivating Elite Athletes: Communicating to Improve
         Performance
Topic 4A & 4B Strength: Principles, Planning, Testing and Prescription
Topic 5A & 5B Development and Testing of Endurance Training
Topic 6A Olympic Psychological and Practical Preparation Procedures
         for Coaches and Athletes
Topic 6B Skill Refinement and Skill Teaching: A Workshop in Applied
         Biomechanics
Topic 7A Planification et périodisation des programmes d'entraînement
         et de compétition
Topic 7B Control of the Training Process

The CAC Coaching Scholarship and Coaching Apprenticeship programs
provide additional training opportunities to selected recipients.
Coaching scholarships are awarded each year to experienced Canadian
coaches who wish to undertake Master's or doctorate study in sport
sciences at a Canadian university or who wish to work towards Level 4
or 5 certification.

In addition to the regular academic workload, scholarship recipients
are expected to complete a practical coaching internship under the
direction of a tutor coach. Part of the requirement for completion
of the program is the preparation of a coaching article suitable for
use in CAC publications. In this way the coaching information
sharing process is enhanced.

The National Coaching Apprenticeship Program provides grants to
Canadian coaches to study advanced coaching theory and practice under
the tutelage of a master coach. The aim of the program is to develop
more national and international class coaches for Canada who will be
able to prepare Canadian athletes for international level competition.
The relationship of this program to the NSGB's coaching education
program should be well established; the NSGBs may wish to design
their Level 4 and 5 certification programs in conjunction with some
aspects of the apprenticeship program.

Each year a limited number of grants are awarded to selected
apprentice coaches to enable them to study advanced coaching on a
full-time basis under master coaches in their respective sports.
Apprenticeships are awarded for a minimum period of three months to
one year and may be credited towards Level 4/5 accreditation on
approval of the NSGB and the NCCC.

A Coaching apprenticeship includes three areas of concentration:
coaching practice - practical experience in the coaching of high

calibre athletes under the tutelage of the master coach; coaching theory - the study of the theory of training and competition, under the guidance of the master coach; and sport science - the study of physiology, psychology, biomechanics and related sport sciences, usually in a university environment.

The apprentice coach is expected to complete a learning program which is individually tailored to meet his or her needs. The master coach directs the learning program, tutors the apprentice on all aspects of coaching, and provides feedback to the apprentice on his or her coaching techniques. Quarterly reports are submitted by the apprentice and master coaches that reflect the progress being made towards the learning objectives.

Graduates of the apprenticeship program are expected to continue with a career in coaching. Reasonable assurance of a job opportunity in coaching upon completion of the apprenticeship must be provided.

The above examples represent some of the major "informal" means of disseminating information to Canadian coaches. When combined with the National Coaching Certification Program per se it is evident that those coaches who wish to avail themselves of these multivariate offerings are in a strong position to become well-informed and up-to-date.

University sport scientists contribute variously to Canadian sport development via: applied sport research; membership on technical planning committees and sport research committees; coaching certification committees; staffing coaching conferences; articles for CAC and sport specific technical publications; athlete testing and interpretation of test results; staffing training camps; and support service role on national teams.

Section 2.

2.1 The Shift in Emphasis from Levels 1-3 to Higher Level Coaches.
Level 1-3 Certification.
There will be increasing emphasis on maintenance during the next five years, following completion of the three levels by approximately 56 sports. There will be some need for revisions to existing programs as a means of refining and improving the courses and also to account for important new information. There will also be need for developing and implementing upgrading courses which will provide enrichment and motivation for those coaches who do not wish to progress to higher levels. There will be a slight decrease in time, energy and financial support by CAC.

Levels 4-5.
The recently introduced Sport Canada Sport Recognition Policy (1985) addresses the following questions: the definition of "sport" for federal funding purposes; the criteria for acceptance or recognition as a National Sport Organization; the high performance ranking of Olympic and non-Olympic sports and the general significance of those rankings for federal funding purposes; the relative significance of participant and membership bases of NSOs and their significance for federal funding purposes.

It is clear that, as a result of this policy, not all sports will automatically have a five-level coaching program. Several in the lower recognition categories will essentially stop at Level 3.
For those sports eligible to benefit from this level of the program there will be increased emphasis on development and implementation of the top two levels during the next five years. A disproportionate amount of time, energy and finances are required for these highest levels which are intended for the preparation of national and international calibre coaches.
CAC technical consultants will be committed to working closely with the sport committees in the design and implementation of programs and it is expected that they will offer considerable guidance regarding the very important utilization of sport scientists in the creation of content material and the application of this information during coaching courses, and at times when the coach is working with his own athletes at home.

2.2 Development of the "Credit" System as a Means of Integrating "formal" and "informal" Coaching Programs.
A task listing of NCCP curriculum for levels 4 and 5 has been developed to assist sports in the planning, development and implementation of their advanced level certification program.
The content of the coaching tasks has been outlined comprehensively by subject matter experts in the areas of planning, physiology and psychology. The technical area will be the responsibility of the NSGB who could use a variety of presentation options to implement the content:
1. Technical courses, designed by the NSGB
2. Home study assignments, designed by the NSGB
3. Apprenticeship programs, designed by the NSGB
4. Special education projects, designed by the NSGB
5. National Coaches' Seminar, designed by CAC
6. Special seminar series, designed by CAC
7. Coaching visitations to candidates by master coach
Some sports may wish to organize technical courses for a group of candidates while others may wish to utilize the individual approach of an apprenticeship program or a selection of individual modules (1-7) to fulfil the various coaching tasks, i.e. a "credit" system.
The Credit System.
Sixteen tasks have been identified at Level 4 and 17 at Level 5. These tasks could be completed by Level 4/5 candidates as "credits" towards final completion of their Level 4 or 5 certification subject to satisfying the content and evaluation standards of each task. "Crediting" candidates with completed coaching tasks does not preclude NSGBs from designing formal technical courses at Levels 4 and 5. If they choose this option, the course would simply be evaluated for an appropriate number of credits.

Examples of the Level 4 tasks follow:

Planning
1. Plan, conduct and evaluate practice
2. Plan, conduct and evaluate a year-round periodized training program
3. Plan, conduct and evaluate a training camp
4. Plan, conduct and evaluate a competitive tour
5. Plan long-range career plan for athlete
6. Design talent I.D. system
7. Select sport science resource people

Physiological Development
1. Plan, conduct and evaluate physiological training program for elite athletes
2. Evaluate training elements - speed, strength, endurance
3. Plan nutritional requirements

Psychological Development
1. Conduct goal setting
2. Develop strategies for mental preparation
3. Plan, conduct and evaluate psychological training programs

Technical Development
1. Teach advanced technical skills
2. Teach appropriate tactics and strategy
3. Analyze individual and team performance

2.3 Training of High Level Coaches.
The training of high level coaches in Canada has relied on a variety of supplementary courses and experiences in addition to the coach's personal practical background in the absence of a formal educational program for the upper certification levels.
Level 4 and 5 certification levels were expected to have filled this need by now but national sport governing bodies have been slow to develop higher level coaches due in part to fulfilling the developmental needs of the lower three levels.
As an impetus to this need and to assist in the development of core sport science areas for the advanced levels, the initiation of a residential one-year diploma course, in conjunction with the University of Victoria, is planned for September 1986.

National Coaching Institute.
This first "National Coaching Institute" will formalize the advanced course content for six sports who can provide suitable tutor coaches at this site.
The diploma course will consist of a core of sport science content developed and taught by subject matter experts who have had experience in applying the material with elite athletes.
The tutor coach will be responsible for imparting the technical content as developed by the national sport governing body both in formal lectures/tutorials and in practice with the athletes and teams on site at the university.
Future plans for expansion of the program after this initial "pilot" year will consider additional sports and institutes in other locations
By moving towards the concept of full-time courses of study for recognized qualifications as pre-requisites for employment as elite coaches, Canada is attempting to implement the ingredients of a

profession in coaching.

2.4 Development, Implementation and Evaluation of the Practical Component of the Coaching Model.
The description of the apprentice-master coach relationship in the Apprenticeship Program and the Diploma course of the National Coaching Institute represent the best practical experience and learning environment for the practical component of coaching.
The practical component in the Canadian model has been one of practical coaching experience at the lower two levels with coaches attempting to impart the information gleaned from their recent technical courses.
Technical courses have been designed to teach how to coach not just what to coach; but because of the limited weekend time requirement of Levels 1-3, little coaching practice or assessment is included until Level 3.
National sport governing bodies have been required to include self-assessment techniques and completion of training diaries at Levels 1 and 2 and are required to conduct practical assessments at Level 3 prior to full certification.
This practical evaluation has varied from the traditional approach of paper and pencil assessments on coaching interactions to the video-taping of candidates for private analysis at the end of the day.
A computer-assisted analysis program is currently being developed for use in the analysis of coaching effectiveness.
The "Process of Coaching" has been researched by "The Centre for Performance Analysis" at the University of British Columbia utilizing the video analysis of coaching interactions with the Canadian women's basketball team. This research project will result in a more objective assessment process in the practical component for application to the training of coaches particularly when integrated with the research on performance analysis.

Section 3.

3.1 Short and longer term tasks for the future include ongoing evaluation and long-term planning.
A major evaluation of the program is being undertaken. The National Coaching Certification Council has appointed a committee to manage this. A Toronto-based consulting firm are evaluating the program based on its goals and mandate. The basic task is to determine if the NCCP is producing the intended results. The work of this group will be complete by June 30, 1986. This major task requires the co-operation of all parties comprising the NCCC.
A significant source of data for this evaluation will be provided by a study by M. Robillard, in which the influence of NCCP courses on coaching behaviour and the feelings of coaches about the NCCP were assessed by questionnaire technique. A random sample of 1,500 coaches were surveyed in this comprehensive study and preliminary analysis of data indicates very positive response to the program and the positive influence of both theory and technical courses on coaching behaviour.
A committee of six active Level 1-3 course conductors are working on

the updating and revision of theory course content and on the delivery of the program. The theory program was previously revised in 1980. This group are working concurrently with a committee which is establishing the basic sports science modules for Levels 4 and 5. Clearly this total task requires excellent co-ordination and collaboration since information emanating from the work of each group is interdependent. The work is planned for completion in April 1987 with course conductors trained and ready to teach the revised courses in the early winter of that year.

While the work described above is primarily linked with coaching certification, preliminary work is underway in relation to clearly defining a long-term plan for coaching development in Canada. There are many agencies involved in various aspects of coaching and the time is overdue for improvement of co-ordination and the clarification of roles. The Coaching Association of Canada has a major responsibility in this venture. The Coaching Development in Canada matrix, discussed later, provides some clarification of the major factors which must be considered if optimum effectiveness is to be achieved during the next decade.

3.2 It is important to utilize the information dissemination, the information exchange and the participant involvement potential of the hardware and software being developed by the rapid growth of the high technology industry. Canada enjoys a prominent position in the communications area and we must capitalize upon this fact and use the technology to better prepare our coaches by providing them with the best information to meet their needs. Communications technology is almost all electronics and software and makes for a natural fit with Canadian expertise.

Several futurists have predicted that communications and personal services could double in a relatively few years. People-related jobs show great growth promise and training itself, since everyone will need constant upgrading of skills, will be a major growth area. These predictions have significant implications for our programs of the future. In this regard, too, there will be need to examine new approaches with the consumer's needs uppermost. Many, perhaps most, of these approaches will need to be interactive and all will need to be entertaining or at least psychologically arousing or they will not be used. It is entirely feasible that future "manuals" will move out of paper and into content and software, much of which can be delivered electronically.

3.3 As Certification reaches a stage of development where most sport bodies have at least three levels of coaching programs, and several have five levels, there will be increased emphasis upon the provision of supplementary information to Level 1-3 coaches through existing CAC publications; through the offering of half-day refresher or enrichment courses; and by development of materials suitable for dissemination via communication media exemplified by Telidon.

For national and international level coaches, professional development opportunities will be offered via the Coaching Scholarship, Coaching Apprenticeship, Special Education, and coach/athlete high performance assistance programs. A collective opportunity for personal enrichment

and information exchange with peers is provided by the annual
National Coaches' Seminar. Coaching-related information is
desseminated regularly through S.P.O.R.T.S. and Coaching Review.
This information which has been presented to this point has focussed
on meeting the needs of the coach. However, the coach is only one
member of the coach/athlete tandem, the most significant pairing in
the sport performance equation. If we can provide the athlete with
information on various topics which will enhance self-development,
then the combination of better-informed athletes, and competent
coaches should enhance the total sport experience. Preliminary work
is underway which should lead to the development and implementation
of athlete self-development programs which can be offered through the
vehicle of the NCCP or which may be disseminated through other
channels.

3.4 Certification Incentives.
The incentive for pursuing certification in coaching has been, to
date, an intrinsic rather than an extrinsic process.
Few attempts have been made by government or sports to insist on
standards of certification for employment or coaching appointments.
However, some sports have included references to coaching qualifications in their coaching advertisements and in the Canada Games, a
quadrennial competition, the provincial governments have applied
various pre-requisites, from Levels 1-3, for their provincial coaches.
The motivation of individuals in various national sport governing
bodies varies from, for example, the soccer coach who knows that a
Level 4 qualification will be the minimum standard required of
provincial team coaches and an opportunity to be selected to a Level
5 training program, to the swimming coach who, without a formal
certification level, is already in a well-paid professional club
position.
This disparity in standards of qualification required is also obvious
at the international level and until such times that the Canadian
government chooses to impose a pre-requisite certification level, a
true incentive for certification will not be in place.
The financial support area has received inadequate attention in the
past. Such support can take many forms, including salary or honor-
arium, the payment of expenses, or the provision of other benefits.
Work is beginning regarding the development of rewards and incentives
for certified coaches but there will be need for sensitive handling
of this issue before certification becomes a common requirement for
coaches.

3.5 The Profession of Coaching.
Statements which follow result from some liberal borrowing from
John Lyle's paradigm paper "Coach Education: Preparation for a
Profession", July 1985.

We are presently some considerable distance from a coaching profession
in Canada. One method of estimating professional development is to
examine attributes of an existing occupational grouping (coaches).
Entry requirements as exemplified by educational demands, length of
training, type of training, qualifications; recognition of the

uniqueness and exclusivity of the individual's skills; the self-
regulation of a code of conduct with appropriate discipline
mechanisms, are some indicators of professional status.
Canadian coaching does not measure up to requirements such as those
described. Training is varied, educational requirements are
unspecified, courses are of minimum duration and unqualified persons
can become recognized as high level coaches.
The status of coaches will continue to be restricted until such time
as better entrance and exit controls are exercised. This is
particularly true at the elite level. There is no significant
organization of coaches which permits self-regulation of conduct.
Minimal time is spent by coaches in the discussion of ethics and
professional practice.
There can be little doubt that the general absence of a systematic
career structure has militated against major progress towards the
establishment of a profession. Progress will continue to be limited
until career opportunities in coaching are incorporated into a
clearly identifiable progressive system.
While it may be some time before sports coaching becomes an
established profession, the work of sports coaches can be professionalized and the occupation established and valued providing some
standards are met and the training requirements are rigorous enough
to earn respect. It is evident that some regulation will be required
to achieve this, and this requires sufficient conviction by potential
regulators to introduce these requirements. It is important that
coaches who aspire to professionalization recognize the need for this
and lend their support.
Regulation which will affect NSGB appointees, representative coaches
and provincial coaches, will influence control and status and will be
closely related to potential career patterns.
The demand for coach education will also be influenced as a result.
Coaching education is the essential basis from which the profession of
coaching may eventually develop. Consequently the development of an
extensive coaching education program is the first essential step.
In the last 12 years, this has been the number one priority. The task
is not yet complete. Without this, talk of a profession of coaching
is meaningless.

SUMMARY AND CONCLUSIONS

The preceding information attempts to provide some background on the
Canadian Coaching Program. The Coaching Development in Canada matrix
provides a good overview of the major areas of the program and provides an excellent snapshot. Views may vary about how many of the
areas are well developed at this time. However, it is safe to state
that, at present, every item is receiving attention though not all
are receiving the support they deserve. The aim is to attend to all
items, optimally.

Let it be stated that there has been no intent, in presenting information on selected aspects of the Canadian Coaching Program, to suggest
that it is a panacea or, "the answer to a coach's prayer". The
preparation of coaches requires more than well-developed, well-

presented coaching courses; more than the provision of good-quality, well-varied, supplementary coaching information; more than simply going out and coaching athletes, no matter how enthusiastic and willing the coach may be.

There are no easy formulas for coaching success and it is not possible to say how coaches should approach their athletes and how they should not. A coach has to be a chameleon, being at times a trainer, a philosopher, a friend, a teacher and much more. Knowledge and understanding of physiological, psychological and mechanical principles is no guarantee of coaching excellence, but ignorance of these important principles is a guarantee of at least partial failure. However, if coaches are well-informed on the many topics related to effective coaching, they have a better chance of being successful coaches than if they are ill-informed.

What we must constantly keep in mind is this rather basic point: the cutting edge in the improvement of performance is practical coaching. Ideally, this is most effective when, at some optimal frequency, athlete, knowledgeable coach, and adequate facility, are brought together in an environment which provides the climate of support required for this to flourish.

Primarily and commonly, this is provided by the club at town, university, school, or corporate level, although it may exist through such entities as specialist squads, regional or national centres or training camps, where the highly specialized demands of today's top performers must be met.

The Canadian Coaching Program attempts to ensure that functioning coaches have the necessary fundamental knowledge and skill that are pre-requisites to their coaching effectiveness and coaching effectiveness has to do with athlete performance.

What of the 1990's? Plato perhaps provided a good answer to this question when he said: "What is honoured in the country will be cultivated there."

References

Rea, W.H. (1969) Task Force on Sports for Canadians. Queen's Printers, Ottawa, Ontario.

Coaching Association of Canada (1979) Curriculum Design Series. Ottawa, Ontario.

Sport Canada (1985) Contributions Program 1986-1987, pp 6-7.

Lyle, J. (1985) Coach Education: Preparation for a Profession. Glasgow.

Coaching Association of Canada (1986) Programs Services & Policies. Ottawa, Ontario.

COACHING DEVELOPMENT IN CANADA

	DEVELOPMENTAL LEVEL COACHING objective: development of the athlete				HIGH PERFORMANCE COACHING objective: peak performance	
	Level 1	Level 2	Level 3	U P G R A D I N G	Level 4	Level 5
EDUCATION • development • implementation • promotion	• theory • technical • practical supplementary programs • provincial seminar, local coaching seminars, Coaching Review	• theory • technical • practical	• theory • technical • practical		• credit system: technical courses, seminar assignments, "mini apprenticeships" • National Coaching Institute(pilot) • National Coaches Seminar/ COA Seminars supplementary programs • Special Education Projects, S.P.O.R.T.S. periodical	
FINANCIAL SUPPORT • payment (salary&honorarium) • expenses • benefits	• employment of provincial, regional center and club coaches • club support for certified coaches • support for coaches to attend Canada Games, training camps, provincial competitions • rewards/incentives for certified coaches				• employment of national and training centre coaching staffs • club excellence and card athlete coaching support • rewards/incentives	
ENVIRONMENT • appropriate training and competition • rules and equipment • supportive people	• sport development models: growth and development principles: training and competition appropriate to developmental needs revisions in rules and equipment • education of parents, athletes,club, league and s.g.b. volunteers				• relationships between coaches and volunteers • responsibilities and authority of national coaches	

STATE OF THE ART

SUE CAMPBELL
The National Coaching Foundation

Abstract
The National Coaching Foundation was established by the Sports
Council in 1983 with the support of all other major bodies in
British Sport. It is based in Leeds and there is a staff of 8
people employed under Miss Sue Campbell, the Director. It is not an
Institute of Sport in its own right; instead the Foundation is
establishing a network of institutions to operate its programmes
throughout the United Kingdom. The National Coaching Foundation was
formed to develop a comprehensive coach education programme
throughout the United Kingdom. Its brief was to provide non-sports
specific information at a number of levels to cater for all coaches
from the beginner to the top level national coach.
Key words: National Coaching Foundation, Coach education, Non-sports
specific, Levels.

1. Introduction

Whilst recognising the excellent work that had been done by many
overseas countries, the National Coaching Foundation staff were
aware that they could not simply 'adopt' an established coach
education scheme from elsewhere. The United Kingdom has a complex
sports structure and the Foundation's programmes had to be built
around the existing framework. The National Coaching Foundation
staff spent many of the early days exploring the existing situation
in Britain. The following facts emerged:-

(a) The vast majority of coaches in Britain work in a voluntary
capacity in sport and therefore any services provided by the
National Coaching Foundation would have to be easily accessible,
inexpensive, and not too time consuming.
(b) Many coaches had received no formal education for many years
and therefore material would have to be presented in an everyday
language - avoiding 'threatening' jargon wherever possible.
(c) The National Governing Bodies of Sport had each evolved
their own training programmes for coaches. These varied enormously
from the simple to the highly sophisticated. The Foundation's
services would therefore have to cater for all needs, complementing

6 1

and supplementing existing programmes.

(d)   The autonomy of the National Governing Bodies is a vital part of British sport and this could not be threatened by the imposition of a new overall 'controlling' body.

(e)   National Governing Bodies have limited resources (human and financial) to spend on the development of coach education courses and therefore the National Coaching Foundation had to work in partnership with them but rely on its own sources of funding for the development of its services.

(f)   The general provision for coach education in Britain was limited and spasmodic. There were one or two initiatives, the most notable of which were the Northern Ireland Institute of Coaching and the Scottish Pilot Project. The Northern Ireland Institute of Coaching was established in 1980 by the Northern Ireland Council of Physical Recreation, Ulster Polytechnic and the Sports Council for Northern Ireland. It was the first venture of its kind in the United Kingdom and is still operating successfully. The object of the Northern Ireland Institute of Coaching is to develop and advance the level of instruction and coaching of sport and physical recreation in Northern Ireland. The Institute depends for its basic funding on The Sports Council for Northern Ireland, and Ulster Polytechnic. This funding is supplemented by fees and sponsorship. A seconded member of the Sports Council's staff acts as Organising Secretary on a part-time basis and the Institute employs its own secretarial support. Since its inception the Institute has provided a wide range of courses, workshops and conferences suited to the needs of sports' coaches in the province. The Annual Conference has brought together groups of distinguished coaches, administrators and sports' scientists from Europe and North America and is recognised for its valuable contribution to the development of sports coaching. The National Coaching Foundation has fully recognised the work of the Institute and a joint agreement has been reached to ensure the full utilisation of resources in the future. The second major initiative which was underway was the Scottish Pilot Project on the Training of Coaches. In 1981 the Sports Development Committee of the Scottish Sports Council approved the establishment of a pilot project aimed at examining in practice the concept of a co-ordinated, coherent approach to coach education. Over the last few years the pilot project has focused its attention on producing a learning system to help sports coaches understand the common theoretical components which underlie performance. Those working on the project took the view that it was important to take learning to the coaches by developing distance learning materials. These are referred to later in more detail. The National Coaching Foundation has established an excellent working relationship with the project and will be liaising closely with the newly formed Scottish Sports Council Consultative Group on Coaching to ensure the best use of all available resources in Scotland.

2. Structure of the Foundation

2.1 Objectives
Set against this backcloth, the National Coaching Foundation was born and its objectives clearly established:-

(a)   The promotion of the education, instruction and training at national and local levels of honorary and professional coaches and other interested persons in performance-related knowledge applied to all kinds of sport and physical recreation.
(b)   The promotion and dissemination of knowledge in pursuit of the above objective.

In the furtherance of these objectives, the Foundation as directed and approved by its Management Committee shall:-

(a)   assist in the planning and provision of coach education programmes as required and requested by the Governing Bodies of Sport,
(b)   assist in the co-ordination and standardisation of the Sports Councils' coach development courses,
(c)   facilitate and share in the collation, evaluation and dissemination, in written and audio-visual forms, of research and other material from this and other countries of value to coaches,
(d)   organise courses and conferences,
(e)   co-operate with individuals and institutions in order to provide access to resources for coaches,
(f)   assist as required in identifying and progressing research projects of value to coaches, in close co-operation with the Sports Council and other relevant agencies,
(g)   provide an advisory service as required,
(h)   investigate possible sources of additional funding for the fulfilment of the above objectives.

The Foundation has the support of the Sports Council, the Central Council of Physical Recreation, the British Association of National Coaches, the Department of Education and Science, The British Olympic Association, the British Association of Sports Sciences and Sports Medicine, and Institutes of Higher Education.

2.2 The Management Committee
The Management Committee under the chairmanship of Mrs Judith Mackay (The Sports Council) is composed of representatives from the following organisations:-

Central Council of Physical Recreation (CCPR)
British Association of National Coaches (BANC)
The Sports Council
British Olympic Association (BOA)
Sports Sciences
Sports Medicine
The Host Institution (Leeds Polytechnic)

There are observers from the Department of Education and Science, Institutes of Higher Education and the Sports Council present at Management meetings. The work of the committee is to oversee the affairs of the Foundation as set out in the objectives and be responsible for budgets and programmes of work to fulfil those objectives.

The Management Committee has 3 sub-committees:-

(a) Technical Sub-Committee
(b) Research Sub-Committee
(c) Finance and Resources Sub-Committee

Each has its own specific functions.

2.3 Technical Sub-Committee
The Sub-Committee is responsible to the NCF Management Committee for giving consideration to and making recommendations for:-

(a) The NCF coach development services
(b) The implementation of those services
(c) The budget estimates to enable the Foundation's services to be financed.

Membership
Chairman appointed from the British Association of National Coaches representatives on the Management Committee
Vice-Chairman appointed from the British Association of National Coaches representatives on the Management Committee
Two members with coaching expertise nominated by BANC
Three members with expertise in performance-related fields nominated by the NCF Director
Ex-Officio: Chairman NCF; NCF Director (non-voting member)
Invited Observer: Member of Sports Council Development Unit

The composition and membership is reviewed every 2 years by the NCF Management Committee. Additionally, the Sub-Committee may recommend to the Management Committee individuals for co-option for specified periods.

2.4 Research Sub-Committee
The Sub-Committee is responsible to the NCF Management Committee for:-

(a) The identification of research projects relevant to sports coaches, in association with National Governing Bodies and Sports Organisations where appropriate.
(b) Recommending the commissioning and grant aiding of Sports Coaching research projects.
(c) Submitting budget proposals to the Finance and Resources Sub-Committee.
(d) Liaising with the Sports Council's Research Unit and other research groups and organisations in the United Kingdom and overseas.

(e)   Ensuring the dissemination of relevant research findings.

Membership
Chairman
One nominee from BANC
One nominee from the Network Institutes
Two members of NCF Management Committee
Ex-Officio: Chairman NCF; NCF Director (non-voting member)
Invited Observer: Member of Sports Council's Research Unit

The composition and membership is reviewed every 2 years by the NCF Management Committee. Additionally, the Sub-Committee may recommend to the Management Committee individuals for co-option for a specified period.

2.5 Finance and Resources Sub-Committee
The Committee is responsible to the NCF Management Committee for:-

(a)   Providing a means whereby persons or organisations may have the opportunity of making financial and other contributions to the Foundation, and receiving such donations.
(b)   Considering the viability of various commercial ventures.
(c)   Investing those NCF funds which are not immediately required.
(d)   Receiving reports on the accounts and making recommendations relating to the Foundation's budgets to the Management Committee.
(e)   Making recommendations on personnel and staffing matters to the Management Committee.
(f)   Receiving and considering requests from other NCF Sub-Committees and various individuals and organisations who require NCF financial support and recommending appropriate action to the Management Committee.
(g)   Dealing with further items referred to it by the Management Committee.

Membership
Chairman
Chairman or Vice-Chairman, Technical Sub-Committee
Chairman or Vice-Chairman, Research Sub-Committee
Ex-Officio: Chairman NCF; NCF Director (non-voting member)
Invited Observer: From Sports Council Finance/Personnel Units as required.

The composition and membership will be reviewed every 2 years by the NCF Management Committee. Additionally, the Sub-Committee may recommend to the Management Committee individuals for co-option for specified periods.

3. Funding

The Sports Council is at present financing the National Coaching Foundation. The Foundation is also actively seeking other financial assistance to support its work and to ensure its future independence. Funding from the Sports Council has been as follows:-

	1983/84	1984/85	1985/86	1986/87
National Coaching Foundation	£50,000	£129,600	£164,000	£322,000

Income from other sources includes sponsorship and sales of products and services. We anticipate a considerable upturn in both these figures over the next few years.

4. Coach Development Services

4.1 Aim
To provide opportunities for the development of knowledge and skills relevant to coaching, performance and participation at all levels.

4.2 Approach
To provide units of study at various levels which National Governing Bodies of sport, coaches and other interested persons may select, thereby complementing and supplementing technical knowledge provided by and through the National Governing Bodies.

4.3 Levels of Provision
The National Coaching Foundation will provide a linked series of study units structured in broad bands of performance-related knowledge. National Governing Bodies, coaches and other interested persons will select their own progression as need dictates.

4.4 Level 1 - Introductory Study Packs
Many 'new' coaches are concerned with the mastery of the skill techniques of their activity and the method presentation. Introductory study packs (produced in 1985) are available to introduce coaches to all aspects of performance-related knowledge. These packs are simple, diagrammatic and have clear practical applications.

(a) The Coach in Action   - Geof Gleeson with the assistance of Clive Bond
(b) The Body in Action   - Rex Hazeldine/John Cadman
(c) Safety and Injury   - Dr J Aldridge/Norman Pilgrim
(d) Mind over Matter   - Dr J Fazey/Dr L Hardy
(e) Improving Techniques   - Dr A Lees/John Shedden
(f) Planning and Practice   - Rod Thorpe

These packs are being promoted through the Governing Bodies of Sport, the Sports Councils and the National Coaching Foundation itself. Each pack is accompanied by a 20-minutes VHS video tape. The book and video tape will be linked by a manual which allows an individual coach to work his own way through the material or assists a tutor coach to conduct a course for beginner coaches in any of the 6 areas.

4.5 Level 2 - Courses for Coaches

When a coach has been operating for a period of time, (s)he is more at ease with the skill techniques and methods of group control etc. It is at this stage that the coach is wanting to move away from being nothing more than a 'mimic', i.e. copying practices/techniques of others. Without a foundation of performance-related knowledge this is difficult.

(a) Units of Study : It was agreed that the units would come from the same 6 major areas of study as the introductory packs. Each unit is 4 hours of contact time with tutors and 2 hours of personal study. The teams of 'experts' identified all units of study within the 6 major strands which they felt would be relevant and useful to coaches. All core units are available to coaches at a network of institutions across the United Kingdom. The core unit courses for 1986 are:-

1. Structure of the Body. The bone and muscle structure of the body, including joints, their structure and movement. Selected exercises are analysed, and posture and control of movement is studied.

2. Prevention and Rehabilitation of Injury. The course includes study of the nature and causes of sports injuries; prevention methods, including hygiene and diet; immediate treatment; and rehabilitation after injury.

3. Developing Endurance. This course presents methods of endurance training in relation to the body's basic energy systems. Heart, lung and muscle endurance are related to conditioning methods, including circuit training and sport-specific training. Simple laboratory and sports tests are used to illustrate how changes in endurance can be monitored.

4. Nutrition and Sports Performance. An introduction to nutrition, the different types of food (fats, proteins, carbohydrates etc); dietary factors and their effect on performance; energy balance and the assessment of nutritional requirements; "ergogenic" aids.

5. Development of Strength and Speed. Muscle action; strength training principles; safety requirements; strength exercises; the planning of strength testing and training programmes. Speed; sprint training; speed drills; reaction time and mobilization.

6. Introduction to Sports Mechanics. This course is designed to provide the coach with an understanding of the basic mechanical principles underlying sports techniques.

7. Use of Video in Coaching. Video can help the coach observe what is really happening during performance. This course shows how to use video for accurate measurement and analysis of movement, and how to apply the results to training.

8. How Skills are Learned. How people learn skills: in particular, how sportspeople acquire the skills fundamental to their sport. Identifying goals, designing effective practices and planning progress.

9. **Factors Affecting Performance.** Identifying the specific needs to improve skills; correcting errors; helping the performer to cope without side influences; concentration; relaxation; developing a mental image. How to guide the performer to his ideal performing style.

10. **Mental Preparation for Competition.** This course covers how to plan the training for competition, and what steps need to be taken after the competition. Goal-setting in relation to actual achievement; implications for future training.

11. **How to Plan your Programme.** How to apply the knowledge gained from other courses to the planning of short-term (one season) and long-term (e.g. 4-year Olympic cycle) training programmes. Monitoring progress in the closed season and the competition season. Realistic schedules taking account of different sportspeople's lifestyles, time commitment etc.

12. **Effective Coaching.** This course looks at the various styles of leadership and examines the role of the coach. It also compares different methods of presenting and communicating information.

(b) The Network of Institutions has been decided following consultations with Colleges, Polytechnics and Universities. Those institutions involved in the NCF network for 1986 are:-

England: Bedford College of Higher Education; Brighton Polytechnic; Bulmershe College of Higher Education; Crewe + Alsager College of Higher Education; Lancaster Polytechnic*; Leeds Polytechnic; Liverpool Polytechnic; Newcastle upon Tyne Polytechnic; North Staffordshire Polytechnic; Salford College of Technology; Sheffield Polytechnic; Teeside Polytechnic; University of Bath; University of Birmingham; University of Cambridge; University of East Anglia; University of Essex; University of Exeter; University of Kent; University of Lancaster*; University of Oxford*; University of Southampton*; University of Technology, Loughborough; University of Warwick; West London Institute of Higher Education (Venues marked * offer a limited number of courses).

Wales: North East Wales Institute of Higher Education, Deeside; South Glamorgan Institute of Higher Education, Cardiff; University College of North Wales, Bangor; University of Wales, Swansea.

Scotland: Aberdeen College of Education; Dunfermline College of Physical Education, Edinburgh; Scottish School of Physical Education, Jordanhill College, Glasgow.

The National Coaching Foundation have provided a student resource pack to support each course. These packs were originally written by one person nominated by the technical committee. Following the courses in 1985 a complete review was undertaken with all tutors who had taught on the courses. As a result, revised student packs and tutors packs have been prepared for 1986. It has been agreed that the National Coaching Foundation will not be setting up its own formal assessment of students but that this will be done through National Governing Body examinations. It is felt that the purpose of the courses is to help people become better coaches in their own activity, not sports science experts.

It has been necessary to build in an effective monitoring process to evaluate the packages and courses accurately. This is being done by a research assistant based at Loughborough University.

Many National Governing Bodies are 'locking' the courses into their own awards so that they become an integral part of their own schemes.

4.6 Level 3 — Supplementary Courses

Once a coach is operating at this level, (s)he usually has a clearer understanding of coaching techniques and many aspects of performance-related knowledge. It has been agreed that these courses will be 20 hours in length and resource materials are being developed in consultation with the relevant experts and organisations. Courses will be coach-centred, identifying particular coaching responsibilities and problems and providing information to assist with their problem solving. The course content will include a considerable amount of practical work including the use of laboratories and specialised equipment. The initial 8 courses will be:-

Communication Skills
Stress Control Techniques
Mechanics of Sport
How to find out more
Working with Teams
Peak Performance
Competitive Sport and Young Children
Sports Injuries Prevention and Primary Care

Initially a series of pilot projects will be run in November 1986 and refined before being included in the full national programme in 1987.

Coaches attending these courses will have to be endorsed by their own governing body of sport.

4.7 Distance Learning Materials

Alongside the various units of study at Levels 2 and 3 being provided by the Foundation, the Scottish Sports Council audiotapes mentioned earlier cover many of the same topics thus providing coaches with excellent additional support.

Each module of study consists of an audio cassette tape and workbook. The material has been designed to be as practical as possible and throughout the modules great care has been taken to relate theory to practice. The tapes have been produced with the assistance of the Scottish Council for Educational Technology whose expertise in open learning has been invaluable. To date the following series are available:-

Psychological Preparation for Competition. Dr R Cox, Lecturer,

Dunfermline College of Physical Education (10 tapes)
The Coach. John Lyle, Lecturer, Dunfermline College of Physical Education (6 tapes)
Goal Setting. Nanette Mutrie, Assistant Director of Physical Education and Recreation, University of Glasgow (2 tapes)
Communication Skills and Coaching Styles. Jim Wylie, Lecturer, Dunfermline College of Physical Education (13 tapes)
Working with Teams and Groups. Dr Malcolm Reid, Assistant Director of Physical Education, University of Aberdeen, and Peter Clarke, Lecturer, Scottish School of Physical Education (2 tapes)
Safety and Injury. Greg McLatchie, Consultant Surgeon, Hartlepool General Hospital and First Medical Officer of the Martial Arts Commission, and Donald Macleod, Consultant Surgeon, Bangour General Hospital and Honorary Surgeon to the Scottish Rugby Union.
The Body and How it Works. Dr Craig Sharp, Co-Director, Human Motor Performance Laboratory, University of Birmingham.
Training the Body. Andrew Maile, Lecturer, Scottish School of Physical Education.
Testing of Fitness. Andrew Maile. Available September 1986.
Nutrition and Sports Performance. Dr Myra Nimmo, Queen's College, Glasgow.
Acquiring Skills. Dr Bob Sharp, Lecturer, Scottish School of Physical Education.
Planning your Training. Available November 1986.
The Use of Video in Coaching. John Lyle and the Television Unit of Dunfermline College of Physical Education (Modules on this subject will include video tapes). To be produced in association with the National Coaching Foundation. Available December 1986.

4.8 Level 4 - Special Provision for Top Level Coaches
The National Coaching Foundation is working closely with the British Association of National Coaches throughout the programme but is particularly closely linked with National Coaches at this level. The National Coaching Foundation assists BANC to run national in-service courses to 'refresh', 'up-date' and 're-vitalise' coaches according to their needs. The Foundation also offers 2 grant programmes at this level.

(a) Special Provision Grants for Experienced Coaches. The National Coaching Foundation considers applications from experienced coaches for grants under a number of categories, for example:-

To undertake period of investigation and study in specific areas related to coaching.
To obtain access to facilities and expertise to assist with specific coaching problems.
To establish links with coaching-related organisations overseas for the exchange of knowledge and expertise.
Other approved projects which the National Coaching Foundation deems of value to coaching.

The transmission of the information obtained to other United Kingdom

70

coaches is an important component of this programme.

Special provision grants for experienced coaches: 1984, 1 allocation, £500; 1985, 17 allocations, £7,000.

(b) Research Grants. The research activities of the National Coaching Foundation can be currently categorised as follows:-

1. Supported and Joint Research. Research projects may be proposed which benefit coaching in general, or a sport in particular. Under such circumstances this research may be supported in whole or in part by the National Coaching Foundation, or a joint sponsoring venture may be undertaken with other research funding bodies.

2. Commissioned Research. The National Coaching Foundation may commission research into specified areas. The main requirement of this research will be the generation of applied knowledge specifically related to coaching. In the first instance, commission research projects will be aimed at supporting the coach development programme of the National Coaching Foundation.

3. Co-ordination of Student Research. Undergraduate or postgraduate sport-related research projects essentially provide an academic training in applying research techniques to sport. The National Coaching Foundation will encourage such students to work in areas of value to coaches by making known coaches' needs, collating research ideas, and making these available to institutions undertaking research projects in the United Kingdom. This will be done in the first place through the network institutions.

4. Research by Coaches. The National Coaching Foundation will assist experienced coaches to undertake investigations which will aid them in solving particular coaching problems. The National Coaching Foundation will liaise with the appropriate National Governing Body of Sport.

The National Coaching Foundation will consider applications for research projects in categories 1 and 4 above. Possible research areas include:-

    training methodologies and monitoring of training
    training and competition environments
    motor learning and skill development in high-performance athletes
    competition strategy and tactics
    programme planning for high-performance athletes
    social aspects of high-performance sport
    coaching theories
    comparative high-performance sport systems
    sport safety
    sport psychology, sport physiology and sport biomechanics.

All research must be designed to provide information which can be readily applied. The transmission of research results to practitioners is an important component of this programme.

To date 12 projects have been assisted under the Joint/Supported

Research Programme:- 1984, 8 allocations, £15,100; 1985, 10 allocations, £18,000.

5. Information Services

The Information Service of the National Coaching Foundation is available to a large and disparate audience of coaches, teachers and researchers in all aspects of sport at a variety of levels.
Information Service key functions:-

To provide a co-ordinating role for information on all aspects of coaching
To systematically process all relevant information
To evaluate, adapt and "package" information according to the needs of the particular user group ("bridge the gap" between researchers and coaches)
To disseminate information by a variety of means.

Potential Services

publications in the form of resource packs/study packs
subscription service
in-house databases
on-line information retrieval from NCF databases, e.g. bibliographical information
on-line search service for external databases
current awareness bulletin - on-line and published copy
audio-visual productions

Some of these services are being viewed as long term objectives. A number of projects have already begun:-

(a) "Coaching Focus". "Coaching Focus" was launched in April 1985 as a subscription service for coaches. The first issue discussed the topic of 'Drugs in Sport'. Sponsorship from NatWest Bank enabled 10,000 copies of the first issue to be printed, each with an insert giving details of how to subscribe. A bibliography has been prepared to support this issue. "Coaching Focus" issue no. 1 has been included in the NCF Information Pack and additional copies have been sent to the following:-

National Governing Bodies of Sport - Directors of Coaching
Regional Governing Bodies of Sport
150 journals, magazines and Press contacts
Institutes running NCF Courses for Coaches programme
Sports Council's Drug Abuse Advisory Group and Drugs and Schoolchildren Working Party members.

Copies have been circulated to members of the following organisations:-
British Association of National Coaches

The second issue of "Coaching Focus" was published in October and discusses the topic of "Competitive Sport and Young Children".

To date, 1,000 coaches and organisations have registered as subscribers. Governing Bodies of Sport have been offered a discount bulk subscription for members of their Coaching Associations.

(b) Enquiry Service. The NCF responds to requests for information received by letter, telephone or personal visit. Requests may be of a general nature, i.e. for information on the work of the NCF; or may require some element of information retrieval and preparation where the enquiry requires more detailed assistance.

(c) Computer/Library Software. A systems analysis and design is underway to enable the NCF to build up specialist databases of information. This will include information on research projects; specialists/experts available for consultation; and bibliographical records.

(d) On-Line Services. SPORT database: The NCF is a registered user of the SPORT database provided by the Coaching Association of Canada. A number of on-line searches have been conducted. The service is not yet being used to full potential because of the relatively high costs involved. PRESTEL: Information on the NCF is now available on British Telecom's Prestel service. Details of NCF publications, services and courses are given on 'pages' provided by the Sports Council. A response frame system has been set up whereby users can order copies of NCF brochures etc using the Prestel system. The NCF has registered as a Prestel MAILBOX USER, which is an electronic mail system.

6. Problems Encountered

Some of the major problems we have encountered in implementing a Coach Education Programme are:-

(a) Overcoming entrenched attitudes and prejudices of administrators and coaches.

(b) Persuading coaches that they do need an 'education' programme. Many have coached for years with no formal qualifications and they see no need to undertake any 'new' training.

(c) Funding required to mount coach education programmes is considerable. Distance learning modules for example require substantial investment.

(d) Language — much of the information required for coaches lies in the areas of sports science. Unfortunately, the material is often couched in a particular 'jargon' which is not recognisable to the average coach! Material has to be presented simply. One way of overcoming some of these problems is to provide good visual aids.

(e) Tutors — it is vital to the success of any scheme that the right kind of leadership is developed. Tutors to coach coaches need special training and the right resource materials to support their work in the field.

(f) Getting the right balance - it is particularly important to help coaches recognise that there is a need to balance the theory and practice of coaching. There is no substitute for working under and alongside experienced coaches in the practical area. Theory provides a coach with the tools but it is only by learning the craftsmanship needed to use these tools that a coach will become successful. Good coaches never stop learning and are always willing to share ideas with others.

7. Future Plans

Our future plans obviously centre around the continued expansion of our coach development services. We will be working hard to encourage and assist National Governing Bodies of Sport to 'lock' our modules into their programmes.

One major development on the horizon for the Foundation is the move towards formalising the working relationship with the Institutions of Higher Education. The present ad hoc arrangement of centres was seen as an interim measure and it was agreed that a permanent network was required to implement the National Coaching Foundation programmes. The network will have a crucial part to play in the development of coach education. It will assist with:-

(a) Development of coach education programmes - courses, individual tutorials, projects
(b) Development of resource bases for coaches - videos, articles, books
(c) Development of information services for coaches
(d) Development of applied research programmes
(e) Development of provision for top level, experienced coaches - seminars, conferences.

The National Coaching Foundation headquarters will form the nucleus of the network and be responsible for policy, finance and administration of the network. NCF National Coaching Centres will be established in each region of England and in Wales, Northern Ireland and Scotland to co-ordinate the NCF programme within its region/country. Further NCF Regional Coaching Centres will be selected in each region to complement and supplement the services to coaches. The NCF network will build on plant and expertise which already exists rather than attempt to create new institutions.

8. Conclusions

The Foundation has made a good start largely thanks to the enormous assistance we have been given by the Sports Council, the British Association of National Coaches and the Institutes of Higher Education. There is still much to be done to consolidate the various programmes and to assist the National Governing Bodies of

Sport take full advantage of our services. We know there are many difficulties ahead but we are confident that with the support of the coaches we will achieve our objectives.

There is no doubt that sport and leisure will have an ever increasing part to play in our lives in the future. Many changes are occurring in society which require us to re-examine the meaning of words like 'work', 'leisure', 'physical education' and 'sport'. We must remain flexible in our planning and ensure that we make whatever adaptations are necessary to accommodate new trends.

One thing which will never change is the value of sport in its broadest sense in shaping human development. I believe it to be a most powerful tool and I am convinced that if that tool is to be placed in the hands of coaches, then we must ensure that they are highly skilled craftsmen and women. The Foundation's job is to ensure that every coach has an opportunity to learn all aspects of his/her craft and that all coaches are given the support they need and deserve.

Section II

The Nature of Coaching

DIMENSIONS OF AN ETHICAL CODE FOR SPORT COACHES

E.F. ZEIGLER
Faculty of Physical Education, The University of Western Ontario

Abstract

This presentation is based on the underlying premise that there is a
considerable need for those involved in highly competitive sport to
understand and develop a greatly improved approach to ethics.
Attention is directed specifically to recommending dimensions or
components that should be included in an ethical code for sport
coaches as part of their background preparation and subsequent
certification. The make-up of an ethical code is described with
attention given to the possible distinctions among standards,
principles, and rules that can be included. The following topics
are considered in the development of an embryonic code for possible
further development: (1) the bases upon which professional coaching
services are made available (to whom and by whom?)--e.g., is there a
mal-distribution of services? (2) the ethical nature of the
coach-athlete relationship--e.g., what constitutes trustworthiness?
(3) the possible conflicts that may arise between the coach's
(individual and collective) obligations to athletes and to third
parties--e.g., should a coach report his/her own athlete to a meet
official if the athlete has taken an illegal drug? (4) the coach's
responsibility to society--e.g., the professional obligations
coaches should have to their profession--e.g., for service, to carry
out research) and (5) the ensuring of compliance to a code of
ethics--e.g., the reporting of misconduct on the part of a fellow
coach.
Key words: Ethical Code, Ethical Creed, Sport Coaches, Profession,
Professional Ethics, Professional Obligations (Standards,
Principles, and Rules)

1. Introduction

The discussion here is based on a presumably logical sequence of
questions that would need to be answered by an individual or group
of practitioners who accepted the task of developing an embryonic
code for the consideration of the members of a professional society
operative within a recognized political unit and geographical area.
The following, then, are the questions which the writer will strive
to answer as precisely and succinctly as possible within the
confines of a paper in a conference proceedings:

(a) What is ethics?
(b) What is a value?
(c) What is an ethical code?
(d) Is this the same as an ethical creed?
(e) What is a profession in the 20th century?
(f) What has been published about the professionalization of the field of coaching and the possible need for a code of ethics?
(g) Should coaches develop a code of ethics as soon as possible?
(h) How can ordinary norms be related to professional norms or obligations?
(i) What might be a reasonable approach to the categorization of these professional norms or obligations?
(j) Is a secondary categorization within the heading of professional obligations possible and/or desirable?
(k) What are the major areas of concern in the development of an ethical code?
(l) What are some examples of provisions that could well be be included in each of the major areas of concern?
(m) What conclusions may reasonably be drawn from this discussion?

2. Definition of Terms

The first 4 questions (a-d above) will be answered under this heading as follows:

(a) Ethics is defined variously as "a pattern or way of life" (e.g., Christian or Muslim ethics); "a listing of rules of conduct or moral code" (e.g., medical ethics); or an "inquiry about rules of conduct in a society or culture" (i.e., meta-ethics).

It can be explained further that ethics has a direct relationship with values, to "right" and "wrong" as applied to individual or collective acts and to "good" and "bad" as applied to the effects of acts.

(b) A value can be explained roughly as something that is regarded as "worthwhile" and "good" by a person or group. For example, the values of a democratic society might be as follows: (i) governance of law, (ii) autonomy or freedom, (iii) protection from injury, (iv) equality of opportunity, (v) right to privacy, (vi) concern for individual welfare, etc.

(c) An ethical code may be defined as "a systematic collection of rules and regulations (i.e., what's right and wrong, and good and bad) determined in relation to the values espoused in a given society." It should be noted that values expressed as norms often take the form of laws.

(d) The answer as to whether a code is the same as a creed is both "yes" and "no." A creed can be defined as a short idealistic (in the non-philosophic sense) statement of belief, while a code is a longer set of more detailed regulations.

3. What Is a Profession in the 20th Century?

To this point the discussion has related to the subject of individual ethics. In this paper, however, the intent is to consider professional ethics as applied to coaching. Thus, the following is a brief attempt to define a profession in the last quarter of the 20th century:

(a) A profession can be defined as an occupation which requires specific knowledge of some aspect of learning before a person is accepted as a professional person.

(b) It can be argued, however, that there is no generally acceptable definition today—i.e., it is impossible to characterize professions by a set of necessary and sufficient features possessed by all professions—and only by professions (Bayles, 1981, p. 7).

(c) Also, there are categories of professions as follows: consulting, teaching, research, performing, etc. Coaching would presumably be a combination of consulting and teaching.

(d) The following may be considered as three necessary features of an occupation that can also be designated as a profession: (i) a need for extensive training; (ii) a significant intellectual component that must be mastered; and (iii) a recognition by society that the trained person can provide a basic. important service.

(e) Additionally, there are some other features that are common to most professions as follows: (i) licensing by state/province or professional body, (ii) establishment of professional societies, (iii) considerable autonomy in work performance, and (iv) establishment of a creed or code of ethics.

4. What Has Been Published About the Professionalization of the Field of Coaching and the Possible Need for a Code of Ethics?

If there is agreement that a young person in our society should be so educated that there is ample opportunity for him or her to develop rationality as a life competency, it is essential further that such ability be available for use with the many ethical problems that arise in all phases of daily life. Thus a more basic concern in the present discussion is that the young adult be able to apply such competency to the ethical problems that arise subsequently in the course of professional service to a chosen field.

I am not arguing that we (in sport and physical education) as a profession are any better or any worse that most other professions in regard to the application of professional ethics to our endeavors. Perhaps it would simply be best to state that our western culture is confused in this matter, and it has just happened that way in our development. This tangle of ethics has developed because of a diverse inheritance of customs and mores from the other lands, and we have simply added our own brand of confusion to this ill-suited mixture of moral systems.

Where does that leave the profession of sport and physical education? The answer at this point must be, "In trouble!" Nevertheless, if our profession is to survive and to continue to grow, it must serve society more effectively in the years immediately ahead. To do this, our profession, along with all other professions, must be attuned to the all-important values and norms that have been established within the culture.

It is obvious that we need to take a hard look at ourselves, admittedly a difficult assignment. Responding to current heavy criticism of highly competitive sport is indeed a humbling experience. Further, in some ways we are part of the teaching profession, and yet ideally sport and physical education has a broad mission that extends from infancy to our oldest citizens be they "normal," "special," or "accelerated."

We do have many of the attributes of a profession (e.g., extensive training period; significant intellectual component to be mastered; and some recognition that the trained person can provide a basic important service to society). However, sport and physical education has not done as well as some of the highly recognized professions in developing and enforcing carefully defined professional obligations that the practitioner must follow to remain in good standing with his or her fellows and with society.

In considering what we do have in the field that might be considered to be professional ethics, initially we must be careful to distinguish between a creed, or "statement of professional beliefs" and a code, or "set of detailed regulations of a more administrative nature" (Bayles, 1981, p. 24). In competitive sport, for example, the National High School Athletic Coaches Association in the U.S.A. has developed what might be called an embryonic code. A similarly brief code--with some overlap--has been adopted by the Minnesota High School Coaches Association.

In Canada the Coaching Association, as part of the National Coaching Certification Program, has adopted what is called a coaching creed. It too is very brief and contains some elements that might more correctly appear in a code. However, that is the extent of this development, and there is probably no coach at any level who could repeat all or even the essence of these statements.

In physical education, which is unfortunately usually viewed only within the domain of the education profession, several efforts have been made in the United States over the years to define what our ethical concerns should be. However, at present there appears to be no concerted effort underway to rectify a situation that is glaringly inadequate.

Several textbooks have been made available by Shea (1978), Fraleigh (1984), and Zeigler (1984), the latter book being divided equally between discussions of personal and professional ethics. However, there are very few courses in North America in sport and physical education ethics offered (10-15?), and practically none that treat the subject of professional ethics for the teacher/coach in our field. (I do not know what the situation in Great Britain and the rest of the Commonwealth is in this regard, but I am not aware of other texts along this line than McIntosh's (1979) excellent volume called Fair Play.)

The field of recreation has made some (but not substantive) headway on a continuing basis in this area. A brief code of ethics was developed by the American Recreation Society a generation ago, and the Society of Municipal Recreation Directors of Ontario in Canada constructed a code in the 1950s as well. These codes typically receive lip service, and the societies most certainly do not enforce compliance with the codes' tenets.

In summary, therefore, we can report only very meager beginnings in an aspect of the allied professions that most certainly warrants significant attention at this time.

5.   Should Coaches Develop a Code of Ethics?

The review of the meagre amount of development and accompanying literature on the subject of coach/teacher ethics described above, as well as investigation carried out in the past several years (Zeigler, 1983a, 1983b, 1984a, 1984b, 1984c, 1985a, 1985b, 1985c, 1985d) has led me inevitably to the conclusion that the coach as a professional person striving for public recognition will increasingly have obligations to the public, to his or her profession, and to his or her clients. In addition to the necessary features for a profession as indicated above (e.g., extensive training), the establishment of a creed or code of ethics was included as another feature that was common to most established professions. History has made clear that such ethical codes appeared only after one or more professional societies within a developing profession had been established for a period of time.

Accordingly, it is logical to propose that the time has now come for the various coaching associations extant to set about such a task carefully and extensively on a cooperative basis. This would simply be taking one more important step forward in the total professionalization process. Such a detailed code, as opposed to a short creed that could easily turn out to be "window dressing" (such as medicine's Hippocratic Oath), would not seem to be sufficient at this time. Such a code, as is being recommended, would be a system of norms describing what should be the case in an individual's professional practice as a coach.

6. How Can Ordinary Norms Be Related to Professional Norms or Obligations?

It is important to understand that the term "norm" has several different meanings. Used in this sense it does not mean an "average," as one understands the term in the social sciences. It has more the meaning of one of a series of standards of virtue that are expected to prevail in the society or culture. Thus persons in this society can be expected to be honest, fair, etc.--in other words they should possess these desirable traits. These would be considered to be ordinary norms as opposed to professional norms.

Further, it is also to be expected that the society's ordinary norms will have a definite relationship to the norms or obligations expected in a specific profession. Bayles (1981) explained that ordinary norms can have four possible relationships to professional norms. By adapting these for the present discussion, we might suggest something like the following:

(a) Identical to: a coach should be honest,
(b) Specifications of: a coach should be honest with his or her athlete,
(c) Functionally related to: a coach should be honest when advising an athlete about his/her mental state prior to an important contest,
(d) Independent of: a coach may occasionally need to be tell a "white lie" when making an unusually difficult decision about staff or personnel selection (i.e., employing a separate system of ethics) (pp. 16-17).

7. What Might Be a Reasonable Approach to the Categorization of These Professional Norms or Obligations?

Coaches may be functioning as professional, semiprofessional, or amateur practitioners, as coaching educators, as coaching researchers or as coaching administrators. (For the present, we should probably limit our discussion to those who earn their living in the field.) Thus, in any effort to list or enumerate the variety and large number of professional norms with which an intelligent and dedicated coach may be confronted, it will be necessary to postulate an underlying approach to the categorization of such obligations. On the face of it, a good starting point is to seek to answer two questions: (a) what should one do? and (b)) what should one not do? The responses to the former question would be considered as obligations; they are prescribed. Responses to the latter question would represent actions that a professional should not take. The former would be considered right and should result in a condition or state that is good. The latter would be considered wrong and would presumably bring about a bad result.

Of course, there are always choices to make in life where the situation and any action to be taken are not clear-cut. Thus if one category is that of obligations, a second category of norms could be designated as <u>permissions</u>. In this case, where action is debatable, and possibly right or wrong resulting in a good or bad state of affairs, the professional coach is offered the freedom to make a choice.

8. Is a Secondary Categorization Within the Heading of Professional Obligations Possible and/or Desirable?

A secondary categorization of professional obligations involves three specific sub-headings that are designated as <u>standards</u>, <u>principles</u>, and <u>rules</u> (Bayles, pp. 22-23). This approach should be very helpful to members of any profession (i.e., embryonic, developing, or established) in the process of developing or upgrading its ethical code.

The stricture regarding the particular obligation is preceded by a designation of the <u>standard</u> of virtue and/or vice involved. Then the approach moves from the general to the specific in that the ensuing <u>principle</u> allows for discretion and the accompanying <u>rule</u> is most specific.

More specifically, standards present desirable or undesirable character traits to be sought or avoided; principles state responsibilities that allow for discretion in the fulfillment of standards and may be balanced or weighed against one another; and rules explain duties that prescribe specific conduct and allow for very little discretion. As Bayles explains it, "principles can explicate standards, justify rules, and provide guidance in their absence" (p. 24).

The following might well be one example of how the above schemata could work:

(a) <u>Standard of Virtue or Vice</u> (for the practitioner): a coach should be unselfish and beneficient in his/her dealings with an athlete.

(b) <u>Principle of Responsibility</u> (this allows for individual discretion): a coach should use his/her power over an athlete carefully--not as a means to some other end.

(c) <u>Rule of Duty</u> (this must be followed): an athlete should never be forced (i.e., made to feel) that he/she must compete because a third party's reputation is at stake (e.g., the owner, the coach, the sport psychologist).

9. What Are the Major Areas of Concern in the Development of an Ethical Code for Coaches?

One way to learn about some of the major areas of concern that ought to be in a profession's ethical code is to examine other such codes in existence. For example, there is "Ethical Standards of

Psychologists" as developed originally and revised by the American
Psychological Association (1977). There is no denying that this is
an excellent statement with a fine preamble. It has been prepared
carefully over a considerable period of time with numerous revisions
along the way. Interestingly, the initial preamble seems to be
almost actually what has been defined in the present paper as a
creed (see Definition of Terms above). This code contains nine
principles to which the members of the Association have subscribed.
These principles relate to the following aspects of the profession:
(a) responsibility, (b) competence, (c) moral and legal standards,
(d) public statements, (e) confidentiality, (f) welfare of the
consumer, (g) professional relationships, (h) utilization of
assessment techniques, and (i) pursuit of research activities
(Ibid.).

As good as the prevailing APA code is, it does not appear to clarify
sufficiently among standards, principles, and rules as Bayles has
recommended. His plan (i.e., the format of standards, principles,
and rules) represents a significant improvement over the prevailing
arrangement. The APA's code simply lists nine excellent principles,
but makes no effort to categorize or arrange them as sequentially as
could (should) be done. Also, the APA has not sufficiently
delineated among standards, principles, and rules. The result is a
lack of clarity as to where one leaves off and the other begins. In
other words, the ethical standards that have been developed make an
effort to "throw a covering blanket" over the entire discipline and
profession. This is fine, but the task should be designed more
specifically to cover the duties, obligations, and responsibilities
of each of the sub-professional groups concerned (i.e., teaching,
clinical, research).

10. What Major Areas of Concern Can Be Recommended?

I agree that the listing of nine "principles" in a seemingly random
order without categorization into major areas of concern is perhaps
a satisfactory beginning. Nevertheless I believe that such a
statement can be strengthened by further clarification. Consider,
for example, the subsuming of the "principles" listed above under
five major areas of concern as follows:

   (a) Bases upon which professional services are made available.

   Example: Is there a mal-distribution of services?

   (b) Ethical nature of counsellor-athlete relationship.

   Example: What constitutes trustworthiness?

   (c) Conflict-resolution when conflicts arise between
   counsellor's obligations to athletes and to third parties
   (e.g., his or her employer, the state or province).

   Example: Should a coach report his/her own athlete to his/

her employer or the team owner if it is known that the athlete
has taken an illegal drug?

(d) Professional obligations to society and to his or her own
profession.

Example: Should a coach risk doing harm to his/her own
profession's reputation by carrying out his or her
duties in such a way that fellow coaches and the public view
him or her as an unethical person?

(e) Ensuring compliance to the profession's established ethical
code.

Example: Should a coach report a colleague who has
undoubtedly been unethical in his/her actions so that possible
action may be taken against him/her by the professional
society?

11. What Are Some Examples of Provisions That Could Well Be Included Under Each of the Major Areas of Concern?

The following are some examples of provisions (i.e., standards,
principles, and rules) that could well be included under each of the
major areas of concern (Table 1 immediately below):

Categories	Standards	Principles	Rules
a. Bases upon which professional services are made available	A coach should be _fair_ and _just_ in providing his/her services	A coach should ensure that all team members receive adequate coaching	A team member needing help must receive it as soon as possible

Example: A coach shows bias toward a team member
and coaches him/her as little as possible.

b. Ethical nature of coach-athlete relationship	A coach should be _honest_ in his/her treatment of an athlete	A coach should never treat an athlete as a means to an end	An athlete must never be forced to take an illegal or unethical action because of fear of loss of income

Example: A coach urges an athlete to continue playing
by stating that a scholarship will be lost otherwise.

87

c. Conflict resolution when conflict arises between coach's obligations to athletes and third parties	A coach has an obligation to be _truthful_ in dealing with third parties	In checking eligibility of a team member, a coach should be most careful not to permit an inaccurate statement to be entered	A coach must never knowingly sign an eligibility form in which an athlete has committed perjury

Example: A coach knows that an athlete's eligibility has been used up elsewhere, but signs the form nevertheless in which an athlete has perjured himself/herself.

d. Professional obligations to society and to profession (i.e., duty to serve the public good)	A coach should be _loyal_ to societal values and those of the profession	A coach has a duty and responsibility to preserve and enhance the role of the coaching profession	A coach has a duty to upgrade and strengthen his/her knowledge by attending one or more coaching clinics or symposia annually

Example: A coach gives the profession a bad name by obviously falling behind on the rules and strategy of his/her sport.

e. Ensuring compliance with the established obligations of the professional ethical code	A coach should practice his/her profession with _honesty_ and _integrity_	A coach should encourage his/her team members to play fair within the letter and spirit of the established rules	A coach who permits his/her player to cheat shall be reported and should be excluded from the profession if found guilty

Example: A coach guilty of flagrant unethical practice shall be reported to the ethics committee of the professional society and to the administrators of the league in which his/her team is playing.

Table 1. Examples of Provisions for an Ethical Code

12. What Conclusions May Reasonably Be Drawn From This Discussion?

In this paper there has been a sequential discussion and analysis of the developing professionalization of sport coaching. In addition to a brief review of literature on the topic, a rationale and format for an ethical code has been presented. Having arrived at this point, the following conclusions may reasonably be stated:

a. That there is some recognition by society that a qualified sport coach can provide a basic, important service.

b. That there is a significant intellectual component to be mastered, and therefore an extensive training is required before a person becomes qualified as a professional sport coach.

c. That coaches are moving very slowly toward true professional status based on the following accomplishments:

   i. Establishment of professional societies
   ii. Conferences and symposia held to improve the knowledge and competency of coaches
   iii. Publication of a variety of semi-scholarly ("professional") and scholarly journals
   iv. Discussions held and articles and books published on the subject of professionalization over a period of time
   v. Considerable autonomy in work performance

d. That, to promote sound, long range development, a specific creed for sport coaches should be developed, and that this should be followed by a subsequent expansion to a detailed ethical code as soon as possible.

e. That programs of voluntary registration/certification at all levels (i.e., local, regional, national, and international) be developed as soon as possible. Future development of required licensing for practitioners would necessarily have to take place on a state-by-state (province-by-province) basis.

f. That, in the development of such registration/licensing procedures, every effort should be made to avoid narrow discrimination on the basis of "professional/disciplinary labels" and training (i.e., unwillingness to accept obviously comparable course experiences from another profession/discipline as part of certification requirements). What must be guaranteed, of course, is that an acceptable level of knowledge, competency, and skill be determined, and that all who practice professionally possess such ability on a continuing basis.

In conclusion, may I reiterate what I have sought to convey throughout this paper. I feel that there is an urgent need to give this topic serious consideration in the development of sport coaching.

References

American Psychological Association. (1977) Ethical Standards of Psychologists. Washington, DC: American Psychological Association.

Bayles, M.D. (1981) Professional Ethics. Belmont, CA: Wadsworth.

Fraleigh, W.P. (1984) Right Actions in Sport. Champaign, IL: Human Kinetics.

McIntosh, P. (1979) Fair Play. London: Heinemann.

Random House Dictionary of the English Language, The. (1967) New York: Random House.

Shea, E.J. (1978) Ethical Decisions in Physical Education and Sport. Springfield, IL: C.C. Thomas.

Zeigler, E.F. (1983a) Cross-cultural applicability of a model for applied ethics in sport and physical education. A paper presented at the Big Ten CIC Symposium, The Ohio State University, Columbus, Ohio, Oct. 14.

Zeigler, E.F. (1983b) Strengthening our professional arsenal. In Proceedings of the Nat. Assoc. for Phys. Educ. in Higher Educ. Champaign, IL: Human Kinetics.

Zeigler, E.F. (1984a) Ethics and Morality in Sport and Physical Education. Champaign, IL: Stipes, 1984.

Zeigler, E.F. (1984b) A triple-play approach to ethical decision-making in competitive sport. A paper presented at Central Michigan University, Oct. 25.

Zeigler, E.F. (1984c) Applied ethics in sport and physical education. Philosophy in Context, 13, 52-64.

Zeigler, E.F. (1985a) The urgent need for sport and physical education ethics. A paper presented at the University of Saskatchewan, Canada, March 17.

Zeigler, E.F. (1985b) Sport ethics in world perspective. A paper presented at the Ethics and Athletics Conference, Louisiana State University, April 7.

Zeigler, E.F. (1985c) The development of an ethical code for sport psychologists. A paper presented to the Sport Psychology Academy of the Amer. Assn. for HPERD, Atlanta, Georgia, April 18.

Zeigler, E.F. (1985d) Merging the triple-play approach and a jurisprudential argument in sport and physical education ethics. A paper presented at the University of Windsor, Ontario, Oct. 17.

TO TEACH THE COACHES OR TO COACH THE TEACHERS

CATHERINE M. O'BRIEN
Department of Physical Education, University of Sydney, Australia.

Abstract
This paper will explore the distinctions between the teacher, who is
also coaching, and the coach, who also teaches children. Teachers are
often pressed into coaching service at schools, without formal training
in coaching, while perhaps having had some experience as an athlete.
Trained coaches and their administrators often decry the lack of knowledge and skills of the sport these teachers possess. Coaches, on the
other hand, are guilty of not using proper teaching/learning techniques.
While the definition of the differences between these teachers and
coaches is not always clear-cut, the process involves examination of
training procedures for the art of coaching/teaching, the importance
of sport-related background, the role involvement and philosophy of
coaching.
    Our coaching accreditation schemes and physical education training
courses both teach essential aspects of coaching. This paper will
demonstrate that work in teacher-training should effect special consideration for the teacher-trained coach, and that separate requirements
for coaching can be established for them. The rationale for all
schools to require teachers/coaches of sport to be accredited for
school sport assignment is thereby justified. Points of reference
from Australian and American experiences will be used.

BEHAVIORAL DETERMINANTS OF COACHING EFFECTIVENESS

S. GORDON
Department of Physical Education and Sport Studies, University of
Alberta

Abstract
This study examined the influence of coaching behavior (independent
variables) on dimensions of athlete satisfaction (dependent variables).
Perceptions of athlete satisfaction were the study's measures of
coaching effectiveness. Two versions of the Leadership Scale for
Sport (LSS) and a Personal Opinion Inventory (POI) were administered
to one hundred and sixty-one male Canadian University (CIAU) soccer
players. Coaching effectiveness (athlete satisfaction) was related
to the congruence between what athletes 'see' and what they 'want'
and specifically to Training and Rewarding behavior. Results also
suggest that successful coaching is not necessarily synonomous with
effective coaching.
Key words: Effective coaching, Coaching behavior, Athlete satisfaction, Congruence.

1. Introduction

The Multi-dimensional Model of Leadership, developed by Chelladurai
(1978), acknowledges the dynamic relationship between situational
factors and the characteristics of both leaders (coaches) and subordinates (athletes). To operationalize this model Chelladurai and
Saleh (1980) developed the Leadership Scale for Sport (LSS) a forty
item inventory which assesses five dimensions of coaching behavior.
These categories of behavior are defined as follows:
   Training and Instruction Behavior(13 items) - behavior aimed at
improving the performance of athletes by emphasizing and facilitating
hard and strenuous training, clarifying relationships amongst team
members through structuring and coordinating team activities.
   Democratic Behavior(9 items) - behavior of the coach that allows
greater participation by athletes in decisions relating to the
establishment of, for example, group goals, practise methods, game
tactics and team strategies.
   Autocratic Behavior(5 items) - behavior of coaches who tend to set
themselves apart from athletes and make all the decisions pertaining
to team affairs on their own.
   Social Support Behavior(8 items) - behavior of coaches that indicates a genuine concern for all athletes and their welfare. Also,
behavior that fosters a positive group atmosphere and warm inter-

personal relations between team members.

Rewarding behavior(5 items) - coaching behavior that provides positive and rewarding reinforcements for athletes through recognition of good performances.

Different versions of the LSS can elicit athlete responses on a five point Likert type scale ranging from 'always-never' on preferred and perceived behavior by pre-fixing the same forty items by "I prefer my coach to . . ." (preferred version) or by "My coach . . ."(perceived version). An important assumption in operationalizing the model is that the consequences/outcomes of the leadership process (satisfaction and performance) are facilitated and enhanced when athlete preferences/perceptions of coaching behavior are congruent.

The purpose of this study therefore was to determine the preferences and perceptions of coaching behavior of a sport specific group of athletes; and second, to relate the discrepancies in those responses to measures of athlete satisfaction with their coach.

2. Procedures and method

2.1 Sample
Responses to two forms of the LSS and an athlete satisfaction inventory (Personal Opinion Inventory-POI) were received from one hundred and sixty-one 'starting' players representing eighteen male Canadian Intercollegiate Athlete Unions (CIAU) soccer teams.

2.2 Inventories
Two athlete versions of the LSS were used to obtain athlete preferences and perceptions of coaching behavior. The POI consisted of thirty-seven items and represented seven dimensions of athlete satisfaction, i.e., satisfaction with personal and team performance, coach expertise, coach social skills, role clarity, role acceptance and team involvement. Responses ranging from 'very satisfied-very dissatisfied' on a five point Likert Scale reflected athlete perceptions of coaching effectiveness.

2.3 Statistical Treatment
Individual and team average scores were calculated by collapsing LSS and POI item responses into respective behavior and satisfaction dimensions. Their relationship was subsequently analysed using SPSS and MIDAS.

The latter was used to calculate dyad scores between preferred and perceived responses to the LSS and it is important to point out that congruence measures were treated as absolute scores (or differences) and not signed differences. The magnitude, but not the direction of differences in preferences or perceptions was considered most important to satisfaction. Also, consistent with both Chelladurai's (1984) and Yukl's (1971) approach to discrepancy measurement, athlete satisfaction was proposed to be maximal in conditions of least discrepancy (congruence).

Each of the five behavior congruence scores was subsequently related to each of the seven satisfaction dimension scores using simple correlations.

3. Results and discussion

3.1 Behavior and Satisfaction Responses
Means from the LSS and POI data, with a possible range of 1-5 are illustrated in Table 1.

Table 1. Behavior and satisfaction means: LSS and POI data

LSS version	5 Behavior Category Means (SD)				
	Training	Demo.	Auto.	Soc. Sup.	Reward
Athlete Preferred	4.11 (.49)	3.14 (.56)	2.32 (.60)	3.21 (.56)	4.05 (.63)
Athlete Perceived	3.49 (.61)	2.81 (.59)	2.83 (.60)	2.89 (.73)	3.60 (.73)

	7 Satisfaction Dimensions (SD)						
	Pers.P.	Team P.	Exp.	S.S.	R.C.	R.A.	T.I.
Means	2.75 (.97)	2.95 (1.07)	3.51 (.66)	3.76 (.85)	3.97 (.72)	3.66 (.87)	3.55 (.70)

Except for Autocratic behavior the soccer players 'preferred' more of each category of behavior than they 'perceived'. Athletes were less satisfied with performance factors than with the other five satisfaction dimensions which was to be expected with a won-loss percentage (success) range of 6.3%-95% for all teams over the season.

When team means for satisfaction dimensions were related to each other and then grouped according to three won-loss groupings (0-30%; 31-75%; 80%+) over half of the total significant differences were found in levels of satisfaction with team performance. Predictably, the most successful teams were significantly more satisfied with team performance than intermediate and poorer teams. However, these data also revealed that some 'losing teams' differed significantly from 'winning teams' in satisfaction with personal and team performance and in particular coach expertise, social skills and role clarity. This evidence suggests that non-successful athletes recognize and appreciate effective coaching regardless of results.

All seven satisfaction dimensions intercorrelated and the most significant correlations suggest that satisfaction with athlete roles in a soccer team (role acceptance) is closely associated with satisfactory clarification of roles (role clarity) and levels of athlete input (team involvement). Perceptions of overall coaching effectiveness (athlete satisfaction) are therefore significantly related to the quality of athletic participation and influence in general team affairs.

3.2 Congruence scores
Least discrepancy scores, obtained by subtracting Athlete Perceived behavior from Athlete Preferred behavior were negatively related to ALL satisfaction dimensions as illustrated in Table 2.

Table 2. Significant Relationships: Coaching Effectiveness/Congruent
Behavior Scores

Satisfaction	Training	Demo.	Auto.	Soc.Sup.	Reward
			5 Behavior Categories		
Personal Performance	-.07	-.05	-.15	-.13	-.15
Team Performance	-.24**	-.17*	-.14	-.05	-.14
Coach Expertise	-.47**	-.19*	-.23**	-.14	-.23**
Social Skills	-.21**	-.27**	-.32**	-.22**	-.22**
Team Involvement	-.14	-.07	-.08	-.07	-.03
Role Clarity	-.48**	-.12	-.20*	-.13	-.17*
Role Acceptance	-.24**	-.12	-.15	-.06	-.09

*p < .05   **p < .01

The pattern in this analysis strongly suggests that congruence scores
are significantly related to higher levels of athlete satisfaction
(perceptions of coaching effectiveness). This is particularly evident
in Training behavior where congruence scores were significantly
related to five of the seven satisfaction dimensions. Also important
is that low discrepancy scores in all five behavior categories were
significantly related to satisfaction with coach expertise and social
skills (Social Support p < .06) while none of the correlations for
personal performance and team involvement were significant. Perhaps
in regard to the latter finding athletes believe that their satisfaction in these two dimensions is primarily a function of their own
initiative.

4. Implications for coaching

The analyses on behavioral data emphasizes Training behavior and
Rewarding behavior in determining athlete perceptions of coaching
effectiveness. Coaches therefore, who exhibit technical competence,
positive feedback in a direct but supportive and friendly manner are
more likely to be regarded 'effective' by athletes.
    While 'effective' coaching probably includes elements of success,
actual success did not influence athlete reports of satisfaction with
coaching expertise and athlete role factors (role clarity, acceptance
and team involvement). Successful coaches therefore are not necessarily effective coaches.
    Finally, when athletes 'see' what they 'want' in terms of coaching
behavior they are more likely to report satisfaction with the coach.
Coaches would be well advised therefore, to assess and periodically
check their verbal and non-verbal coaching behavior and communication. Consistent, appropriate and comprehensible coaching behavior
both enhances and facilitates athlete perceptions of coaching
effectiveness.

References

Chelladurai, P. (1978) A multi-dimensional model of leadership in athletics. Unpublished Ph.D. thesis, University of Waterloo.

Chelladurai, P. (1984) Discrepancy between preferences and perceptions of leadership behavior and satisfaction of athletes in varying sports. Journal of Sport Psychology, 6, 27-41.

Chelladurai, P. and Saleh, S.D. (1980) Dimensions of leader behavior in sports: Development of a leadership scale. Journal of Sport Psychology, 2, 34-45.

Yukl, G.A. (1971) Towards a behavioral theory of leadership. Organizational Behavior and Human Performance, 6, 414-440.

COACHING EFFECTIVENESS : A SYSTEMATIC APPROACH

W.W. EWENS
Department of Health and Sports Studies, St. George Institute of
Education, Australia

Abstract
Coaching effectiveness depends on the application of sound education
principles. The generally accepted sequencing of the Pre (subject)
experiences, subject vocabulary, manipulation of vocabulary and
problem solving or creative use of the vocabulary is appropriate in
movement education, especially sport. Sports modifications should be
defined as a lead-up activity placing basic skills in a competitive
situation or modified game which is a breakdown of the sports. Sport
is best defined in terms of skills, rules and tactics. Sports
education is as much concerned with decision making as skill
performance.
Key words: Sequencing, Sport definitions, Decision making.

1. Sequencing, Sports Experiences

Sport is an area where the outcome criteria has been paramount.
Sports socialization (or education) has been plagued with an
obsession, by significant others, to win at all costs. The bottom
line for most administrators, coaches, teachers and, for that matter
parents, is playing and winning the "real game". This obsession with
winning has created a situation where those with natural talents
succeed in spite of the system. However, those who are unable to
quickly master the fundamental physical, social and psychological
elements of a sport are left by the wayside. Equally disturbing is
the disillusionment of the early maturers who taste success through
physical superiority rather than skill, but fails later when the
other children's maturity equals theirs.
Far too many potential sports participants are denied a meaningful
experience because little attention is given to process. Developing
sequential learning experiences has either been ignored, or at best
developed on some ad hoc basis.
The most popular approach to sequencing experiences has been to
introduce some form of variation to the sport. Terms such as mini,
modified, lead up, and minor games have been used. Regrettably
these terms have never been defined conceptually or operationally.
Even if they had, the notion of variation on the sport falls short
of a meaningful continuum of experience. If one is to develop some
form of sequential learning experiences in sport it is necessary

to identify stages within the continuum. Other disciplines have
developed procedures that have logic and appear viable for sports
development.

The concept involves:

1. Pre (subject) experiences
2. Subject vocabulary
3. Manipulation of that vocabulary
4. Problem solving or creative use of the vocabulary

This might best be illustrated by a comparison of sport with
mathematics and writing.

Phase	MATHEMATICS	WRITING	SPORT
1	Pre number	Pre writing	Pre sport Basic movement
2	Number sequencing	Written word vocabulary	Complex skills
3	Number manipulation (+, -, x, -)	Sentence structure	Lead up Games
		Composition	Modified sports
4	Problem solving (Accounting, Finance, Stock)	Creative writing (Novel, play, documentary)	Sport (Cricket, hockey tennis)

FIG. I   SEQUENTIAL LEARNING

If one accepts this proposition of sequencing then it is imperative
to understand the role and purpose of each phase.

Phase I Pre-Sport Experiences: Basic Movement
Sport depends on a number of basic movements such as running,
dodging, falling, kicking, hitting, throwing and catching. Without
a reasoned level of ability in all, or a selected group of these
basic skills, further progress in sports education is impossible.

Phase 2 Sports Vocabulary
The basic need in Phase 2 is to establish some specificity of
purpose. The use of particular implements in particular situations.
Cricket bats and cover drives, rugby balls and lateral passing,
netballs and sling passes, dynamic balance and slide tackle in
soccer. In other words the particularization of basic skills.

The extension of this first step is to develop complex skill
activity which combines a number of skills in an appropriate
sequence.

Relationship judgements are a vital aspect of this phase. For
example, in cricket the ability of a batsman to play a stroke and
flow into a run pattern or a softball fielder's selection of
appropriate reactions to a grounder or fly ball. Confidence in the

98

use of skills in sports specific situations without decision making overload is essential to sound fundamentals.

Sports educators, in the main, have failed to appreciate the need to give learners opportunities to execute these combinations without competitive pressure. Players incapacity to progress, in many cases, can be attributed to an inability to effectively combine individual skills into a sequential movement pattern.

Phase 3 Manipulation of the Sports Vocabulary
Two major problems may arise at this level, one is to ignore it altogether and move directly to the sport. The second is to remain at the first level of the phase for too long a period. I suspect, at least in Australia, the former is a problem of community based coaching while the latter is something the school programmers need to address.

Earlier I referred to a lack of definitions related to the variations of a sport. I believe this can be overcome by operationally defining these variations. In doing so I would use only three categories:

1. <u>Lead up games</u>: Games which provide opportunities for learners to use a number of skills in a competitive situation. The games evolve as a <u>build up</u> from the basic skills. Lenel's (1969) concept of 1 on 1, 1 on 2 .... X or Y, is an excellent example of how lead up activities provide opportunities for elementary offensive/defensive interactive strategies to be practised. The Lead-up game should be seen as the elementary manipulation of the sport vocabulary which extends the learners insights into the tactical use of skills.

2. <u>Modified Sport (Games)</u>: Games whose origins are a major sport played be adults. The sport is <u>broken down</u> to accommodate the level of the participants. The breakdown must be such that skills and tactics of the sport are practised, the offensive/defensive interactions recognisable, scoring procedures comparable and the spirit of the sport retained.

3. <u>Minor Games</u>: Games which involve any or all of the basic skills of running, falling, hitting, kicking, throwing and dodging in a unique way. The games have <u>no specific</u> rule or tactical association with a major sport and therefore are games in their own right.

If one accepts these definitions then games can be examined against them and used effectively at an appropriate level within the sequence. This would give more purpose to the games selection and avoid serious problems such as using minor games as a substitute for either a lead-up or modified game. Minor games, by definition, are a mix of skills and tactics, some which may positively reinforce a sport while others are either neutral or negative reinforcers. For example, continuous cricket develops fielding skills, is almost neutral for bowling but encourages poor batting techniques. Even the name is inappropriate. Specificity of purpose therefore requires an understanding of the experiences and outcomes offered players.

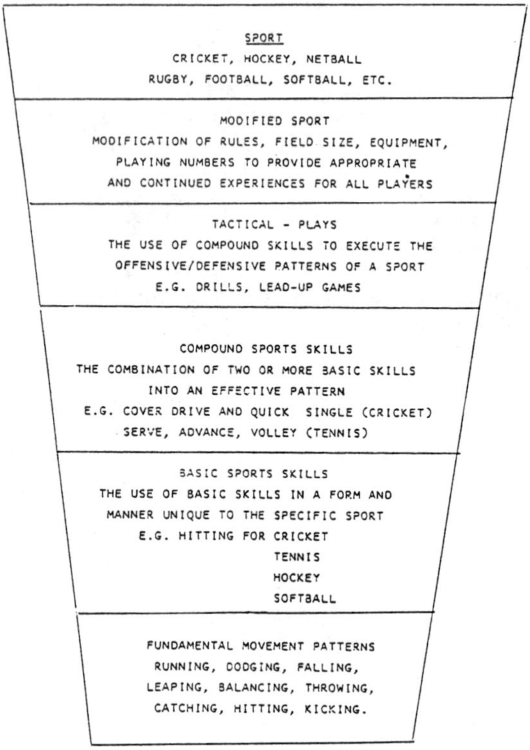

```
                        SPORT
              CRICKET, HOCKEY, NETBALL
           RUGBY, FOOTBALL, SOFTBALL, ETC.

                   MODIFIED SPORT
       MODIFICATION OF RULES, FIELD SIZE, EQUIPMENT,
          PLAYING NUMBERS TO PROVIDE APPROPRIATE
         AND CONTINUED EXPERIENCES FOR ALL PLAYERS

                  TACTICAL - PLAYS
         THE USE OF COMPOUND SKILLS TO EXECUTE THE
         OFFENSIVE/DEFENSIVE PATTERNS OF A SPORT
              E.G. DRILLS, LEAD-UP GAMES

                COMPOUND SPORTS SKILLS
       THE COMBINATION OF TWO OR MORE BASIC SKILLS
                INTO AN EFFECTIVE PATTERN
       E.G. COVER DRIVE AND QUICK  SINGLE (CRICKET)
           SERVE, ADVANCE, VOLLEY (TENNIS)

                 BASIC SPORTS SKILLS
         THE USE OF BASIC SKILLS IN A FORM AND
         MANNER UNIQUE TO THE SPECIFIC SPORT
              E.G. HITTING FOR CRICKET
                      TENNIS
                      HOCKEY
                      SOFTBALL

            FUNDAMENTAL MOVEMENT PATTERNS
             RUNNING, DODGING, FALLING,
            LEAPING, BALANCING, THROWING,
             CATCHING, HITTING, KICKING.
```

FIG. II DEVELOPMENTAL SEQUENCING

2. Elements of Sport

The necessity to give meaning and specificity to the practices and
drills is vital. To do this sport must be defined operationally.
Traditional definitions have been skill oriented, for example cricket
involves batting, bowling and fielding or netball consists of
running, passing, guarding and shooting.
    While this approach provides a basic fabric for the sport, it
fails to recognise the dynamics associated with the playing of the
sport.
    More appropriately sports should be seen in terms of skills,
rules and tactics. The interplay of these three elements provide
the dynamic nature of sport.

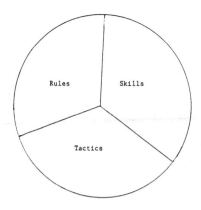

FIG. III ELEMENTS OF SPORTS

By using this approach coaches can give purpose to their coaching
sessions. Each drill can have a specific aim. The aim can be
directed at one element or a combination of two or all three.

The number of players who lack understanding of rules and how to
apply them is a serious weakness of coaching programmes. Furthermore
this approach provides opportunities for practise of both the
offensive and defensive aspects of the sport.

Clearly as players become more proficient drills will involve
more advanced rule and tactical concepts; however, like any
sequential learning the development of sound basic skills is
essential to effective utilization in complex decision making
situations.

The following diagram illustrates some elementary drill
objectives.

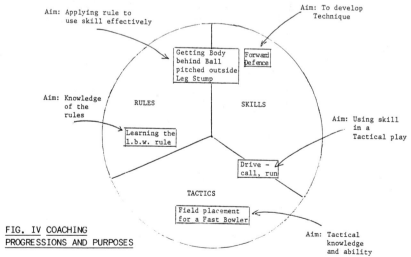

FIG. IV COACHING
PROGRESSIONS AND PURPOSES

3. Decision Making

The notion of gradually increasing the number of options available is an important learning experience often neglected or at best treated in a haphazard manner.

Sport is as much a matter of selecting a viable option as it is exhibiting "good form". Coaching must provide opportunities for players to have these decision making skills in simulated sports situations. Let me illustrate how this might be done. The ability to take or defend against the quick single is a cricket fundamental. An elementary 2 or 1 situation would give a batsman experience in stroking the ball and completing the run, the fieldsman the practice in fielding and returning the ball to the bowlers end.

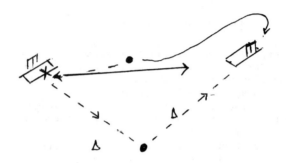

FIG. V 2 ON 1 DRILL

In this situation each player has only one decision to make. The batsman to hit and run, the fieldsman to gather and throw.

Introduce a second batsman and a wicketkeeper to give a 3 on 2 situation and you increase the alternatives. The batsman not only has to consider his own safety but that of his partner. The fieldsman has to decide between two targets.

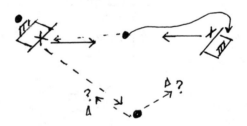

FIG. VI 3 ON 2 DRILL

Complexity is increased by adding another fieldsman (4 on 2).
The fieldsmen now have to co-operate. Who can get into the best
position to effect a run out? (Who attacks the ball? Who backs up?).
They will need to consider lines of flight, interception points,
transfer of weight, balance etc. Given a further condition of the
batsmen calling the traditional "Yes", "No" or "Wait", the practice
provides all the elements of the quick single play in the "real"
situation.

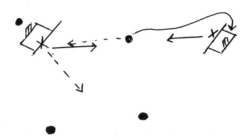

FIG. VII 4 ON 2 DRILL

While I have used cricket to illustrate how the decision making
process is experienced in more complex tactical situations it is
valid for any sport. Drills, which can be made into lead-up games,
should reflect the dynamics of game and the decision making options
involved in given "plays".

4. Conclusion

The purpose of this short paper was to highlight the need for
coaches to review their methods in light of generally accepted
teaching principles. In particular it highlights the need to:
(i)   consider process as well as outcomes,
(ii)   logically sequence learning experiences,
(iii) define sport operationally,
(iv)   recognise the importance of the decision making process.
The credibility of coaching and coach education will depend upon
the use of sound teaching strategies based on appropriate
educational principles.

References

Ewens, W.W. (1975) Sport for the young. Biennial ACHPER Conference,
    Perth.
Ewens, W.W. (1980) Sport for the young: Need to match practice with
    theory. 50th Congress ANZAAS, Adelaide.
Ewens, W.W. (1984) An approach to Coaching cricket (unpublished).
Ewens, W.W. (1986) Sports Modification - help or hindrance. XVI
    ACHPER Conference,Launceston.
Lenel, R. (1969) Games in the Primary School. Oxford Uni Press.

A CONCEPTUAL MODEL OF THE COACHING PROCESS: THE COACHING ASSOCIATION OF CANADA'S LEVEL THREE THEORY OF COACHING

I. R. HASLAM   School of Physical Education and Recreation
                 Brock University

L. ADAMS   School of Physical Education
                 Brock University

Abstract

Coach education programs often emerge on the basis of an ad hoc arrangement of content and methods that have but minimal concern for the truly generic needs of both coaches and athletes. The Coaching Association of Canada's national coaching certification program attempts to bridge the gap between theory and practice across three components and at five levels of delivery. This paper uses a conceptual model (Mason and Ventre, 1966) to analyze the level 3 theory of coaching course which is the highest level multi-sport theory course in the program at this time. What has developed is a process of coach education which has the potential to meet the practical and personal needs of all coaches.

Key words: Coaching process, Biophysical, Mental preparation, Program planning, Coping strategies, Growth and development.

Introduction

Ten years ago to this very week Canada had the privilege of hosting the twenty-first Olympiade of modern times and became a world stage for the top international athletes of the era. The preparations for the games went far beyond the facility development and operational organization and included a number of federal and provincial initiatives in the area of athlete and coach development. A variety of 'arms length' federal government agencies were established in the early 1970's one of which was the Coaching Association of Canada (C.A.C.). Part of the C.A.C.'s mandate was to train and develop coaches and with this in mind the National Coaching Certification Program (N.C.C.P.) was formed. This paper will briefly explain the nature, role and function of Canada's national coaching program and undertake a conceptual analysis and explanation of the level 3 theory of coaching course which is the most recently introduced (1981) and the highest level multi-sport component of the program.

Canada's National Coaching Certification Program

The N.C.C.P. embraces three distinct yet interrelated components
including a practical, technical and theoretical requirement.
The practical coaching experience is the actual time spent coaching
a team. Many sports will consider the requirement to have been
met at the first level of the program, for example, after one
year of coaching. This period of time can either be a season
of coaching or a calendar year of coaching. The technical requirement is the attendance at a recognized coaching course which involves at least 14 hours (at level 1) of instruction by a course
conductor who has been trained by the particular sport governing
body. These are uni-sport courses and are offered by the Ontario
Soccer Association, for example, on behalf of their national
affiliates, i.e. the Canadian Soccer Association. The theory
of coaching component is a multisport course that is designed
to introduce the coach to a variety of sport science topics to
assist in the planning and implementation of their programs.
The focus is on the pooling and sharing of ideas and information
across a number of sports as coaches join together in small group
situations to discuss the applicability of sport science issues
to their sport. The instructor of the course has attended a course
conductor training workshop through the provincial ministry responsible for sport development. In Ontario this would be the ministry
of Tourism and Recreation.

   The N.C.C.P. is guaged on five levels that correspond to
geographical levels of coaching involvement. The first level
of technical, theoretical and practical experiences are designed
to meet the needs of the community level or local level house
league coach. The second level of the program across all components is designed to meet the needs of the regional coach.
This coach might be involved with travel teams who engage in
competition throughout a given region of the province. The third
level of the program is designed for the provincial level coach
who has aspirations of coaching in provincial championships or
even working with provincial teams in the Canada games or national
championships. The fourth level of the program is geared to meet
the needs of coaches who are coaching athletes at the national
level of competition and with aspirations of international competition. At the fifth and final level are the international level
coaches who coach Canada's national teams at the World Championships, Commonwealth and Olympic Games.

   The delivery of the program involves all three levels of government in Canada including the federal, provincial and municipal
departments responsible for leadership development in sport.
Sport Canada, the national sport governing bodies and the coaching
association of Canada have shared responsibilities for the development of material at all levels and with the implementation of
levels 4 and 5. The provincial and territorial governments and
the provincial sport governing bodies are responsible for the
implementation of levels 1 through 3. Municipalities help with
the marketing and hosting of leadership clinics and workshops

in communities across Canada. Finally, a National Coaching Certification Council which is comprised of officials from all the aforementioned partners plus the interprovincial sport and recreation council is the advisory body to the program.

A conceptual model

An educational program at any level of service must be based upon a statement of goals and objectives to facilitate intelligent decision making relative to the content, methods and sequence of the process. The national coaching certification program in Canada is no exception. To facilitate an explanation and analysis of the level three theory of coaching a conceptual framework (Mason and Ventre, 1966) that illustrates the relationship between program ends and means will form the basis of the ensuing discussion. It is hypthesized that **what** we include in the program at this level is only valuable if it relates directly to **how** we teach the course, **when** we change the course and most importantly **why** we conduct the course the way we do (see Figure 1).

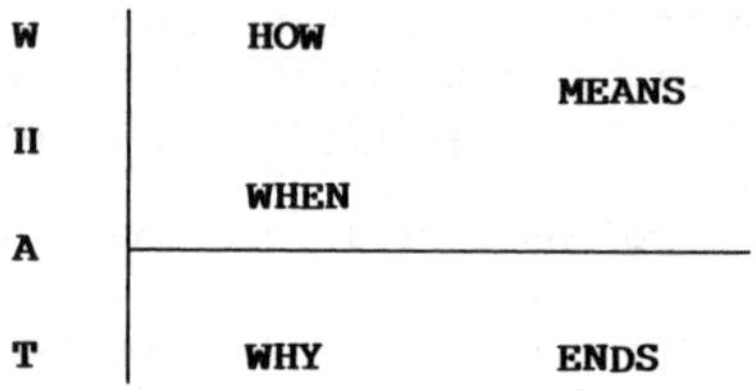

```
W       HOW
                    MEANS
II
        WHEN
A       ─────────────────────────
T       WHY          ENDS
```

Fig. 1   A conceptual framework for an analysis of the level 3 theory of coaching

A conceptual analysis of the level 3 theory of coaching

Administrative context
The level 3 theory is a 35 hour course designed for coaches who have completed the requirements of the first two theory levels and are fully certified at level 2 in all areas. There are three multiple choice tests in the course, a compulsory attendance at all sessions requirement along with the submission of a yearly training plan.

Course Content (WHAT?)
Biophysical content

Level one theory introduces coaches to the concepts of practice planning such as energy systems, use of space and creating a suitable learning environment while the Level two content looks at planning for the competitive season. Conceptually, the coaches are asked to examine in level 2 the changing roles of the given energy systems as the season progresses.

In the level three course coaches are provided with biophysical information that should be incorporated into a year round training program. Very early in the program coaches are trained to conduct and interpret selected field and lab like tests of physiologic function. Coaches are encouraged to utilize tests as an evaluation tool which will provide information about the athletes status in a given energy system in relation to his teammates and also in relation to some desired end point of physiologic function. This information allows both the coach and the athlete an opportunity to evaluate the existing training program and to make any necessary adjustments to bring the athlete back in line with pre-stated goals. Another benefit of the testing program is that coaches are able to provide exercise prescription that is appropriate in terms of intensity duration and frequency. As the athletes energy systems respond to training, exercise can be changed in terms of mode (continuous vs. interval) and intensity (% of VO_2 max). Power and capacity of each of the energy systems is also examined as they relate to performance requirements at an elite level.

In level three coaches are also provided with information about strength training, flexibility training, nutritional planning and biomechanics. In all cases the emphasis for the participant is to organize material into a yearly plan that will meet the needs of a preelected target group that has been identified by the coaches themselves. As such, implementation of the material is veiwed as a problem solving exercise. Instructors take the position that there is enough information in the thirty-five hours of instruction to produce an adequate training program. However, the problem for the coaches is being able to pick out the material that is appropriate to their sport, the age of the competitor, the level of competition, and of course the goals the coach and athlete have agreed upon. The role of the instructor, then is to act as a facilitator for planning and problem solving so that coaches can implement their programs in a real life setting.

Socio-psychological content

Coaches entering the level 3 psychology section have had an introduction to selected issues in the area including the notion of self concept development through sport, communication skills, what motivates athletes, anxiety and athletic performance and the progressive muscular relaxation (P.M.R.) technique. At level 3 the content includes a selection of topics in the general area of mental preparation including visual imagery, mental rehearsal, additional relaxation strategies including centering techniques and controlled breathing (Orlick, 1980, Tutko and Tosi, 1976, Vanek and Cratty, 1970), as well as attentional control strategies (Nidiffer, 1977, 1978, 1981) and mental simulation procedures. Rushall's (1979) precompetition and competition coping strategies form the basis of additional units in this section of the course

followed by growth and development material based upon the writings
of Mazill, Ash and Smoll (1978) and Thomas (1977). Finally, a
planning and problem solving unit that is extremely important
to the organization of the theoretical aspects and which is
designed to bridge the gap between theory and practice. These
sections are based upon the work of Bompa (1983) whose classic
test the Theory and Methodology of Training outlines the concept
of periodization in training program design. The content of the
level 3 theory is organized for teaching purposes on the basis
of three broad areas that deal with the **evaluation** of concepts,
the **organization** of concepts and the skills needed for the **implementation** of the material.

Evaluation would include the gathering of data primarily on
motivation levels in sport, arousal levels in relation to athletic
performance and attentional styles. The material also includes
discussions and ideas on strategies a coach could use for
administering questionnaires, analyzing and interpreting data
as well as interviewing and counselling athletes on the results.

The second area for consideration is the organization of an
athletes psychological training program in relation to the physiological, technical and strategical requirements of the yearly
training plan. Actual mental training techniques are built into
the yearly plan with dates and times set aside for periodic monitoring of training effects. The yearly training plan is broken
down into three phases of the season (at the most basic level)
including a pre-season, in-season and post-season period. The
coach takes a particularly active role in the explanation of the
concepts and the techniques of evaluation of mental profiles during
the pre-season and then in collaboration with the athlete determines practice procedures and priorities for the season. Actually
during the season the athlete practices the various techniques
on their own, away from the training site, thus taking very little
time from the physical, technical or strategical training components. Constant communication is maintained between coach and
athlete on the regularity and perceived effectiveness of the techniques as well as feelings toward the training. A written log
of mental training schedules is maintained by the athlete that
outlines and charts the volume, intensity, duration frequency
and type of mental training activity.

The final focus of the level 3 theory psychology component
is the ability of the coach to implement a mental training program
for athletes and in this sense a variety of skills unique to this
material is practiced during the course. For example, the ability
to introduce the concept of mental training techniques; the ability
to counsel athletes in relation to a selection of tests that are
available through the program; the skill of adminstering and analyzing the data for each athlete; the challenge of actually conducting and undertaking a relaxation or visual imagery session; and
finally the ability to teach athletes how to design and refine
pre-competition and competition coping strategies. Thus the
psychology component of level 3 theory teaches a selection of
basic mental preparation concepts, outlines strategies for

organization of mental preparation in the yearly training plan
and teaches coaches a variety of skills required to implement
this material.

Course methods (HOW?)
One of the strengths of the N.C.C.P. at all levels of the theory
component is the emphasis on adult learning techniques in that
the atmosphere for learning created by these strategies produces
a continual sharing and pooling of information across all sports.
Ideas from some coaches that have introduced various techniques
with their athletes helps other coaches to visualize the possibilities of these techniques for their own sport. Still other
coaches share and discuss strategies that didn't work and try
to understand why they failed and what they would do again under
the same circumstances. In themselves these strategies make for
a rewarding and fruitful experience for the coaches personally
and if the coaches are excited about the content and ideas they
are more likely to get their athletes excited about the material.

Scientific findings (WHEN?)
The program content is heavily influenced both directly and
indirectly by the emergence of up-to-date research findings that
have application to the purpose and intent of the N.C.C.P. The
direct interface occurs at the federal level as consultants who
are responsible for the program liaise with their provincial
affiliates to determine the impact of the content on coaches and
athletes. If material is considered to be irrelevant or out of
date it is subject to scrutiny by selected sport scientists across
Canada and changes are made directly to the support literature
and teaching strategies. However, the program content is probably
more influenced indirectly by the marvellous array of sport science
journals that reach both the course conductors who teach the
courses and the coaches who have finished the program or are continuing through the various levels. The Science Periodical on
Research Technology and Sports, Coaching Review, Coaching Science
Update, the Sport Bibliography published by S.I.R.C. as well as
the sport specific journals published by many of the national
sport governing bodies all serve to keep both coaches and course
conductors informed and up-to-date.

Purpose of the course (WHY?)
Perhaps the most important question in the development of any
educational experience is the question of purposes and objectives.
Even today in Canada there is disagreement among sports scientists
over the content of the program largely because of a misunderstanding, perhaps, of the purposes of the course. Some would
argue that the focus is on the coaches study of the disciplines
of the sports sciences because without a thorough knowledge and
understanding of the concepts implementation would be difficult.

Still others look at the coach as a teacher and one who is not training in the specific disciplines of the sports sciences but is very much interested in pedagogy and the application of relevant sport science information. It is on the basis of the last assumption that the present level 3 theory of coaching is presently being taught. The question of how to implement the latest advances in sport scientific knowledge is far more important to the coach and ultimately to the athlete than knowledge of how the sport scientist arrived at these recommendations.

With this in mind the material was structured to meet the needs of a coach working with a particular level of athlete. In the case of the level 3 theory material most coaches will need to spend some time (minimum 3 times per week) during the week with athletes who are sufficiently serious about their sport to undertake the level of training emphasis in both the biophysical and socio-psychological areas. These athletes would be classified in a competitive + stage of sport development and would likely have demonstrated their potential at the local and regional levels and who are now in contention for representative honours at the provincial level. Age per se has little influence on the nature of the athlete in that all sports have different types of elite competitors; rather, it is the ability level of the athlete that determines the relevance of the material.

A further theoretical assumption would be that the level 3 theory coach has been through level 1 and 2 theory courses and has therefore experienced a developmental sequence of content with one unit of material building on the next. In short, the accumulative knowledge of coaching theory through the N.C.C.P. alone is in excess of 70 hours of instruction. The expectations of this coach are therefore quite high.

Summary

The C.A.C.'s national coaching certification program was outlined in this paper and a conceptual analysis undertaken of the level 3 theory of coaching course. The course represents a magnificent example of an integrated multi-disciplinary educational program for coaches involved with elite athletes that can be conducted to good effect in a multi-sport setting as well as in a single sport course.

It should be noted that the perceptions of the program and of the course as previously explained are the views of the authors and not necessarily of the C.A.C.

References

Bompa, T. O. (1983) Theory and Methodology of Training. Dubuque, Iowa, Kendall/Hunt.

Mason, R. and Ventre, P.G.L. Elements of Physical Education. Thistle, Leeds, England.

National Coaching Certification Council (1979) National Coaching Certification Program Level 1 Theory Manual, C.A.C., Ottawa.

National Coaching Certification Council (1979) National Coaching Certification Program Level 2 Theory Manual, C.A.C., Ottawa.

National Coaching Certification Council (1981) National Coaching Certification Program Level 3 Theory Manual, C.A.C., Ottawa.

Nideffer, R. M. (1981) The Ethics and Practice of Applied Sport Psychology. Movement Publications, New York.

Nideffer, R. M. (1977) The Inner Athlete. Thomas Cromwell, New New York.

Orlick, T. (1980) In Pursuit of Excellence. Coaching Association of Canada, Ottawa.

Rushall, B. S. (1979) Psyching in Sport. Pelham Books Ltd., London.

Tutko, T. and Tosi, U. (1976) Sport Psyching. J. P. Tarcher, Inc., Los Angeles.

Mazill, R., Ash, M. and Smoll, F. (1978) Children in Sport: A A Contemporary Anthology. Human Kinetics Publishers, Champaign, Illinois.

Thomas, J. (1977) Youth Sports Guide for Coaches and Parents. AAHPER, Washington, D.C.

Seidentop, D. Physical Education and Introductory Analysis. W. C. Brown, Dubuque, Iowa.

Yanek, M. and Cratty, B. (1970) Psychology and the Superior Athlete. MacMillian, Toronto.

Section III

Structure and Content

COACH EDUCATION - STRUCTURE, CONTENT AND QUALITY CONTROL

REX HAZELDINE
The National Coaching Foundation

Abstract
One of the major problems in establishing any coach education programme is quality control. With common theory material this is particularly important if we want coaches to adopt a positive approach to learning. There are several aspects of any programme which require control:

(a) The technical content which needs to be analysed in terms of relevance to coaches, the level at which the coaches operate and the various needs of different sports.
(b) The appointment and subsequent training of tutors. There are many specialists in the performance-related arts and sciences who have the required technical expertise but there is still a need to provide orientation courses to consider the style and method of delivery to sports coaches.
(c) The presentation of written material and audio-visual aids is crucial to the success of any scheme. The reader or audience needs to be stimulated by their experience to want to learn more.

The practical difficulties facing the National Coaching Foundation in setting up its coach education programme are used to elaborate the various points raised above and some attempt is made to identify practical solutions to the problems encountered.
Key words: National Coaching Foundation.

1. Introduction

The primary aim of the coach education programme is to provide all coaches access to a body of knowledge which is not necessarily sport specific but which has relevance to performance at all levels.

The initial exercise of identifying a body of knowledge must recognise the multifarious nature of coaching and must incorporate the current developments in sports science. There is growing agreement concerning the more apparent kinds of knowledge required for the practice of coaching. However, in developing the technical content in a coach education programme, detailed evaluation is required in terms of its relevance to coaching, its sensitivity to the level of operation and the sport specific factors. A balance must exist in the programme between performance-related sports science, educational responsibilities, conceptual issues and the technical requirements of the various sports.

This paper, in illustrating ways in which the service is created, implemented, developed and assessed, provides an insight into the mechanics of a national scheme for coach education.

2. Considerations

A number of major considerations were taken into account prior to devising the services for coaches:-

(a) The nature and content of the Governing Body award schemes already in existence.

(b) The amount of time and resources that many coaches working on a voluntary basis would have available.

(c) The structure and content of the scheme has to allow for the different levels of coaching expertise and experience, together with the diverse needs of the various sports.

(d) In the implementation of the scheme, consideration has to be given to the availability of appropriate experts to staff courses.

(e) The requirement for support material in terms of written resource packs and audio-visual aids.

(f) A national scheme has to be flexible and adaptable.

3. Planning

In co-ordinating coach education throughout the United Kingdom, the National Coaching Foundation decided to operate through a network of Institutes of Higher Education. This system enables direct use of resources nationally, but the widespread nature of the network presents something of a challenge to the Foundation in terms of quality control of its services.

The Foundation developed a 4-tier structure on which to base its technical services. The design of the inaugural programme and the support resource material was evolved in co-operation with members of The British Association of National Coaches, The National Governing Bodies of Sport and the British Association of Sports Science.

4. First Level

At the first level of provision, foundation units were devised to provide opportunities for coaches to acquire a fundamental understanding of basic principles of performance-related knowledge. Introductory Study Packs were produced for 6 units of study:-

(a) The Coach in Action
(b) The Body in Action
(c) Safety and Injury
(d) Improving Techniques
(e) Mind over Matter
(f) Planning and Practice

These Level 1 Introductory Study Packs were written by coaches and sports scientists - in some cases in actual partnership. With a considerable number of these publications now in circulation, feedback from all sources will be noted, recorded and taken into account and the resource material will be revised and re-written. Audio-visual material and workshop manuals are also being produced to accompany the Introductory Study Packs and to improve the efficiency of the material at this level. The underlying principle at the first level is to help the coach move towards positive and safe activity.

5. Second Level

At this level, with the underlying principle of moving towards understanding, core units were constructed to present coaches with opportunities to develop a cognizance of a common body of knowledge. Inter-related packs of information were offered as a number of separate units which coaches could select as required. Twelve units (e.g. Nutrition and Sports Performance, Development of Strength and Speed, Mental Preparation for Competition, and How to Plan your Programme, etc) are at present based in a network of 30 institutions across the United Kingdom. Each unit comprises a course of 4-6 hours using lectures and practical workshops.

Resource packs to support the Level 2 courses have been designed to supplement and provide resource material for this programme of tutored courses. These publications also provide a basis of common theory material and to a certain extent a means of controlling and standardising the content of the courses within a national network structure. The authors of these resource packs were selected for their professional knowledge and expertise in the particular area of study together with substantial coaching experience or a close liaison with coaches. At the conclusion of the first programme, review seminars were conducted for each set of courses. Tutors from the network centres met to appraise the cogency of the course and its resource material. The revision and re-writing of the resource packs then took place, incorporating comments and criticisms received from coaches and governing bodies.

The essence of the Level 2 courses is tutoring so the appointment and training of tutors becomes a vitally important factor in National Coaching Foundation quality control. The inceptive appointment of tutors was drawn mainly from personnel within the Institutes of Higher Education, according to their relevant disciplines, e.g. anatomy, nutrition or in the specialised application of related disciplines (exercise physiology or sports psychology). In approving the appointment of tutors, the National Coaching Foundation was looking for coaching expertise itself or close contact with coaching, as well as a working knowledge of their own subject.

Presentation of information, style and method of delivery to sports coaches is also a vital function within the programme and a tutor's pack has been written for each course with guidelines for such presentation. In addition to outlining the general approach required, specific information for each course, inclusion of practical work and recommendations for further study are included. The tutor's pack also contributes to a measure of consistency and standardisation across the courses. The tutoring factor still requires considerable development in the future because, although the majority of specialist tutors have the academic and technical expertise, there is an obvious need to provide training courses that will study fully the pedagogy for sports coaches. It is planned that these training courses will be supplemented by seminars, workshops and conferences for tutors.

The complete programme of courses has been monitored through a research project conducted by Loughborough University on behalf of the Sports Council. The findings of the monitoring will be incorporated into future planning.

The basic aim of the research is to assess the effectiveness of the coach education programme and to concentrate on the certain key areas of enquiry:-

(a) Recruitment of coaches including the publicising of courses, how and to whom courses are promoted, links with the regional and national bodies, assessment of those sports responding to the scheme and reasons for co-operation.
(b) Consideration of the specific needs of the regions.
(c) Possible links with other coaching or similar schemes.
(d) Timing, structure and location of courses.
(e) Assessing the reception and perceived effectiveness of courses in the eyes of coaches, Governing Bodies and BANC and determining the criteria that relate to the different perceptions of coach education courses.
(f) The effectiveness of the information given on the courses, curriculum, content, level and 'pitch' of information, presentation; practical/theory, general versus specific approach, relevance to particular sports.
(g) The use of Institutes of Higher Education as a resource base for coaches with reference to staff expertise, research facilities, testing of performers, dissemination of sports coaching information and use of student clubs.

With reference to this final area of enquiry, it should be observed that the very nature of a network scheme implies a dependence on the network centres to provide a quality contribution to coach education. The current economic situation and ever stronger trends towards research based initiatives in the Institutes of Higher

Education and the pursuit of academic excellence indicates that in the immediate future institutions as a matter of policy will not readily provide a service for sports coaching. The National Coaching Foundation in forming the nucleus of the network and being responsible for policy, finance and administration will also need to inject and influence an interest and commitment to coach education within the institutions and to initiate and co-ordinate more fundamental research in the area.

6. Third Level

At Level 2 the core elements of coaching theory were identified and presented to coaches and Governing Bodies by a 'market stall' approach through the network centres. Early discussion indicated that Level 3 courses, with an underlying principle of moving towards innovation, should be coach-centred, identifying particular coaching responsibilities, coach problems and providing information to assist with problem solving, e.g. stress control, peak performance, sports injuries. It was thought that the presentation of this information could be offered in several ways - specialised in-depth related knowledge or grouping coaches with 'like' concerns to study particular aspects of performance - e.g. body management sports, gymnastics, diving, trampolining coaches doing a more detailed study of biomechanical analysis. Another approach could provide a synthesis of material already learnt and assist coaches to translate the information presented at Level 2 into skilled practice. This would involve practical workshops which, for example, could consider monitoring performance including physiological, psychological and medical evaluation.

In order to develop the most effective presentation of this level, pilot projects would be held and carefully monitored at a number of centres before being implemented in a full national programme. National Governing Bodies would be required to endorse applications from coaches so that on the completion of the pilot projects their opinions will be reflected in the future planning of the full scheme.

7. Fourth Level

Level 4 was designed to provide a support service for all senior coaches when and if required. It is based on close liaison between the Foundation, the Governing Bodies, the British Association of National Coaches and, of course, individual coaches. The service includes undertaking special research projects related to coaching, providing access to relevant facilities and expertise to assist with specific problem solving, giving access to latest research findings and information from home and abroad, and arranging for coaches to undertake periods of investigation or study. Seminars, workshops and conferences are organised to provide an exchange of ideas and the opportunity to examine coaching topics. The interaction between the Foundation and senior coaches not only enables an appropriate service to be provided at this level but also valuable feedback from experienced coaches on future indications and initiatives needed for coach development.

8. Conclusion

Currently, the functioning of the National Coaching Foundation relies on a system of voluntary co-operation. Close liaison with Governing Bodies, Directors of Coaching and coaches is essential to introduce and familiarise them with the programmes and resources which the Foundation is providing. Attractive, well written material and high quality audio-visual aids are an essential requirement of the resources, incorporating a balance between sound relevant content and an appealing presentation.

The National Coaching Foundation will need to continue to gain agreement among coaches about what they need to know and will face the challenge of attracting coaches to theoretical courses and resources. This can only be achieved by a programme of coach education which has evidence of relevance and quality in every aspect. Further, by linking its information service for coaches with its technical programme, the Foundation seeks to promote a coach education programme in the fullest sense by attempting in the first place to stimulate coaches to seek more information in their field and to provide an efficient fabric for the dissemination of that knowledge. It is undeniable that a coach requires a detailed and intimate knowledge of the sport but there must be a balance between technical requirements and a knowledge of relevant coaching theory. A better understanding of the theory should bring a greater mastery of the practice.

COACH EDUCATION AT THE MASTER'S LEVEL - A CANADIAN EXPERIENCE

MICHAEL R. HAWES
Faculty of Physical Education, University of Calgary, Alberta, Canada

Abstract
In 1977 a Federal Government Green Paper identified the most critical technical problem facing Canadian Amateur sport as being the "development of coaches for communities, schools,clubs and international athletes". The paper identifies further problems as a " shortage of experienced world class coaches in Canada" and a "lack of available formal instruction for anyone wishing to become a world class coach". The following programme was developed at the University of Calgary to meet these perceived needs but the resulting programme has not been offered due to a lack of funding by the Provincial Government. The impending Winter Olympic Games has resulted in the development of a new Physical Education facilty and it is anticipated that the Provincial Government will approve funds for the programme to commence in September 1987.
The programme is designed to integrate the many disciplinary areas that are perceived necessary for an expert coach to master. Students will study a common core of theory courses applicable to coaching in general which will lead into sport specific courses and ultimately to extensive practica with an expert coach or coaches.
Key words: Coaching, Canada, Master's Degree, Sport

1. Introduction

The place of sport in modern society is a phenomenon of recent origin which continues to gather momentum. The significance of competition between athletes representing their countries is viewed in many different ways - an entertainment spectacle, an arena for ideological propaganda, a placebo for the ills of society, a place for the realization of the lofty ideals of character building, perseverance and training for life, a theatre for showcasing the grace of human movement. Whatever values are placed upon sports events in the international arena at the level of the individual there can be no doubt that the end endeavour of the athlete is the pursuit of excellence. The athlete is seeking to attain ultimate levels of physiological efficiency, to refine complex motor skills to their maximum mechanical advantage and to prepare the mind to allow the human body to perform under the most stressful of psychological conditions. The preparation of an athlete to achieve ultimate levels of efficiency is both an exacting science and a creative art which is mediated through one individual, the coach. The scientific aspects of coaching have been and continue to be subjected to intensive scrutiny by sport scientists in many countries. The problem however, has always been to meld specific scientific knowledge with the creative skills of the coach.

In recent years Canada has been relatively successful in the international sport arena. This success has been in no small part due to a policy of bringing in master coaches from many parts of the world to provide leadership in sport development and to coach national teams. However, until the late 1970's there was no formal educational system to prepare Candians with the necessary theoretical and practical knowledge required to coach at any level. The Federal government, in the White Paper "Partners in Pursuit of Excellence" (May 1979) identified the most critical problem facing Canadian amateur sport to be "the development of coaches for communities, schools, clubs and international athletes". This problem has in part been addressed by the National Coaching Certification Programme (NCCP) which has evolved over a period of years initially establishing a solid base for community level coaches and subsequently offering a more sophisticated and detailed knowledge base for coaches operating at district and provincial levels.

It is appropriate to digress and briefly describe the Canadian sports milieu as it is frequently categorised with the United States and described as the "North American Model". The conduct of amateur sport in Canada is quite distinct from the manner in which it is organised in the United States. The size of the country and the relative smallness of the population contribute to a unique circumstance for sport development . A relatively small population spread over an enormous area is clearly at a logistical disadvantage when it comes to identifying and developing athletic talent and at an even greater disadvantage when it comes to assembling and preparing representative teams. It is not feasible to rely on a few peripetetic coaches to perform these tasks due to the vast distances and travel time required. Canadian society has responded to these circumstances in several ways - by evolving a network of community organised sports (typically ice hockey, soccer, baseball, softball) commencing at ages 5-6yrs and organised and coached by parent volunteers; by development of agencies, clubs and businesses manned by professional coaches on a full or part time basis (typically in sports such as figure skating, gymnastics, swimming, dance) again commencing at 5-6yrs. In contrast to the authors experience in the UK the Canadian school system does not provide the same degree of leadership in sport development. Scholastic teams typically compete in football, basketball,volleyball and track and field but age categories are far fewer than are typically found in the UK and consequently there is less opportunity to be a member of a team, receive coaching from a sport educated individual and to compete on a regular basis. University and College representrative teams are active in most sports typically operating with a philosophy of the pursuit of excellence. However, in contrast to the United States university sports in Canada draw crowds measured in hundreds rather than thousands or tens of thousands for major sports in United States. Thus the entertainment spectacle of college sports has nowhere near the influence on sport programmes in Canada as in the Unites States.

It is clear from this brief summary that there is a considerable amount of sport coaching commencing at a young age and that many of the coach practitioners are voluntary with no formal training as a coach and often little or no competitive background in the sport. While community efforts are appreciated it is clear to those with professional training that these individuals unwittingly have the potential to do more harm than good in developing and nurturing athletic talent and attitudes towards an active lifestyle. These problems have been addressed with good success through the NCCP programme, however the major problem of preparing high caliber coaches stilll remains. As a temporary measure the Federal government implemented the Coaching Apprenticeship Program to provide support for identified coaches to work with Master coaches. While such a programme allows coaches to learn from successful coaches it does not systematicaly address the problem of providing a sophisticated knowledge base for rational decision making in the coaching process.

With this backdrop the Faculty of Physical Education at the University of Calgary decided to develop a Master's Degree in the Art and Science of Coaching specifically geared to coaching the elite athlete. The University of Calgary is situated in the province of Alberta on the Eastern slopes of the Rocky Mountains. The city is predominantly a financial center with strong ties to the oil industry and in recent years has grown rapidly to a population of just over half a million. The city succesfully bid for the 1988 Winter Olympic Games and this has led to a large influx of capital funding for facilities that include the Olympic Saddledome, the World's first indoor 400m speed skating oval, ski jumping and bobsled/luge tracks all of which are within 15 mins of the University. The University as such is very young - a mere 20 years as an autonomous entity. The Faculty of Physcial Education currently does not offer a graduate program although staff members supervise graduate students in Biomechanics, Exercise Physiology and topics in Curriculum and Instruction. In proposing a masters degree in coaching the Faculty previously evaluated their perceived strengths and weaknesses, other offerings at the provincial and national levels and the needs of professionals in the general field of Physcial Education within the province. Independent of the Olympic thrust it was decided that the Faculty could make a major contribution in this particular field. The University of Calgary already has an established faculty capable of providing both the formal education and practical experience alluded to in the Government White Paper. In addition the Faculy hosts a very successful International Coaching Symposium every year to address theoretical and technical aspects of a wide variety of sports. Faculty for this symposium are drawn from many parts of the world - for example Alan Wade and Wilf Paish who need no introduction to this auidence, other include Dr Tom Tutko, Dr. Miroslav Vanek in sport pyschology, Dr. Robert Singer in motor learning and many others. Resident teams in Calgary include the national volleyball and ice hockey teams and the world champion synchronised swimming team (Aquabelles) together with a substantial portion of the national swimming team.

2. Nature and intent of the degree

The intent of the programme is to prepare individuals who are knowledgable and effective coahes with the ability to read and understand relevant research, address problems in their field and who have well developed technical, inter-personal and professional skills. The programme will reflect a professional rather than research orientation. Coursework has been structured to maximise the cross linkage of areas of study rather than to present discrete sub-disciplinary courses. In addition, a substantial practicum component has been included to allow a student to practise the application of knowledge under expert supervision.

Table 1: Art and Science of Coaching Curriculum Model

	Technical Knowledge	Skill Analysis Error Detection Communication	Interpersonal Skills
Knowledge base on Admission	- personal skills - playing experience - coaching experience	- Functional Anatomy - Biomechanical Princip. - Motor Learning	- Intro. Psychology - Sport Psychology - Intro. Sociology - Sport Sociology
Knowledge base on Graduation	- Knowledge & application of advanced skills & techniques pertinent to particular sport - Knowledge & application of advanced strategies	- skill analysis by film & VTR - force analysis - EMG & Electro-goniometry - Biofeedback - Performance models, information theory - Presentation of material - types of instruction, selective attention, whole part whole learning, teaching for training - Practice consider-ations knowledge of bio-mech, principles, practice distribution individual differ-ences in perf. - Feedback - knowledge of peformance & results, augmented feedback, use of A-V aids	- Motivation - behaviorism humanism, social com-parison theory, inequity theory, achievment theory - Performance outcomes - attribution theory - Group processes - Attitude formation and change - Psychology of competition anxiety management, arousal & aggression - Imagery - Behaviour Management - Perception management - Goal seting
Medium	- Practicum including individual study guided by Master coach	- Lecture, seminar practicum	- Lecture, seminar practicum

Table 1 (continued)

	Sport Condition-ing &Athlete Selection	Philosophy & International Knowledge	Professional Knowledge	Research Reading
Knowledge base on Admission	- Biology - Physiology - Exercise Physiology - Human Growth & Development	- Philosophy of Sport & Physical Education - Sport History	- Administration of Sport & Physical Education Prog-rammes	- Tests and Measurement

Knowledge base on Graduation	- Principles of athlete preparation
	  i. muscular system
	  ii. cardio-vascular
	  iii. respiratory
	  iv. energy systems
	  v. nutrition
	  vi. environmental factors
	  vii. ergogenic factors
	- Training principles
	  i. macro & micro cycles
	  ii. tapering, peaking & periodization
	  iii. types of training
	  iv. monitoring progress
	  v. age & sex factors
	- Long range prediction
	  i. anthropometric considerations
		-Theory of games & play
		- Meaning of competitive athletics
		- Role of coach
		- Motivation of coach
		- Ethics
		- State sponsorship model
		- Volunteer model
		- Professional model
		- Issues in international sport
			- Administration & organisation of athletic teams
			- Use of assistant coaches & support staff
			- Public relations & media
			- Funding
			- Sport governing bodies
				- Problems & hypotheses
				- Variables
				- Variance
				- Sampling
				- Research design
				- Types of re-search
				- Measurement
				- Evaluation
				- Statistics
				- Library access & appropriate publications & sources

Medium	- Lecture, laboratory seminar, practicum	- Lecture, seminar	- Lecture, seminar	- Lecture, sem-inar, project

125

3. Role of the graduate

It is envisaged that graduating students will be employed by national and provincial sport governing bodies as coaches of national and provincial teams in Canada and other countries; as technical directors of associations in charge of developing coaches and technical material throughout the country or within various regions; as professional club coaches in a variety of sports; and as coaches within elite programmes at universities, colleges, clubs and schools.

4. The degree programme

4.1 Premises

a) The degree will be geared towards the practise of a profession rather than the study of a discrete discipline. The graduate will be capable of reading and evaluating reserach in terms of content, design and statisitical analysis but not necessarily able to conduct sophisticated research of his/her own.

b) The degree will be offered on a part time basis with courses offered in the evenings and and a minimum expectation of 1 full course per academic year. It is anticipated that many students will opt to complete the programme as full time students.

c) Completion of nominally six full courses will be expected for graduation. One full course represents study over the time period September to April with 78 hours of lecture - this amount may increase with additional expectations of seminars, labs and practica.

d) It is felt necessary that the student be exposed to the full coaching cycle under the tuteledge of a master coach - this would normally be an eleven or twelve month practicum commitment.

4.2 Expectation of the incoming student

a) The incoming student should have completed an appropriate undergraduate degree preferably with an emphasis in the science and social science of sport and physical activity. Applicants with a degree in another field and with particular coaching expertise may be admitted as a qualifying student on condition of completing appropriate undergraduate courses Such courses would be over and above those prescribed in the degree programme and would be determined by an admissions committee. Initial consideration of students would require at least a B average over the last two years of academic work

b) Under normal circumstances an applicant would be expected to have a minimum of two years full time practical experience in the field of coaching to allow full benefit from the practical and theoretical learning situations.

c) The applicant should have demonstrated a successful career in terms of team/individual achievments and communication of skills. In addition the admissions commitee will be looking for evidence of self motivation and ability to conduct individual study.

4.3 Curriculum

The particular curriculum design of the programme is summarised in table 1 with references to expectations for incoming knowledge, learning media and exit knowledge.

There are several elements of the curriculum that require further amplification. The practicum is regarded as the key element of the whole programme providing opportunity to work with and learn from a master coach. It is important that the practicum coach experience as wide a range of tasks as possible under the tuteledge of the master coach. Clearly there are limitations as to how much a coach will delegate to an apprentice coach and each individual will interpret the role in a unique manner. To alleviate this problem where possible the coach will be a faculty member at the University of Calgary and will be a part of the admissions committee. This guideline will limit the variety of sports that may be catered to and the number of students in any given sport at any given time. It is proposed that there will be opportunites, subject to funding and academic scrutiny, for practica to be completed with other coaches eg. national coaches based in Calgary, other parts of Canada or even in other countries.

The course project also requires some explanation. It is characteristic of a Master's programme for the student to demonstrate the ability to approach and resolve a particular problem. In the practical field of coaching the traditional thesis is not necessarily the most appropriate format for expressing this ability. A project will allow greater flexibility in task selection and approach taken - for example a coach may elect to research the available literature pertinent to training for a particular event and to write an extensive paper describing what he/she considers to be the best training programme under a given set of circumstances ; another example would be to contract with the supervising professor to have two or three papers accepted for publication in recognised journals in lieu of a project. The project also allows scope for those who wish to complete a more traditional experimental thesis.

5. Conclusion

This paper has reviewed the content of a programme to be offered at the Master's level in the field of "The Art and Science of Coaching" at the University of Calgary. The programme was proposed and accepted for its academic worth in 1981. The programme has not been offered yet because of a lack of appropriate facilties and the economic vagaries of a Province that relies heavily on the export of oil. However, the forthcoming Olympics has enriched the campus with some of the finest sport facilities in the world and the Provincial Government has commenced building an additional Physical Education complex with activity areas, research laboratories and teaching facilities that has the potential to become a national centre for applied sport research, coach education and a national team training centre in many sports.

References

Towards a National Policy on Amateur Sport (1977) Federal Government Green Paper, Department of National Health & Welfare

Partners in Pursuit of Excellence.(1979) Federal Government White Paper, Department of National Health & Welfare

THE CHALLENGE OF EDUCATING YOUTH SPORT COACHES IN SOUTH AUSTRALIA

IAN ROBERTSON
South Australian College of Advanced Education, Australia

Abstract
Sport for children and youth is a significant social phenonmenon in
South Australia. In this State, with a population of over one million
people, it is estimated that more than 100,000 children and youth and
10,000 coaches are involved in organised sport each year. However, the
extent, quality and impact of this interaction and involvement upon
the participants, in terms of their future participation in sport, has
not been researched until this time.

Between 1979 and 1985, a series of projects have been undertaken in
an endeavour to evaluate the contribution of organised sport towards
the development of children and youth, to identify any problem areas
that need to be addressed and to undertake pilot intervention projects.

The first study involved a stratified random sample of 2,3000
Adelaide children which investigated their socialisation into, through
and out of sport. The impact of sport involvement upon participants
and non-participants, who had dropped out of sport, was compared in
terms of the constructs of self concept, anxiety, attitudes towards
sport and physical activity involvement,and value orientations concerning winning, fair play and aggression.

Sport specific and pilot studies have also considered children's
perceived enjoyment factors towards organised sport; a needs assessment
of school sport coaches and the resource needs of primary schools.

The last, and current, study is considering the attitudes, values
and educational needs of over 1,000 junior sport coaches. The objectives of this study is to increase our understanding of the sport and
educational backgrounds; motivations, expectations, values and attitudes; problems ans perceived solutions; and information needs of these
coaches.

The final stage of the overall project will be in the development of
an educational package for parents and coaches. This package will be
an outcome of the research findings and the experience gained from the
presentation of seminars, coaching courses, the production of audio-
visual materials, and informal discussions with administrators, parents
and coaches from school and community club settings.

The primary aim of the package is to assist adults in their present-
ion of an improved quality sport programme for children and youth. It
will provide information in the form of a video "Winning through Sport'
accompanying brochures which will focus upon critical issues in under-
age sport, and behavioural guidelines by which schools and community

clubs can initiate self help, if needed, to facilitate change.

The 7 year project will conclude in early 1986 when the educational package is to be trialled and evaluated by interested schools and sport organisations.

The above projects have been supported by grants from South Australian College of Advanced Education and private sponsorship.

THE IMPACT OF THE NATIONAL COACHING CERTIFICATION PROGRAM ON THE
STATUS OF WOMEN IN COACHING IN CANADA

N. THEBERGE
Department of Kinesiology, University of Waterloo

Abstract
The National Coaching Certification Program provides training from
introductory to advanced levels of coaching. The NCCP has benefitted
women by providing a clearly structured and accessible means of
learning about coaching. This has partially offset the problems in
gaining entry to coaching that women have experienced because of their
exclusion from the informal contacts and networks in sport than men
enjoy. The Program has also aided women by providing a more standardized means of evaluating applicants' qualifications for a position
than has been available in the past. This increases the likelihood
that qualified women are considered and their applications are given
due process. While these effects of the Program have been important,
the other side of the picture is that the impact of the NCCP on
women in coaching is limited in several ways. These limitations include restrictions on the integration of the Program into the
Canadian sport structure, and additional factors within sport and
outside sport that restrict the mobility of women in coaching. The
paper concludes with the assessment that while the NCCP has improved
the prospects for women in coaching, the most powerful barriers to
women's advancement in this field lie beyond the reach of the NCCP.
Key words: Coaching, Women

   Gender inequality in sport is a topic that has received considerable attention in recent years. While there has been some reduction
in sex differences in rates of participation, in other types of sport
involvement the differences between males and females remain pronoun-
ced. An area that has been particularly resistant to change is
coaching. In both the United States and Canada, the proportion of
female coaches of girls' and women's programs has declined in recent
years, prompting concern to identify the causes of this trend and
steps that may be taken to reverse the pattern (Holmen and Parkhouse,
1981; Abbott and Smith, 1984; C.I.A.U. Women's Representative Committee, 1983).
   This paper provides a discussion of the effects of the National
Coaching Certification Program (NCCP) on the status of women in
coaching in Canada. Introduced in the early 1970's, the NCCP is
structured into five levels of training and certification, from introductory (Level I) to advanced (Level V). One of the more notable

features of the Program is the significant involvement of women. A report produced by Fitness and Amateur Sport Canada (1982) indicates that 35% of course participants are women. Although precise figures on the sex distribution of coaches in specific sports are often difficult to obtain, it is safe to say that in few sports does the proportion of women coaches approach 35 percent. Thus, figures on the involvement of women in the NCCP are encouraging. At the same time, a full consideration of the impact of NCCP on women in coaching must consider additional concerns. These include the implementation of the program, its integration into the Canadian sport structure, and the variety of factors beyond the reach of the NCCP that restrict women's movement into the coaching ranks. The discussion below will indicate that while the NCCP has improved the prospects of women in coaching, its impact is limited in several important ways.

The material presented here is taken from a larger project on the careers and work of women coaches. Research for this part of the project included a review of published materials on the NCCP and field work conducted in 1984*. The field work consisted of interviews with 32 coaches and administrators from across Canada, located in university and secondary school sport programs, private sport associations and federal and provincial government sport agencies.

1. The Implementation of the National Coaching Certification Program

The degree to which NCCP can have a bearing on any aspect of coaching, including the status of women, depends in part upon the extent to which the Program is adopted in Canadian sport. That is, the impact of NCCP depends upon the acceptance of the Program by individuals who are coaching or contemplating coaching, by sport administrators who hire, select and recruit coaches, and by individuals in the sport governance structure. Current assessments of the extent to which NCCP has "taken hold" in Canadian sport are mixed. Conversations with individuals at all levels of sport indicate clearly that NCCP is a "fact" on the Canadian sport scene. Most, if not all, persons are familiar with it and have some ideas about its strengths and limitations. It may be said that the NCCP has developed to the point where the Program provides a point of reference for discussions and assessments of coaching in Canada.

The other side of this, however, is that support for NCCP is by no means universal or unqualified. Nor is it possible to assess systematically the degree of resistance to and reservations about the Program. Similarly, there is no way to estimate the percentage of coaches across Canada who are certified or have taken courses. While information bearing on this issue may be available at the national level and for some sports in some provinces, it is more difficult to obtain data for lower level sport programs. In short, while NCCP has achieved broad representation and support, there are varia-

*This research was funded by the Social Sciences and Humanities Research Council of Canada, under its program on Women and Work.

tions in the representation and support across the Canadian sport
system. Moreover, assessing the degree of representation and support
with any kind of precision would be very difficult and likely impossible.

The limitations on the development and acceptance of NCCP are in
part an inevitable outcome of the structure of sport in Canada.
Canadian sport is organized in the educational system and by private
associations such as sport organizations,clubs and community agencies.
In addition, control of sport is exercised by a variety of groups and
agencies, both public and private. This shared responsibility and
control limits the capacity of any one group or agency (e.g., those
who promote the NCCP) to determine policy direction in sport (e.g.,
the implementation of the NCCP).

The practice of shared responsibility and control over sport also
characterizes the administration of the Certification Program. Responsibility for the development and implementation of NCCP is shared
by the Coaching Association of Canada (CAC), national and provincial
sport organizations, and national and provincial government sport
agencies. In general, this working association is judged to be a
success. It is, however, a loose association in which success depends upon a shared commitment to the extension of NCCP and a good
working relationship among the different bodies. In addition to the
above mentioned differences in the strength of this commitment, there
are differences in the effectiveness of the working relationship
among the various concerned parties.

Effective promotion of NCCP also relies on convincing coaches and
would-be coaches, as well as those who select and hire coaches, that
the Program is worthwhile and effective. Resistance to this message
takes different forms at different levels of the sport structure. At
the lower levels of sport, where potential coaches have little formal
training or knowledge about coaching -- and sometimes little sport
experience as in the case of some parents of youth participants --
the need for an experience such as NCCP may be obvious. Resistance
in this instance may come in the form of lack of interest or desire
to meet the obligations of the courses. Moreover, since may community sport programs have a severe shortage of coaches, they cannot
afford to reject volunteer coaches who are unwilling to take certification courses. The fact that coaching in Canada is largely a voluntary (i.e., unpaid) activity, particularly at the lower level of
sport, is a major limitation to the imposition of any requirements
upon would-be coaches, such as a requirement of certification.

At the higher levels of sport, resistance may come from persons
whose coaching experience and training largely predate the growth of
NCCP. Some of these persons may see little need to fulfill the requirements of the higher level certification courses. This resistance to NCCP among elite coaches in on the decline, however, as persons whose coaching experience largely predates the advent of NCCP
are becoming a minority. As well, many of these coaches have been
involved in the development of course materials and have come to support the program through this experience. In future years as there
is a continuing entry of new and younger coaches, it is likely that
the "old guard" resistance will continue to decline.

Although it is usually the case that adoption of NCCP relies on promotion and persuasion, there are some instances where certification is required of coaches in particular circumstances. For example, some provincial government ministries and departments are requiring Canada Games coaches to have a specified level of certification and some sport governing bodies have similar requirements for coaches at provincial or national championships. Although these examples of certification requirements are the exception rather than the rule, the incidence of such requirements is increasing. It is important to note,however, that Canada Games and national and provincial championships are occasions where governments and sport organizations can exercise some degree of control. In the more regular and ongoing coaching activity that takes place in clubs and sport associations across the country, it is more difficult for such control to be exercised. In the end, adoption and acceptance of NCCP depends much more on effective promotion than on legislation.

Another factor that affects the implementation of NCCP is the accessibility of courses. This refers to both the development of courses and to the availability of these courses across the country. Although the development of courses is taking place with greater speed in some sports than others, it is probably safe to say that in most sports progress is being made and in time most sports will have developed a full set of courses*. The accessibility of these courses, once developed, is another matter. Because of the country's size and the geographical dispersion of its population, the problems of offering any program nationally in Canada are considerable. While the lower level courses may be readily available in more populous areas, outreach to remote areas is administratively difficult and expensive.

A different set of factors influences the accessibility of higher level (III, IV, V) courses. These courses require a greater number of hours than the lower level courses and they are often scheduled over several weekends or an entire week in a location requiring most participants to travel some distance. These time and travel demands pose a problem for persons whose personal and work schedules are not flexible enough to enable them to attend the courses. As well, because of their more specialized content, these courses appeal to a smaller number of persons and consequently must draw from a broad geographical area. As a result, the higher level courses, like the lower level courses in less populous areas, also are often difficult and expensive to administer.

2. Impact of the NCCP on Women in Coaching in Canada

The first point to be noted on this topic is that women are involved in the Certification Program extensively. As indicated above, fig-

---

*The composition of a "full" set of courses will vary among sports. Not all sports will develop level IV and V courses, either because they are domestic sports only (i.e., Canadian teams do not enter international competitions) or because there are too few national coaching positions to warrant course development.

ures reported in the Fitness and Amateur Sport Leadership Survey indicate that women are 35 percent of course participants. These data
show widespread involvement of women in the Program. Thus, if only
for its role in introducing women to the coaching world -- a world
which has traditionally been largely a male preserve -- NCCP must be
judged to be beneficial to the cause of women in sport.

There are some features of the Certification process that have enhanced the prospects of women in coaching. As a program which is
widely promoted and clearly structed, the NCCP provides a readily
identifiable way to learn about coaching. One of the factors that
has contributed to women's underrepresentation in coaching has been
their exclusion from the informal networks and contacts in sport that
men enjoy. These networks have provided men with encouragement, information and opportunities to become involved in coaching. Because
access to NCCP is not tied to the benefits of the "old boys network",
the Program has improved the opportunities for women to learn about
coaching.

Another way that the Program has benefited women is by offering a
more standardized means of evaluating applicants' qualifications
for a position than has been available in the past. The selection of
coaches is usually based on consideration of a variety of factors, including experience, references and performance in interviews. In the
end, however, these decisions are quite subjective. The absence of
identifiable and standardized criteria for the comparative evaluation
of candidates likely has worked to the disadvantage of women, both
because of their exclusion from the networks and contacts in sport
than men enjoy and because of outright prejudice and discrimination.
While consideration of certification levels has not elminated the
subjective component of the selection process, it has rationalized
the process to some extent. By providing at least one standardized
basis of comparison to be reviewed along with other factors, the
Certification Program has increased the likelihood that qualified
women are considered for positions and that their applications are
given due process.

3. Other Factors Affecting the Status of Women in Coaching

While the impact of the NCCP upon the status of women in coaching has
been beneficial, it has been limited because many of the factors that
restrict women's involvement in coaching are beyond the scope of the
NCCP.

One major influence that has discouraged women's entry into coaching has been a powerful tradition of sex role stereotyping and sex
typing of activities. The influence of these processes has been powerful in sport, which has traditionally been viewed as a masculine
activity and has been dominated by males. Moreover, within sport,
these processes have likely exerted a particularly strong influence
upon the entry of women into coaching. Of the possible sport roles
that women might fill (athlete, executive, coach, etc.), the influence of sex stereotyping has been extreme in the case of coaching.
The power and authority over athletes that coaches typically hold, as

well as the technical knowledge about sport that coaches must possess, both are inconsistent with conventional feminine stereotypes*. Thus, it is not surprising that the coaching role has been one of the most resistant in sport to challenges to conventional sex stereotyping.

Another factor limiting women's involvement in coaching is the difficulty of reconciling the obligations of the coaching role with traditional definitions of women's family and home responsibilities. Coaches typcially work long and demanding hours and must be available to travel to competitions. Often the major time period for practices is late afternoon and evening, or around the dinner hour. All of these demands place a particular strain on individuals whose personal and family responsibilities include primary responsibility for home and child care. In most cases, these are women. Thus, women in coaching who have families face a particular set of difficulties in reconciling the demands of their personal and professional lives.

A final factor limiting women's careers in coaching is sexism. The sexism that women experience in sport is but a specific instance of that which they face in other institutional settings. Among the forms that sexism in sport takes are outright bias against selecting and hiring women coaches; a form of victim-blaming that attributes the underrepresentation of women in coaching to women's lack of motivation and interest, rather than to a set of broader institutional and social forces; the exclusion of women from the networks and associations that provide access and pipelines to coaching positions; and the judgement that experience in men's sport provides better preparation for coaching than experience in women's sport. All these factors and other combine to continue the pattern of exclusion of women from coaching.

4. Conclusion

This paper has provided a discussion of some factors that affect the status of women in coaching. The discussion has paid specific attention to the impact of the NCCP on women's coaching careers. It has been argued that despite limitations upon the extension of the NCCP, the Program has improved the prospects of women in coaching. It has also been argued, however, that the impact of the NCCP on women in coaching is limited because many of the causes of women's underrepresentation lie beyond the scope of the Program and in some cases, lie outside of sport. The implication of such an analysis is that efforts to increase the number of women in coaching should be directed to expansion and recognition of the NCCP, and to improving the status of women in sport and in society.

---

*In regard to these characteristics, coaching is rivalled perhaps only by officiating, another sport role that has been resistant to women's entry.

References

Abbott, A. and Smith, D.R. (1981). Governmental constraints and
   labor market mobility. Work and Occupations, 11, 29-53
C.I.A.U. Women's Representative Committee (1983). [Canadian Inter-
   university Athletic Union]. Report of the Committee. Ottawa.
Fitness and Amateur Sport Canada (1982). Women in sport leadership:
   Summary of national survey. Ottawa: Government of Canada.
Holmen, M.G. and Parkhouse, B.L. (1981). Trends in the selection of
   coaches for female athletes: A demographic inquiry. Research
   Quarterly for Exercise and Sport, 52, 9-18.

Section IV

Professional Development

PROFESSIONAL DEVELOPMENT OF COACHES

P. CHELLADURAI
Faculty of Physical Education, University of Western Ontario

Abstract
This response to the paradigm paper, Coach education: Preparation
for a profession (Lyle, 1985), explores the topic of professions and
professionalization, and the extent to which coaching has been
professionalized. The unique features of coaching as an occupation
are outlined. Its progress along along the various attributes of a
profession are discussed with specific examples from the coaching
development programs of Canada and India. Finally, the need to
align coach education with university education is emphasized.
Key words: Coach education, Coaching development, Profession,
Professionalization, Professional development.

1. Introduction

It is indeed a privilege and an honor to be asked to present my
reactions to Coach Lyle's paradigm paper on Coach Education with
special reference to the professional development of coaches. My
task would have been easier if I could disagree with him on many of
the points he has made. Similarity in our perceptions is merely an
indication that the status of coaching is the same in our respective
countries. Thus, my presentation is mostly an elaboration of what
has been suggested by Coach Lyle.

The basic thesis of the paradigm paper (Lyle, 1985) is that:

Sports coaching will not become an established profession, but
the work of sports coaches can be professionalised and the
occupation established and valued. (p. 20)

In developing this thesis further, my paper outlines what a
profession is with a description of its attributes, and what is
meant by professionalization. An attempt has been made to evaluate
coaching as an occupation on selected professional attributes with
examples from the Canadian and Indian systems of promoting and
developing coaching.

2. Profession and professionalization

Bobbit et.al. (1978) have discussed the differences between a profession and professionalization. They noted:

> We can think of a profession, per se, as an ideal type of abstract model of an occupation.... The ideal is at one end of a continuum of occupations that range from nonprofession to profession. Any occupation may be mapped onto this continuum, depending on how it meets certain established criteria. Then virtually all occupations may be thought of as being in some state of professionalization... the dynamic process whereby an occupation moves toward a profession as the ideal type. (pp.103-104)

The distinction between the state of being a profession, and the process of becoming a profession can be best understood by reviewing the significant attributes of a profession. While the attributes of a profession have been variously listed and described, the most common set of attributes would include an organized body of knowledge, professional authority, sanction of the community, and a code of ethics.

2.1 A systematic body of knowledge.
According to Goode (1969), there are two generating traits for a profession: a body of knowledge and a commitment to service. The body of knowledge, in turn, leads to a number of other unique features including:

- developing special competencies, skills and practices of the profession;
- generating more knowledge by carrying out research as well as compiling and distilling the experiences of successful members; and
- transmitting the specialized knowledge and developing the special skills and competencies of the new entrants through a prolonged and arduous period of training.

It is noteworthy that the established professions like medicine and law relied on the universities for not only generating and synthesizing the relevant knowledge but also for imparting that knowledge and associated skills to the new entrants. It is so because the universities are best equipped to carry out these two functions, and because professions like to share in the universities' aura and mystique.

The training in the specialized body of knowledge would be both an intellectual and a practical experience. The status of the established professions is largely based on the number of years of training associated with entry into that profession. It is, after all, a surrogate measure of the quantity and quality of the knowledge to be absorbed. There are those who hold that most high school and college education can be crammed into half the current number of years. But, in the case of a profession, it can be argued

that long periods of training are needed not only to impart all
relevant knowledge and skills to the trainee, but also to inculcate
the attitudes, behavior, and ethical standards appropriate to the
profession.

2.2 Professional authority

The professional has the authority to decide on what service(s)
should be provided to a client, how and when. This professional
authority (or power) stems from, and is limited to the knowledge
base of the profession referred to earlier. More specifically, it
is the knowledge differential between the client and the
professional that determines the extent of professional authority
(Mills & Margulies, 1980; Sasser et al., 1978). Obviously, the
client(s) must first recognize and accept this knowledge
differential before "authority" can exist. Also the power of a
profession is related to the extent to which the profession can
claim monopoly over knowledge. Thus, those occupations that lack
exclusive control over a body of knowledge can best be described as
semi-professions (Hasenfeld, 1983).

2.3 Sanction of the community

A profession secures the sanction of the community to control the
training and admittance of members to the profession. It also
secures the right to monitor and evaluate the activities of its
members, and to reward members for good performance or punish them
for deviations from the technical and ethical standards set by the
profession. Further, the community restrains non-members from
engaging in the activities of the profession, thereby creating a
monopoly. These exclusive rights and privileges are sanctioned only
if an occupation deals with some universal social concerns and
problems of living, and if the community itself cannot muster the
knowledge and competencies necessary to effectively control and
regulate the members of the profession (Jackson, 1970).

2.4 A regulative code of ethics

With a view to enhancing the legitimation of itself, a profession
formulates a set of ideologies including its mission and values.
All professions emphasize the values of service, impartiality, and
rationality. A profession also attempts to control the behaviour of
its members by prescribing a code of ethics. Goode (1970) claimed
that the ideal of service is critical to the concepts of a
profession and professionalism.

A cursory analysis of many occupations would show that a large
number of them fail to meet the above criteria. Etzioni (1969)
designated occupations like teaching and nursing only semi-
professions since:

> Their training is shorter, their status is less legitimated ...
> there is less of a specialized body of knowledge, and they have
> less autonomy from supervision or societal control than "the"
> professions. (p. v)

Nevertheless, most occupations strive toward reaching that ideal of a profession. This striving, as noted earlier, is a process referred to as professionalization. The process of professionalization takes two directions. According to Friedson (1973), the first is:

> a process by which an organized occupation, usually but not always by virtue of making a claim to special esoteric competence and to concern for the quality of its work and its benefits to society, obtains the exclusive right to perform a particular kind of work, control training for and access to it, and control the right of determining and evaluating the way the work is performed. (p. 22) (Emphasis added)

The emphasis here is on gaining the sanctions from the community for exclusive control over the affairs of the profession. It is suggestive of political maneuvering in competition against other occupations. Historically, forming associations and engaging in political activity were necessary conditions for occupations to gain professional status (Wilensky, 1964).

The second direction that professionalization takes is to seek to improve various aspects like the knowledge base, the quality of the training programs, and commitment to the service ideal without reference to the status and power associated with a profession. Obviously, the professionalization of any occupation, including coaching, must take both directions. Prior to elaborating on the status of coaching with respect to professionalization, its unique features as an occupation need to be outlined.

3. Coaching as an occupation

It was mentioned earlier that the community bestows status and grants exclusive rights and privileges to those occupations that deal with some universal social problems and/or problems of living. From this perspective, how does coaching compare with occupations like medicine, law, and teaching. While all deal with people per se, coaching differs from the other three in significant ways. First, coaching deals with sport which is, fundamentally, a diversionary, leisure-time activity. The content of coaching is not anything serious like life in medicine or justice in law. Just like dentistry is accorded less status than medicine because "life can go on without the teeth", coaching will be accorded much less status than other occupations because life can go on without leisure. Secondly, the established professions deal with problems like disease and disorder whereas teaching and coaching are concerned with growth and learning. Society tends to favor those occupations that solve immediate problems; others are taken for granted. Also, coaching is concerned with pursuit of excellence which means that the pool of clients/customers is restricted to a few gifted and talented individuals. Since teaching is concerned with all the young people, it always is likely to get more societal support than coaching. Another distinguishing feature of coaching flows from the previous one. That is, its concern with pursuit of excellence implies that the _outcome_ of winning is the criterion of effectiveness whereas in other occupations the _process_ is also included. The unfortunate part of this concept of control through outcome is that the coach is held responsible for a team's failure, but the athletes get most of the credit for victories. For these reasons, the community is not likely to confer on coaching a status or authority comparable to other established professions like medicine or semi-professions like teaching.

From the foregoing, it is clear that coaching should refrain from any political activity and, instead, strengthen its internal bonds (organize itself into a strong association), and embark on the second aspect of professionalization, i.e., self-improvement.

4. Is coaching an organized occupation?

The concept of professionalization as defined earlier presupposes an organization of occupationally (career) oriented individuals. According to Wilensky (1964), an occupation must be followed full-time by its members, and be organized before it can be professionalized. Thus, it appears that forming an _association_ of a _large number_ of _full-time_ coaches is critical to the process of professionalization.

If we eliminate all those volunteers who engage in coaching as a pastime temporarily, we are left with a very limited number of coaches whose major source of income is through coaching. This would include all the physical education teachers who also coach in high schools, colleges and universities, and all the full-time coaches of the provincial, national sport governing bodies, and professional teams. Further, this number would be considerably reduced if physical education teachers in high schools were considered to be aligned with teaching rather than coaching.

In India, there is an effort by both the central and state governments to create a cadre of full-time coaches. About 800 coaches have been hired by the National Institute of Sports (NIS) which trains and certifies coaches. Each State government has employed or is in the process of employing NIS coaches to be posted in all the Districts and Blocks in the state. National services like the Defense Services and Railways have agreed to recruit NIS coaches. Nationalized banks and industries have also initiated the process of hiring NIS coaches to coach their teams. Apparently, this trend has filtered through to privately owned large businesses and industries. Recently, universities were subsidized to hire NIS coaches and pressure was brought on the state governments to hire NIS trained coaches in all secondary schools under their jurisdiction. Overall, India is ahead of Canada and Great Britain in creating a large cadre of certified and full-time coaches. But, sheer numbers do not contribute to professionalization. Among other conditions to be fulfilled, there must be a strong association for the occupation.

143

This will be difficult since the fraternity of coaches is a conglomerate of segmented groups with different purposes involved with different sports at different levels of competitions, and affiliated with different kinds of institutions. As for different purposes, Coach Lyle outlined a concept of coaching which he said is applicable only to "competitive forms of organized sporting activity involving highly committed and motivated athletes" (p. 2). Keating (1964) had made a similar distinction between <u>athletics</u> and <u>sports</u>. According to Keating, sport is "a kind of diversion which has for its direct and immediate end fun, pleasure, and delight and which is dominated by a spirit of moderation and generosity. Athletics, on the other hand, is essentially a competitive activity, which has for its end victory in the contest and which is characterized by a spirit of dedication, sacrifice, and intensity" (p. 28). Thus, sport and athletics are radically different fields of endeavor though they might use the same physical activity as a medium to reach their respective goals, and utilize the same methodology in teaching the skills. The thrust of this distinction is that divergent groups of people with different attitudes and orientations gravitate toward these two different endeavors. It is not easy to design and operate an organization that meets the needs of these divergent groups.

There is also the segmentation in coaching due to specialization. Members of an occupational group may become segmented as they specialize in specific aspects of their occupation. This is the case with lawyers who specialize in matrimonial cases versus those who specialize in criminal cases (Turner and Hodge, 1970). In a similar fashion, coaches become compartmentalized with specialization in specific levels of competition, in specific types of sport (Open versus Closed sports; Team versus Individual Sports), and with institutional affiliation (high school, university, sport governing body etc.). Further, as Leggatt (1970) pointed out for the context of teaching, "the casualness of entry into and exit from teaching [coaching] associated with high rates of turnover of personnel precludes any but a loosely organized membership group" (p. 165).

There is also the tendency among participants as well as outsiders to confer differential status and significance to those who coach certain sports and/or at certain levels. In Canada, for instance, those who coach football of the North American variety at the university level are held in greater esteem than coaches of other sports. This is, of course, due to the popularity of that particular sport. Such distinctions among coaches of different sports is not, however, conducive to unifying the segmented groups of coaches.

Given these kinds of diversities, it is really difficult, if not impossible, for coaches to organize themselves. It is not surprising, therefore, that in a few countries like Canada and India, the government has stepped in to organize coaches and consolidate them into a viable occupation.

4.1 The Canadian scene
The poor showing of Canadian athletes in international competitions, particularly in Ice Hockey in which Canada was the undisputed superpower, spurred the Government of Canada to set up the Task Force on Sports for Canadians. One of the recommendations contained in the 1969 Report of the Task Force was that the government provide funds and assistance for the formation of a National Coaches Association. Thus, the Coaching Association of Canada (CAC) was formed in February of 1971 as a national non-profit, third-sector organization, that is, a private organization funded solely or mostly by the government (Chelladurai, 1985). In the 1984-85 fiscal year, the government's contribution to the CAC was $2,730,142 --- 78.2% of its total revenue of $3,493,209.

The original intention was to make the CAC a mere catalyst or change agent to activate coaches on the one hand and educational institutions on the other toward the development of coaching. But as the Canadian Olympic Association (1978) has pointed out, the role of catalyst has slowly given way to the CAC's preeminent role in dictating policy and directing various programs to train and organize coaches in Canada. Further, the CAC is constrained to act according to the government's priorities since it receives almost all of its funding from the government. Thus, the CAC is largely seen as an extension of government's involvement in amateur sport.

Despite the above criticism, the CAC is among the most efficient and effective of the government sponsored organizations in Canada. Their past and present programs have been well thought out and have been successfully implemented with the collaboration of national and provincial sports organizations, and provincial governments. In just 15 years, the CAC has become the most dominant force in the development of sport in general, and coaching in particular. Its programs and publications have become the envy of many other similar organizations around the world.

4.2 The Indian scene
As in Canada, it was the government that took the initiative in promoting coaching in India. The process began in 1961 when the Government of India set up the National Institute of Sports (NIS). Under the auspices of the All India Council of Sports, the umbrella organization set up to oversee the promotion and control of sport, the NIS serves to produce high calibre coaches and to enhance the competence of the existing coaches. As in the case of the Coaching Association of Canada, the NIS was set up as an arms-length organization. But because it receives exclusive funding from the government, and because it contains senior government officials including the minister concerned on its governing body, the NIS has become another department of the government. In contrast to the situation in Canada, the Government of India is not defensive about its domination of the NIS.

But such organizations pose a different kind of problem for coaching. Government financed organizations tend to be bureaucratized. While both bureaucracy and professionalism are concerned with efficiency and rationality, the control mechanisms of

the two differ drastically. Since a bureaucracy is more concerned
with consistency and uniformity in its operations, it enforces
through a hierarchy the routinization and formalization of its
activities. In contrast, a profession relies on control by a
colleague group and on standards derived from professional knowledge
which, in turn, are internalized by members. A bureaucracy fosters
compliance and uniform behavior while a profession encourages
independent and innovative actions.

5. Professionalization of coaching

The lack of a strong organization is not the only barrier to the
professionalization of coaching. The following sections outline the
progress that coaching has made along the continua described by the
attributes of a profession, namely, a systematic body of theory,
professional authority, and a code of ethics.

5.1 A systematic body of theory.
Although coaching cannot yet claim its own unique body of knowledge,
there are efforts from various quarters to distill and compile
relevant information from other related disciplines, and to generate
knowledge specific to coaching. In the Canadian context, the
Coaching Association of Canada has encouraged through its
publications the synthesis and propagation of knowledge specific to
coaching. CAC's three publications, namely, Coaching Review,
Coaching Science Update, and SPORTS are targeted for different
segments of the coaching population. In addition, the CAC has set
up the Sport Information Resource Center (SIRC) which provides a
great service to coaches by collecting, storing, and distributing
sport information in desired formats. SIRC, the computer based
storage-retrieval system containing more than 100,000 citations,
has been widely used by students, coaches, and researchers. SIRC
subscribes to over 1,330 periodicals and holds more than 19,000
books. The CAC's contribution in the creation of sport specific
knowledge and its dissemination is recognized worldwide.
     In addition to the CAC programs, there is a parallel effort on
the part of the governments to generate and synthesize knowledge
specific to coaching. Several government granting agencies
including Sport Canada and Fitness Canada have continued to provide
funds for research related to sport and coaching. These research
grants contribute to generating a unique body of knowledge, a
necessary ingredient to professionalization of coaching. These
research funds have typically been allocated to scientists in
Canadian universities, and the related professional associations
like the Canadian Association of Sport Sciences, the Canadian
Association of Health, Physical Education, and Recreation. There is
every indication that this trend will be intensified in the future.
     Despite the above, coaching will not likely gain respect from
outsiders for its knowledge base for two reasons. First, if an
occupation can claim power through knowledge, it must have a
monopoly over that knowledge (Jackson, 1970). Coaching faces a

problem in this regard since its knowledge base is multi-disciplinary. The mother disciplines are not likely to yield their "ownership" of the knowledge. To add to the problem, many sport scientists would prefer to be aligned with the mother discipline rather than with coaching or physical education.

Secondly, insofar as coaching competencies and skills are based more on practical experience than on a body of knowledge, many outsiders can claim the same expertise on the basis of having participated and having been coached in some sport. This would be particularly true of juvenile sports. To use Jackson's (1970) comment on primary schools, it is where "everyone goes to learn what everyone knows". It is unfortunate that the experiences and practices of outstanding coaches are not distilled and compiled for use by others. Since these coaches operate in isolation from each other, there is little opportunity for the accumulation of their experiences.

5.2 Quality and duration of training
In Canada, the National Coaching Certification Program (NCCP), initiated in 1974, offers certification at five levels. The first three levels lead to the status of a provincial coach, the fourth to the level of national coach, and the fifth is reserved for international coaches. Although the CAC instigated the theory and technical courses, they are typically offered by the sport governing bodies. The duration of the courses is 28 hours (14 for theory and 14 for technical) for Level I; 42 hours (21 plus 21) for Level II; and 55 hours (30 plus 25) for Level III. The practical experience required is 1, 5, and 5 years respectively for the three levels. For Levels IV and V, the content and duration of the training varies from sport to sport.

It is claimed that approximately 170,000 coaches have participated in the certification process. It is not clear, however, if those who had previously participated in the program continue to upgrade their certification, and if they continue to be members of the association.

The Apprenticeship and Scholarship Programs assist would-be coaches to pursue their academic studies in coaching at the master's or doctoral level, and facilitate the opportunity for coaches to study high level coaching on a full-time basis under the direction of a master coach. The National Coaches' Seminar, inaugurated in 1979, is targeted for the national coaches and technical directors of the national sports organizations. International speakers present seminars on selected themes.

The Physical Education programs in various universities in Canada provide coaching related training. A recent trend has been for several of these universities to offer specialization in coaching. This augurs well for coaching since the status of an occupation is directly proportional to the length and quality of the training of the coaches.

In contrast to the CAC in Canada, the NIS in India is directly involved in the training and certification of coaches. The NIS offers a Diploma and Master's program in various sports. The entry requirement for the 10-month Diploma program is a university degree or a matriculate with an outstanding performance record in a sport. The entry requirements for the master's program are 1) university degree, 2) NIS Diploma, 3) five years coaching experience, 4) aptitude for research work, and 5) sports proficiency. Typically, a candidate is sponsored by a national or provincial organization or one of the employing agencies like a state sports council. All candidates are required to stay in the quarters provided by the Institute so that classes can be held early in the mornings as well as late in the evenings. The interaction between the sport governing bodies and the NIS in designing the content of the courses has been minimal relative to the Canadian situation.

Two points bear mention about the training programs in the two countries. First, the duration of training is rather short. For instance, in the Canadian system, 130 hours of instruction (65 hours for theory and 65 for technical) would lead to Level III certification. It is true that there is the requirement of 9 years of practical training, but such training is neither controlled nor monitored. In the Indian system, the training is much more prolonged and intense, but it still falls short of the requirements in established professions. As Harries-Jenkins (1970) noted:

> The form of of this educational process which is undertaken by a group member, thus reflects the extent to which the exercise of the occupational skill demands knowledge of the underlying theory, and the form is thus an indicator of the level of group professionalization. (p. 74)

Secondly, in both systems, training is dissociated from the university setting. In Canada, although a number of universities offer their own coaching programs, there has been no conscious and sustained effort toward a collaborative scheme of training and certification. In India also, there has been very little collaboration between the physical education institutions and the coaching development programs. On the contrary, the Government of India set up two national institutions to train coaches and physical education teachers separately. Any linkage between the two institutions is only in a common Board of Governors. This tacit separation of the two occupations results not only in duplication of efforts and dilution of resources, but more importantly, in a rivalry between the two occupations. It has been noted elsewhere that most of the newer occupations are not able to gain any status or respect mainly because of the resistance from allied occupations. Therefore, coaching can not afford to sever its links with physical education entirely.

5.3 Professional authority
Coaches as a group do not enjoy the "professional authority" as defined earlier. It is mainly because coaching cannot yet claim a unique body of knowledge, nor the training programs are suggestive of any in depth knowledge and/or esoteric competencies. Even within sport organizations which should uphold the integrity of coaching,

a coach tends to be treated as an appendage rather than an integral part of the team. For, everybody in the organization "knows" as much if not more than the coach.

Chelladurai (1985) had urged the application of the Parsonian (1960) model of organizational structure for sport governing bodies. According to the model, an organization consists of three vertically differentiated subsystems: Institutional, Managerial, and Technical subsystems. The technical subsystem is the core where the organization's major tasks or activities are carried out. For example, the players, the coach, and his/her assistants would constitute the technical core of a sport governing body. Ideally, since the coach has been hired on the basis of expertise, he/she will be complete control of the team including the recruitment and selection of the athletes. The major concern of the total organization will be to ensure the smooth functioning of the technical system without any hindrance from the outside agents including the other subsystems of the organization. This insulation is provided by the managerial subsystem (consisting of officers like an executive director, a technical director, a secretary/treasurer and/or other office staff). The managerial system ensures the flow of required resources to the technical core and protects it from intrusions. The institutional system, consisting of the Board of Governors or an equivalent, links the organization to the wider social system and justifies and legitimizes the activities of the technical core. The essential point of the Parsonian model is that the three systems are comprised of individual with different sets of expertise and orientations suitable to their respective roles, and that the differentiation of activities should ensure the independence of each subsystem. In our context, it is imperative that the coaches are given the autonomy and authority to act according to their best judgements. A number of universities in North America exemplify this ideal situation. A university is where the professionals dominate the organization and who jealously guard professional autonomy and authority. This professional right is extended to coaches of the university teams. It is to be hoped that the sport governing bodies and other agencies which hire coaches will elevate themselves and the coaches by granting that professional authority and autonomy to their coaches.

6. Conclusion

In the final analysis, the need to, and the direction for reorienting the development of coaching are highlighted by Lyle's (1985) comments "Coach education underpins professional development and ought, therefore, to be a priority" (p. 21) and "Should all practitioners be thought of as part of one hierarchy or should the avenues of training be distinct?" (p. 2). My position is that the notion of coaching refers to leadership in the pursuit of excellence (i.e., competitive sports). The training of these coaches should be much more comprehensive, and extended over a period of time so that all the relevant knowledge can be imparted to the trainees, and the required competencies can be developed. The latter part of the training should be highly specialized (i.e., distinct) to suit the needs of pursuit of excellence in various types of sports and, at various levels of competition. Further, the universities are best suited to provide such extensive and specialized training. The requirements of coach education are, to a large extent, met by the requirements of physical education. Therefore, coaching development programs must use the universities as their training centers.

References

Bobbit, H.R., Jr., Breinholt, R.H., Doktor, R.H., & McNaul, J.P. (1978). Organizational behavior: Understanding and prediction (2nd. ed.). Englewood Cliffs, N.J.: Prentice-Hall

Canadian Olympic Association. (1978). Toward a national policy on amateur sport (Response to the federal Green Paper on amateur sport). Ottawa, Ontario: Author.

Chelladurai, P. (1985). Sport management: Macro perspectives. London, Ontario: Sports Dynamics.

Freidson, E. (1973). Professions and the occupational principle. In E. Freidson (Ed.), Professions and their prospects. (pp. 19-38). Beverly Hills, CA.: Sage.

Goode, W.J. (1969). The theoretical limits of professionalization. In A. Etzioni (Ed.), The semi-professions and their organization. (pp. 266-313). New York: The Free Press.

Harries-Jenkins, G. (1970). Professionals in organizations. In J.A. Jackson (Ed.), Professions and professionalization (pp. 53-107). Cambridge: Cambridge University Press.

Hasenfeld, Y. (1983). Human service organizations. Englewood Cliffs, N.J.: Prentice-Hall.

Jackson, J.A. (1970). Professions and professionalization: Editorial introduction. In J.A. Jackson (Ed.), Professions and professionalization (pp. 3-15). Cambridge: Cambridge University Press.

Keating, J.W. (1964). Sportsmanship as a moral category. Ethics, 75, 25-35.

Leggatt, T. (1970). Teaching as a profession. In J.A. Jackson (Ed.), Professions and professionalization (pp. 155-177). Cambridge: Cambridge University Press.

Lyle, J. (1985). Coach education: Preparation for a profession. Glasgow: Conference '86.

Mills, P.K., & Margulies, N. (1980). Toward a core typology of service organizations. Academy of Management Review, 5, 255-265.

Sasser, W.E., Olsen, R.P., & Wyckoff, D.D. (1978). Management of service operations. Rockleigh, N.J.: Allyn and Bacon.

Turner, C., & Hodge, M.N. (1970). Occupations and professions. In J.A. Jackson (Ed.), Professions and professionalization (pp. 19-50). Cambridge: Cambridge University Press.

Wilensky, H.L. (1964). The professionalization of everyone? American Journal of Sociology, 70, 137-158.

PERFORMANCE APPRAISAL FOR COACHES

TOM H. NORCROSS, Head Fencing Coach JSC, Coaching Director HKAFA
Coaching Department, Jubilee Sports Centre, Hong Kong

Abstract
Purpose of Paper
Coaches acquire qualifications which give them a foothold on the
coaching ladder. How far they progress up that ladder depends on
their ability to learn from experience. Coaching qualifications
provide knowledge of the game, coaching method, and background
knowledge for support. They do not provide a means of self assessment of performance and effectiveness.
The Jubilee Sports Centre has been using performance appraisal since
1982 and all coaches employed full time have been appraised under the
system. The System used, normally appraises executives in commerce
and industry, but we believe that this is the first instance of it
being used to appraise coaches.
The purpose of this paper is to examine the experience of applying
performance appraisal to coaching, assess its effectiveness, and
examine the possibility of devising a system more relevant to
coaching.
Content
The following headings indicate the areas for examination and
discussion.
What is Performance Appraisal and how does it work?
Strengths and weaknesses of the System used by JSC.
Devising a system specifically for coaching.
Proposal for implementing Performance Appraisal as a part of in
service training in Britain.
Key words: Introduction, Appraisal systems, Faults, Coaches
appraisal, Method, Qualities.

1. Introduction

The normal pattern of development for a coach is to obtain the
appropriate qualifications and then to work in the field, gaining
experience as he goes along. Some become run of the mill, some
become good and some achieve greatness as a result of their
experience and the effort they put into self improvement.

I believe that more coaches could become good and perhaps achieve
greatness, if they were given some in service development assistance.
In service training for those coaches employed by Governing Bodies
is haphazard, and for the free lance coaches it is frequently non

existent. At the Jubilee Sports Centre we have gone some way towards developing our coaches by subjecting them to performance appraisal.

2.   Performance appraisal

Performance appraisal is a widely used tool in commerce and industry for measuring and improving performance. As far as we are aware, the JSC is the only place where it is used for measuring the performance of coaches.

For those who are not familiar with performance appraisal, I will explain broadly how the system we use works, although it must be said that there are almost as many systems as there are people being appraised, however there are some general principles.

The early use of performance appraisal from the thirties through to the fifties aimed at giving feedback. By the late fifties changes were taking place because it was felt that managers were reluctant to give adverse feedback to subordinates. The value of letting people know where they stood, when in so many cases the individual was just getting a demotivating thumbs down, was called into question. This resulted in a change in performance appraisal to what is widely accepted today. A more participative approach with a strong element of self appraisal. A problem solving approach in which both the appraiser and the appraisee identify the problems associated with the job in the previous year and together work out solutions to them, with the onus on the appraisee to provide most of the solutions. The rationale for this was that the appraisee was more likely to implement action plans that he or she had devised.

3.   Job description

The starting point for any system is the job description. At the JSC the Manager agreed the job description with each coach and then reviewed it a week or so later to ensure that both parties were satisfied that it fairly reflected the job.

The first item in the descriptions is the Accountability Objective, which attempts to summarise the responsibility of the job holder in one simple sentence. Mine says, "To plan and implement a fencing programme in Hong Kong, which will foster the development of fencing to full potential." The description goes on to document the nature and scope of the job, listing responsibilities and work areas. Much of this is summarised in the most important part, which is a list of Principal Accountabilities. As the job descriptions are personalised to each coach, I can only tell you what my accountabilities are.

(a)   Technical Consultant to the H.K.A.F.A.
(b)   Coach to National Squad.
(c)   Training of Coaches and Officials.
(d)   Budgetting fencing programme.
(e)   Training full time assistant.

These accountabilities are the core of the job description and it is on these that performance is judged. If the job description is done correctly, the coach should have a clear idea of what is expected of him.

4. Operation

Performance appraisal is usually carried out over a one year cycle. At the beginning of the year the appraiser and the appraisee agree targets for the coming year for each of the accountabilities. The agreed targets should be accompanied by agreed measures. This is not an easy task as much of the work of a coach is not easily quantifiable into objective measures.

The actual appraisal takes place at the end of the year when targets are reviewed, and if they have not been met, then the reasons are analysed. The reasons may be factors beyond the control of the appraisee or performance failure. If the targets have been over achieved, a similar analysis takes place, and again this may be due to circumstances beyond control, better than expected performance or perhaps the targets were set too low originally. It is at this stage that the coach must critically examine his own performance and if he is not able to do that, then performance appraisal will be of little vaule to him. There should be interim reviews of performance during the year at whatever periods are felt necessary.

This is the broad outline upon which many appraisal system are based, but I want now to look at some of the problems we experienced, which will give a better idea of how it actually works and some of the pitfalls to be avoided if a system is to be set up specifically for coaches.

5. Interview

It will by now be obvious that the appraisal interviews are the key to the success or failure of the exercise. In the early days of the JSC the appraisers were insufficiently trained in conducting these interviews, and did not have expertise or experience as coaches. This latter item aroused resentment among the coaches as their careers were being judged by people without real knowledge of the job. The appraiser is the immediate superior so that at JSC the Manager appraises the Head Coaches who appraise their assistant coaches and secretaries. The interviews should be conducted along the lines of the two parties taking a somewhat detached look at the performance of one of them, analysing successes and failures and the reasons why. If criticism has to be made, it should be confined to performance and in no way should it be made of the personality of the appraisee. This makes some demands on the interviewer and will require training.

6. Faults

The appraisal system which we adopted had one major fault which has now been removed. This was that the results of the appraisal were linked to salary awards. This prevented the appraisal from being an objective assessment of performance, and made it into an exercise for the appraisee in getting the best possible salary award.

Another, less serious, problem area was that the system made no allowances for outside influences beyond the control of the coach or the centre. Much of the coaches work depends on the co-operation of the outside agencies not the least of whom are the Governing Bodies of the various sports. The coach may agree targets for a year but if the outside agency decide that they do not want to carry out that particular project then the appraisal of the coaches performance suffers.

Another aspect of the system we use, which is of dubious value, is the awarding of performance points. This tends to reduce the objectivity of focus from the quality of performance onto gaining the best possible score. Coaches by their nature are highly competitive individuals and as soon as a scoring system is introduced they will want to score as high as possible. This could make them less objective about their perforamnce. If performance appraisal is to work for coaches, then the appraisee must enter into it in a genuine spirit of wanting an analysis and evaluation of his performance, and the appraiser should make every effort to encourage this attitude.

The positive aspect of the allocation of points is that it does give a fixed measure which can be compared from year to year for the individual, and from person to person within an organisation. This can be a powerful motivational tool to improve performance.

There are however further problems with points ratings, not the least of which is that of subjectivity. The rating scales are open to different interpretations by different appraisers and how do you standardise ratings of qualities such as drive, integrity, maturity and determination. This negates the use of scales for comparing individuals within an organisation.

7. A system for British coaches

Despite these faults I do believe that performance appraisal could be a powerful aid to improving the quality of coaching in Great Britain or anywhere else. I envisage an appraisal service being available to a coach anywhere in the country and perhaps it would be compulsory for those coaches working full time for Sports Governing Bodies.

I see the appraisers coming from the ranks of BANC which contain a wealth of coaching expertise and the Association has the administrative structure to run the service and to train the appraisers. I think the appraisers should receive a professional fee for their services and I would like to see this come from the Sports Council as an input to developing the standard of coaching in Britain. The Governing Bodies might also be persuaded to contribute, particularly if their own coaches were being appraised. I would not want to

preclude coaches of proven seniority and experience who were not
members of BANC from being appraisers, but I would expect them to
undergo the necessary training.

It should be possible to provide a network of appraisers country-
wide so that a coach anywhere could have access to an appraiser. The
coach does not have to be in regular contact with his appraiser and
two or three meetings a year would suffice.

Most coaches in Britain are one off individuals and are not a part
of a large organisation. This is an advantage in that there is no
need to compare them with other individuals so that the need for a
rating system almost disappears. This can only help the creation of
the desired atmosphere of the coach genuinely seeking to improve his
performance.

8. Critical incidents

Many of the qualities of a successful coach are impossible to rate on
numerical scale and if I was devising a system of appraisal for
coaches I would not use any form of rating scale at all. I feel that
the method of appraisal which assesses "Critical Incidents" is more
appropriate to the sort of appraisal I would like to see.

Critical incidents are occasions when the appraisee performs
particulary effectively or when he or she performs ineffectively.
These incidents are recorded by the appraiser or the appraisee or
both, and are then discussed and assessed at the appraisal interview.
The appraiser should help the coach to analyse the reasons for effective or ineffective performance. The pattern of critical incidents
for the whole period may be reviewed and interpreted as follows:

(a) Poor performance incidents grouped in a short time period may
indicate personal or other outside reasons for their occurrence.

(b) Poor performance incidents spread throughout the period may
indicate poor training, insufficient experience, lack of motivation,
or lack of understanding of what is expected.

(c) Poor performance incidents early in the period which decrease
show that performance is improving.

(d) Good performance incidents either grouped or spread throughout the period indicate better than expected performance.

(e) No incidents, or very few, indicates satisfactory performance.

This method of appraisal is less frequently used than the systems
involving rating, but coaching is an unusual job which does not lend
itself readily to the more popular methods of appraisal. I must
admit however that we have not yet tried this system at the JSC.

9. Qualities to be measured

The critical incidents should be discussed in relation to the qualities the appraisal is trying to measure, which should be defined by

the job description. Coaching jobs vary considerably. We at the JSC tend to be more in the role of development officers rather than purely coaches, but there are many coaches who see their role at the other extreme, in that their work starts and finishes when they step on and off the pitch.

I think the qualities that a coach performance appraisal should be trying to measure fall into two broad caregories. These are:

(a) Effectiveness as a coach.
(b) Effectiveness as an administrator.

The coach has many roles to fulfill if he is to be effective but I suggest that these could be grouped into three main areas, in order to keep the appraisal relatively simple. These are communication, skill analysis and motivation. If the critical incidents were examined under these areas, they would I believe cover all the aspects of a coaches relationship with his athletes.

The amount of administration a coach has to do will depend on how he sees his role as a coach, but there will be some administration necessary and his effectiveness as a coach will depend on his efficiency as an administrator. The administrative role of the coach should be clearly defined in the job description.

10. Summary

Performance appraisal is a valuable tool for assessing job performance which can be applied to coaching in a way that will help appraisees to analyse and improve their work. The BANC has the necessary expertise and administrative structure to set up a nationwide system, and to provide training for the appraisers. The Sports Council could provide the finance for such a system. The system should be devised to measure the qualities relevant to coaching and should not use any form of rating. The critical incidents method of assessment is suggested as suitable for appraising coaches.

References

Clive Fletcher and Richard Williams (1985) Performance Appraisal and Career Development. Hutchison & Co (Publishers), LONDON.
Marjo van Boeschoten (1978), Personnel in Change edited by Manab Thakur, John Brislow and Keith Carby, pp 68-78.
John W. Humble (1965) Performance Review. Improving Management Performance. British Institute of Management, pp 23-27.
Kenneth Blanchard, Ph. D. and Spencer Johnson, M.D. (1981) The One Minute Manager. Partnership and Candle Communications Corporation.

ACCREDITATION FOR A POST-GRADUATE PROFESSION

P. McNAUGHT-DAVIS and **G. McFEE**
Chelsea School of Human Movement, Brighton Polytechnic

Abstract

To make the topic of the nature of coaching more manageable, this paper focuses on coaching in Great Britain. It argues for a recognition of coaching as a profession -- and as an all-graduate profession. From an analysis of John Lyle's (1985) paper discussing accreditation, a model is developed for a post-graduate certificate in coaching based on Brighton Polytechnic's BSc(Hons) Sports Science degree (also designed to be applicable to other comparable degrees, and to entry from established coaches). The proposal emphasises a meeting of theoretician and practitioner. It incorporates a period of 'clinical practice' in which the actual coaching process is experienced under the aegis of the governing bodies of the various sports.

Key words: Coach accreditation. Professions.

Introduction.

In this paper we address a set of problems about the nature of coaching: what coaching is, and what coaches do. But, to make a complex issue more manageable, we begin from the situation currently obtaining in Britain, as we see it. Our goal is a discussion of the training of coaches for the future; we are not directly concerned with the status of coaching as at present -- although some remarks in the paper bear on that topic. Later in the paper we also attempt some constructive work in the form of an elaboration of a potential post-graduate certificate in coaching, designed to go 'end on' with our own BSc(Hons), Sports Science.

First we clear the ground by clarifying the object of our discussion; why we perceive this need for a centralisation of coaching -- why we think it is right to speak of coaching as a profession. And also, we discuss the objections to and difficulties of such a professionalisation raised by John Lyle in his important paper 'Coach education: preparation for a profession' (1985) which serves as a paradigm for this element of the conference.

Coaching as a profession.

We first consider the idea of a 'profession'. For clearly, we are not speaking here of 'professional' in contrast to 'amateur'; that is, the contrast is not directly between the paid and the unpaid. Rather, it is that between professions on the one hand and trades and the like on the other. In this sense, many occupations are no doubt professional, in that they are done for pay; but that does not make the activity a profession. In contrast, medicine is a profession, even when conducted on a voluntary basis. This paper argues that it is time for coaching to 'come of age', to become a profession and, looking to the future, to aim to be an all-graduate profession. It is these issues that we want to elaborate here.

It seems right to say that we are drawing on the 'common sense' idea of what it is to be a member of a profession, which is caught by the 1933 definition of professions provided by Carr-Saunders and Wilson (1933) which concerns the possession of specialised intellectual skills and a body of theory acquired over a long period by those socialised and trained in it. It is only in this sense that we speak of the professionalisation of coaching, although the sense that interests us (that is, being a member of a profession) is clearly not unrelated to the other sense: that of being paid for one's activity. It is perhaps too obvious a point to make here, but one could be a 'professional' in the second sense (for example, a professional footballer, to take what seems to be a fairly transparent example) without being a 'professional' in the first sense.

What is identified here is some kind of knowledge base for professions. It does not seem far from the mark (Toulmin, 1972: p.262) to see professions as institutional embodiments of disciplines (although that might lead us to some more detailed reflection on the nature of a 'disciplne'). Certainly, we would expect members of professions to be exchanging information, arguing, " ... presenting their results through a variety of publications and meetings, competing for professorships and presidencies of academies, seeking to excel while still vying for others' esteem". (Toulmin, 1972: p.262) It is the structure of these activities which gives rise to recognisable and distinct professions and sub-professions. And seeing the matter as a disciplinary one is really remarking on the possibility of identifying a:

> ... community of teachers, researchers and students,
> committed to a path of studies towards some mutually
> comprehensible and valuable goal; the goal being
> subject to redefinition, but only by the methods of
> orderly and rational discourse through which the path
> to the goal itself is tranversed.   (Cavell, 1981:
> p.269)

If we look at those two ideas, that of the kind of knowledge-base we associate with a discipline and of the kind of institutional activity which turns such disciplines into professions, it seems that both are beginning to be present in the case of the coaching of sports activities. Of course, to speak of a 'discipline' here may be slightly misleading, for there is no one academic source for the kinds of knowledge-base characteristic of coaching. But then, the same is true of, for example, medicine -- so we are quite happy that what we are calling a disciplinary base need not locate itself within one particular academic discipline, providing those other conditions are fulfilled.

At this stage, the need for the professionalisation of coaching might be questioned. But here it seems that the logic of the argument for such a professionalisation is irrefutable. If we are to gain public recognition for the kind of basis in knowledge we have, we will need just that kind of perceived professional status if we are to avoid 'professionalised incompetence'; that knowledge must be perceived as relevant and useful knowledge. But secondly there is the matter of status associated with professions. If we are to have a concrete career structure for coaching (and here again the question of 'professional' versus 'amateur' -- that is, of payment -- arises) we will need to establish the institution of the profession in some deliberate way.

Coaching as an all-graduate profession.

If, then, it is accepted that coaching is an emergent profession, and that the movements towards the establishment of a coaching profession involve the development of the various institutions, one might go on to ask the nature of that development. We raise here three related considerations which should lead us to think of our emergent coaching profession as ultimately an all-graduate profession.
1. The first derives from the position in respect of other professions. Either they are all-graduate (for example, medicine, law) or they are presently regulated in some kind of way, below graduate level (for example, physiotherapy); and most of these presently desire graduate status, and are therefore constructing for themselves (in collaboration with institutions of higher education) under-graduate courses of post-graduate certification. It is true that some bodies have sought to establish a professional structure below graduate level -- for example, the Institute of Leisure and Amenity Management (ILAM). Even in such cases, we must think, first, of their process of regulation as involving the setting up of certain academic or quasi-academic qualifications. Second, the likelihood (deriving from discussions with ILAM) is of their looking to graduate qualifications in the near future. And third, the developing situation with respect to coaching is that an increasing number of the young people entering coaching are already graduates (in Sports Science or Sports Studies, for example). Thus it no longer seems plausible to argue for a less than graduate level for our emergent coaching profession.
2. The second consideration is a kind of elaboration of that last point. For if, increasingly, some coaches are graduates and some

not, we can expect an uneven kind of career structure, with some coaches finding themselves 'second class citizens' in respect of job opportunities, promotion and the like.

A typical history of the processes of 'professionalisation' has recently been written in another context, and we can do no better than to quote it here (Murphy, 1986):

> Initially those recruited to the occupation come from other occupations. In time the question of training arises. The first people to take the formal training are likely to be people already at work in the occupation. In time, the occupation and its training schools become better known, and young people are recruited. In time, the training may seek to become associated with universities and other establishments.

[That is what, really, is our present situation: the question simply is of the nature of that association.]

> At this point, there may be a wave of late seekers of professional training: those who adopted the occupation and also who now seek qualifications in order to more firmly establish themselves within the occupation. They may also feel the pressure exerted by new entrants to the occupation, who arrive with new and more widely accepted qualifications.

If this is, as Murphy urges, a typical history of an emergent profession, it seems right that we should set our sights on some model which pitches the coaching qualification appropriately, both for the intellectual needs of prospective coaches and for the needs of coaching as such -- and this must surely be at the graduate level. A parallel case here which may illustrate the point is the transition which has taken place around the Greek word idiotes (see Silverlight, 1986), for this word did not originally mean 'fool': rather, it picked out the distinction between 'private' citizen and one involved in politics. But, with changes in the Greek political structure it came to mean 'a layman', someone inexpert; and therefore, eventually, 'a fool'. A similar kind of slide in status is very likely for those who remain laymen in a climate of professionalisation. If this is to be avoided in the case of coaching, then the profession will need to structure itself appropriately. And increasingly nowadays (and this was the first consideration that mentioned above), 'appropriately' has meant 'at a graduate level'. The case of teaching, for example, seems a clearly relevant one.

3. The third consideration which leads us ultimately towards the idea of an all-graduate profession is that a new kind of coach is developing -- one whose interest in coaching comes from interests other than a direct involvement in the sport, whose interest lies first and foremost in the psychology of coaching, or the physiology of coaching. If such valuable people are to be integrated into the coaching profession, then it is essential

not only that their importance be recognised, but also that due importance be given to those who take the other routes into coaching. And this partly reiterates the second consideration: insofar as it is possible, we don't want any 'second class citizens' here. And this means equal status within the profession. One wonders if that can be attained without at least some kind of broad-based qualification -- which must surely be at graduate level.

If then the need for the establishment of a profession is granted, and the view is accepted that ultimately this should become an all-graduate profession, one might still wonder what precisely the profession does. Here, again, we can do no better than to quote Denzin (1968; quoted Murphy, 1986):

> Occupations transforming themselves into professional groups develop special codes of ethics, engage in formalised recruitment patterns, establish formal institutions to transmit the knowledge of the occupation, develop social organisations to ensure the perpetuation of the profession through time, and finally take on the characteristics of self-governing, autonomous institutions; in short they claim ... a license to carry out certain actions and a mandate to define what is proper conduct of others towards their work.

As well as summarising the character of professions, this view leads us naturally into a consideration of the objections which might be raised to the professionalisation of coaching, for certainly some of the activities picked out in the quotation from Denzin seem presently to fall within the remit of the governing bodies of various sports. So there is an important question there about the relationship of governing bodies. Additionally, the kind of institution that Denzin describes has only a doubtful connection with the voluntary character of much contemporary coaching in Britain. It is to such topics that we must now turn.

Problems for accreditation.

A suitable way to proceed is through a consideration of the objections to professionalisation to be found in John Lyle's excellent position paper (1985). Some of the major difficulties identified there are as follows:
(1) lack of a clear conceptual base: "... content is dictated by custom and with few exceptions is very sport-specific (p.11);
(2) the role of governing bodies (sport specificity): "... a completely decentralised arrangement in which largely autonomous governing bodies have operated independently in offering courses to prospective coaches" (p.9);
(3) the question of the voluntary: " ... the diminishing of voluntary effort which has followed the introduction of the (accreditation for coaches) scheme" (p.10);
(4) the route to top coaching positions: "Custom seems to indicate

that top-level coaches, in the main, have shortened pathways into such (top) positions, and that this transition reflects performer experience or master/apprentice experience rather than certification" (p.18);

(5) professional associations: "One significant feature of established professions is the power and influence of their professional associations" (p.19). Could this be established in the case of coaching?

It should be said initially that these are all topics about which Lyle has perceptive and well-informed things to say. We wish to raise them in order to comment, sometimes briefly, on how the difficulties he identifies might be overcome (and here often our comments reiterate, in a different form, his own), but also to generate a set of questions to which our own proposal is intended to be an answer.

Let us consider each of these five important points. With respect to the first it must be acknowledged that there is no clear conceptual base for coaching as presently understood, because the coaching qualifications as they stand tend to be validated by specific sports, and hence whatever conceptual base they have is dictated by that sport. As will be seen from our proposed coaching qualification, we hope to circumvent this objection in two ways: first, by introducing an element of what we call 'clinical practice' in which the actual coaching process is experienced under the aegis of the governing bodies of the various sports. In this way, we hope to maintain the present system whereby the coaching qualifications are validated -- and that means accepted -- by the governing bodies of those sports. But second we believe that there is some plan towards a conceptual base for coaching, that there are numerous concepts which have application in more than one area -- in particular we think of notions from the psychology of sport here, among others.

In respect of the second point, there are two related, relevant ideas. First, as above, we think of the accreditation of coaches still being done through the governing bodies of the various sports, and we would see that accreditation as based on the 'clinical practice' period. Secondly, we think that there is room for integration of the various coaching awards into one unified scheme, without the governing bodies losing their present autonomy. As will be obvious, our preferred solution is that the qualifications be given by some other body -- in our case the CNAA -- but where the governing bodies of the various sports accept those qualifications by giving the course some kind of accreditation or status. This accreditation process might well be 'orchestrated' through the Sports Council or the Central Council for Physical Recreation. (Does something similar happen in respect of ILAM?) We feel then that these objections (numbers 1 and 2 above) can be met and indeed are met by the kind of proposal which follows in this paper.

In respect of issue number 3, it seems that there are some nettles to be grasped here. The future may require something less than the kind of democratised picture of coaching offered earlier in the paper: voluntary coaches may not have time for the sort of course we propose -- but two points could be introduced to minimise the difficulty. Firstly, the course should/could utilise their previous experience (for example, by counting that experience in the relevant sport as part of their 'clinical practice'). And secondly, the course should be constructed so that it can be taken in parts -- that is, there should be part-time modes, a modular structure, perhaps the possibility of 'distance learning' and so on. Still, this will lead, in the future, to second class status of some voluntary coaches. This unfortunate consequence cannot really be avoided, but it does to some degree reflect the current situation.

In the paradigm paper, Lyle (1985: p.10) speaks of "sports leading". In respect of issue number 4, this strikes us as, in some ways, a nice idea -- if one with a slightly 'dated' feel about it -- part of the 'amateur' ethos. (This idea can be seen very clearly, in a dramatised version, in the film Chariots of Fire, where the assumption is that a master/apprentice relationship will produce the kind of effortlessness central to sports participation -- a view contested by the only serious coach in that film.)

It strikes us then that this point about the route is no longer viable in the present climate of sport. There is a need, it seems to us, for more than just experience -- the Olympic success of, for example, East Germany might be taken as illustrative here. But what is this 'more'? We hope that a more detailed sketch for the proposed certificate in coaching -- if we could give it -- would illustrate the sorts of things we have in mind. Clearly some of this knowledge could have been got 'on the job' -- but is that particularly likely? We suspect not, and consider our model to offer a way forward for coaches here.

In respect of the last point (number 5), it seems to us very important for some kind of professional organisation for coaches to develop, since we agree that such a body has traditionally been associated with professional status. In order that such an organisation seem viable, a little more will need to be said about the conceptual base mentioned above. But suppose one accepted, as Lyle seems to, the need for such a professional association if coaching is to become a profession. Well, this represents another reason for instituting just one structure for coaching, one scheme of accreditation. It seems to us that it is time we had this: just as it is time for a similar thing in the case of physical education (see N71:1982).

To summarise, then, we think our proposal can deal with the first three points from Lyle's paper, although we need to say more about the first one. We think of the fourth point as a constraint, but something which it is high time was overcome; and we think of the fifth one as good idea which we would hope could be instituted in the future.

Proposal: Post-Graduate Certification in Coaching (PGCC)

Let us look briefly, then, at the sort of conceptual base that we see for coaching. Our proposal for coach certification is designed to fit 'end-on' to our present BSc(Hons) Sports Science degree, and thus 'tops-up', in a particular way, the knowledge and experience common to these students. Naturally, with another base-degree, there would be a need to remove some 'units' of work from the certificate if that work had been adequately covered in the first degree, and to replace these units with aspects of our BSc unfulfilled by the particular undergraduate course. So we begin with an outline of our BSc.

Successful applicants are committed to one particular sport (the 'specialist sport') and have good academic qualifications -- although not necessarily a scientific background. Year 1 offers a foundation in the relevant biological, physical and chemical sciences, psychology and sociology, together with an introductory study of the practice and theory of sport. A quantitative methods course provides a mathematical, statistical and computer-base from which students can work, and hence enables the fulfillment of scientific aspirations on their part as well as ours. Whatever their level/background, students who start Year 2 are required to have shown themselves able to handle a science degree.

Core sports sciences (exercise physiology, biomechanics, anthropometry and sports psychology) feed directly into an Applied Sports Studies component running through the whole degree (see Figure 1). The student's general practical experience of sport is widened by exposure to courses in aquatics, team- and net- and individual sports; their specific 'specialist sport' continues to be a focus for the application of theory to practice.

In the final two terms, students choose two specialist options from among the following: environmental physiology, haemotology, biomechanics, motor control and arousal, and performance of sports groups. In addition, they complete individual studies in the form of a dissertation and an ongoing analysis of their specialist experience (log book). Over the first seven terms of the course the social perspectives of sport are studied, which act as contextual to their central studies.

If this is our BSc, we must ask ourselves the question, "What does the prospective coach need to know, and to be able to do if he/she has already successfully pursued the BSc(Hons) Sports Science degree?" In reply, we identify three related major areas of knowledge and expertise: <u>first</u>, specifics concerned with the coaching of one (or more) particular sports, including knowledge of the organisation and administration of the particular sport(s); <u>second</u>, the general ideas about the nature and practice of coaching; <u>third</u>, theoretical knowledge from sports science and from related theoretical disciplines -- for example, medicine and social theory. Each of these three areas is reflected in an element of the course as proposed.

As envisaged, the PGCC would run on a full-time basis for one year or, in some part-time mode, over a number of years. In both cases it would include a six-month professional practice (governing body-based), what we have called 'clinical practice', to learn organisation and administration, as well as have guided practice in coaching at as many performance levels as possible. As mentioned earlier, previous experience could count against

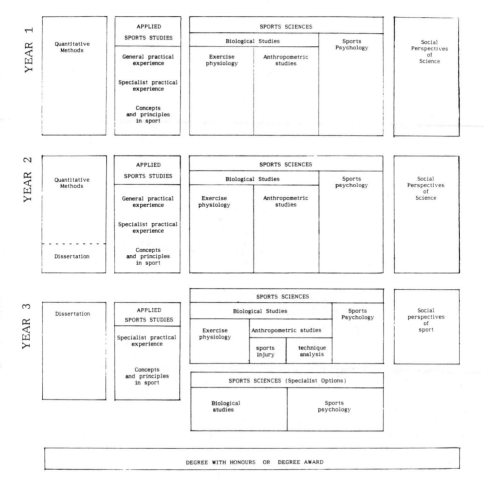

Figure 1:

Outline of B.Sc.(Hons) Sports Science,
Brighton Polytechnic

some of this professional practice.

In the full-time mode, the preceding six months of 'institution-based' aspects would develop two of the areas mentioned above. It would include a course -- to be taken by all students -- on the practice of coaching, where the techniques, methods and aids to coaching are examined, analysed and applied. Under this heading too, we would consider methods for the assessing of performance (see Figure 2).

The second of the 'institution-based' areas would be the theoretical aspects of sports management and administration (which might involve the leadership and performance of sports groups (the organisation, ethics and politics of sport, and managerial strategies), an introduction to sport medicine (where students might be concerned with prevention, rehabilitation and immediate action), and some theoretical input from the sports sciences, where this seemed appropriate. We envisage this theoretical component as offering approximately nine elements or units (see Figure 2). Students from our BSc would take all three units concerned with management and administration, all three units concerning the sports medicine and, at most, one of the sports science elements -- as seemed appropriate given the student's background. (For example, a student who had not done biomechanical techinique analysis as his specialist option would need to do it as part of the theoretical components for his PGCC.) Indeed, it is from this part of the course particularly that units could be credited when considering students with degree backgrounds other than those from our BSc. And typically, we would expect first degrees to account for, say, three such units.

Much of the 'institution-based' material would be presented by students and in an applied manner, using groups of students/ children/outside teams as necessary. It is seen as a positive advantage that many sports will be seen by all students, irrespective of specialism, because we feel that, in the past, it has been the isolation of one sport from another, and from the institutions of education and research, that has held back the level of British sports performance.

Here we identify, as a crucial role for a course such as that we propose, the bringing together of two groups, identified broadly as 'academic' and 'coach'. Thus we see it as an advantage that, in addition to our BSc Sports Science, there is a great deal of sport taking place in our institution alongside the BSc, and in particular in the BEd(Hons) Physical Education. (This is of particular relevance, of course, since teacher education is a profession too.) Thus we see our proposal as located in a suitable ambiance for the developing of an emergent coaching profession.

The National Coaching Foundation has achieved a working link between the specialists in the sports sciences and practicing coaches, in ways congruent with those mentioned here -- and thus has started the ball rolling (!). However, as those of us who have taught some NCF courses will be well aware, there are major constraints of time and background knowledge on those courses as they operate at present. There is little doubt that such courses and, especially, their extension into a third level,

```
┌─────────────────────────────────────────────────────────┐
│                  PRACTICAL COMPONENT I                  │
│            Governing Body Based ('Clinical practice')   │
│                                                         │
│  (a) practical coaching at various levels.              │
│  (b) central management and administration.             │
│  (c) organisation of tournaments/events.                │
└─────────────────────────────────────────────────────────┘

┌─────────────────────────────────────────────────────────┐
│                 PRACTICAL COMPONENT II                  │
│                    Institution Based                    │
│  (a) organisation of effective coaching.                │
│  (b) technical aids to coaching.                        │
│  (c) assessment of performance.                         │
│  (d) sports concepts.                                   │
└─────────────────────────────────────────────────────────┘

┌─────────────────────────────────────────────────────────┐
│                  THEORETICAL COMPONENT                  │
│                                                         │
│  (a) management and administration:                     │
│        1. leadership and performance of sports groups   │
│        2. organisation, ethics and politics of sport    │
│        3. managerial strategies.                        │
│  (b) sports medicine:                                   │
│        1. prevention -- analysis of aetiology of sports │
│                          injuries                       │
│                       -- prevention strategies          │
│        2. rehabilitation -- physical; psychological     │
│        3. immediate action -- first aid; tape techniques│
│  (c) sports sciences:                                   │
│        1. physiological -- structure related to function│
│        2. biomechanical  --  technique analysis and     │
│                              training                   │
│        3. psychological -- psychology of performance    │
│                            preparation                  │
│                         -- stress management            │
└─────────────────────────────────────────────────────────┘
```

Figure 2:

Outline of Post-Graduate Certification in Coaching

N.B.: BSc(Hons) Sports Science graduates to do PC I; PC II;
TC (a) and (b); and, at most, one from TC (c).

will continue to break down the barriers between theorist and practitioner. However, in the longer term, we see a real profession growing <u>only</u> from the established academic base.

Conclusion.

How should we extend this model? Two ways seem important. First, additional detail should be filled in. At present we are not really in a position to do this, although on some matters we have something clear to say. Although we have not elaborated these points (in what is already a long paper), the second major elaboration we see as necessary is a working-out of how to apply and extend our model beyond our own BSc. We have mentioned briefly how the modular structure in the theoretical component might allow for the replacement of some elements with appropriate material from the degree courses; in addition we have implied that some 'remission' in respect of the 'clinical practice' might be credited to those with an established background in coaching. And certainly our first priority here would be to build a course appropriate for currently practicing coaches, for it is to us a matter of the greatest importance that our proposal should be seen as clarifying the nature of coaches in a way which ultimately reflects on what practicing coaches themselves feel they should know. That is to say, coaching should be seen as a genuine meeting-place for theoretician and practitioner.

In discussing this topic with colleagues and friends, we have regularly been asked "Who wants such a qualification?". We should see the answer to that question as three-fold. Firstly, any present coaches should want the professionalisation of coaching. And we hope we have given reasons why that professionalisation requires a programme drawn at least broadly along the lines that we suggest. Second, those wishing to progress as coaches should look for an opportunity to offer prospective employers etc. something objective and demonstrable in respect of their abilities. Finally, we think young people should welcome the opportunity to have recognised and consolidated coaching qualifications. And of course, we wish to re-emphasise that our hope for an all-graduate professsion for coaching is one directed towards the future -- towards those young people presently coming into coaching at various levels.

References

<u>B.Sc.(Honours) Sports Science</u> (consolidated Document) 1984, CNAA, London.

Carr-Saunders, A.M. and P.A. Wilson (1933) <u>The Professions</u>, Clarendon Press, Oxford.

Cavell, S. (1981) <u>Pursuits of Happiness</u>, Harvard University Press, London.

Denzin, N.K. (1968) Pharmacy: incomplete professionalisation, <u>Social Forces</u> Vol. 6, Part 3.

Lyle, J. (1985) Coach education: preparation for a profession, Conference '86, Glasgow.

Murphy, W. (forthcoming 1986) Professionalism and recreation provision in local government and industry, in The Politics of Leisure : Conference Proceedings Volume Four of the Leisure Studies Association 1984 Conference, Brighton: 'Leisure: Politics, Planning and People', Leisure Studies Association.

N. 71 (1982) The Education and Training of Specialist Teachers of Physical Education: Report on Short Course N71, DES/NATFHE, London.

Silverlight, J. (1986) 'Words', The Observer, Feb.16, p.60.

Toulmin, S. (1972) Human Understanding (Vol.I) Clarendon Press, Oxford.

Section V

Workshops and Supporting Papers

THE COACHING STRATEGIES IN SPORT SKILLS

J. BERTSCH, M. DURAND
Laboratoire de psychopédagogie, INSEP, Paris (FRANCE)

Abstract

The purpose of this paper is to compare the effectiveness of different teaching strategies used by coaches when teaching a complex motor skill. 4 graduate coaches had to teach a coincidence anticipation task to 6 students (9 years old). They were unrestrained. Results show the use of two major strategies : the first one, focused on the lecture of ball trajectory and the second one emphasizing the required precision of the response. Data analysis show that the coaches interventions focused on the ball trajectory allow the students to improve their performances in the criterion task.

Key words : Coaching, Effectiveness, Feed-Back, Guidance, Motor Learning, Strategies, Tasks requirements, Teaching.

1. Introduction

The coaches interventions have an influence on the learning of the athletes. Bloom (1969) claims that the quality of teaching amounts to a quarter of the students' learning. What is that quality ? According to JENSEN (1980), an analogy between teaching and the performance of open sports could be made ; the coach is an information processor and each of his interventions results in an information processing : informations samples, selection of adapted responses and control of these outcomes in order to modify them. As the successful performer in open sports, he must constantly monitor and adjust to the changing environmental display. The clinical diagnosis model described by HOFMANN (1983) emphasizes on the discrepancy between the response desired by the coach and the learner's responses.
Hence, the coaches' ability to correctly ascertain the learner's problems and allow that assessment to inform subsequent decisions about the prescriptive part of

teaching, appears to be a major determinant of his effectiveness. The behaviors of coaches result of a continual flow of decisions making before, during and after the course ; the coaches' flexibility during the course being the most important.

Among all the set of decisions he has to make, one seems major : the contains of the learning sessions. This paper deals with the choice of the learning tasks, the necessary consistensy the teacher has to etablish between them and the nature of his interventions. Each motor skill presents different requirements, either it is an open or a closed skill, either it containts high or low uncertainty, either this one is spatial, temporal and so on... Some authors claim that a teacher can facilitate the construction of new informations processing strategies by reducing of the task's demand during the early stage of learning. Durand, Famose, Bertsch (1985) show that the acquisition of a motor skill in a coincidence- anticipation task depends of the sequencing of the learning tasks. Thus, in open sport skills, the coaches' ability consists in adapting the level of the task's requirements to the nature and the level of the subject's ressources and in developping a strategy of consistensy between the criterion task and the learning tasks.

2. Method

2.1 Subjects
Participants were 4 graduate experimented coaches, teaching usually open skills in field hockey (2), tennis (1), table tennis (1). They have to teach in an experimental micro-teaching unit to 6 students. The learners were 24 children (12 male and 12 female) ranging from 9.3 to 10.1 years old, from a french elementary school. They were randomly assigned into four groups (3 male and 3 female in each group).

2.2 Apparatus
A rectangular target (20 cm wide x 60 cm high) was fixed at the center of a semi-circular display (diameter 260 cm). On this display, white and blue bands were painted alternatively and scored from -41 to +41. The target was scored zero. A circle (diameter : 60 cm) was drawn at the center of the display to delimit the striking area (see figure 1).

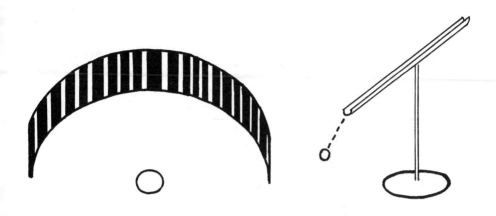

Fig. 1   The experimental display.

2.3 Procedure and design
During a 50 minutes session, the coaches had to promote
the acquisition of a criterion task. This one involved
the subjects to strike bounding tennis ball into the
target with a hockey stick. The balls were delivered by
the mean of a 200 cm long metallic throwing ramp. During
the session, each coach was totally unrestrained from the
learning tasks, the material to use and to set up. Just
the goal was specified : to increase the learners performances in the criterion task. Before and after the
course, each learner was tested : he was asked to perform
2 blocks of eight trials in the criterion task.

2.4 Measures of performances
One dependent factor was scored : average error scores
(absolute error). All the sessions were filmed and the
time recorded by a video-system with one or two cameras.
Post hoc analysis of the movies was supported by a multi-
dimensional observation system (variant of the ALT-PE
observation system of SIEDENTOP, BIRDWELL and METZLER,
(1979) and of the OBEL/ULg observation system described
by PIERON (1983)) dealing with intent and content of the
feedbacks provided by the selected coaches, and by an
analysis system of the interventions about the tasks
requirements. Further the nature of the learning tasks
was analyzed.

3. Results and interpretation

3.1 Performances of the learners
Post hoc comparisons show no differences between the four groups at the pre-test. Student t for dependent groups was calculated.

Table 1.   GROUP MEANS FOR ABSOLUTE ERROR (A.E.)

			G.I	G.II	G.III	G.IV
					GROUPS	
AE	Pre-test	BlockI	29.62	30.04	33.00	31.66
	Post-test	BlockII	23.00	26.60	36.12	31.33
		2 Blocks	26.31	28.32	34.56	31.50
AE	Pre-test	BlockI	12.00	32.66	31.00	26.95
		BlockII	20.25	30.39	29.37	25.37
		2 Blocks	16.12	31.52	30.18	26.16

The performances increase significantly in the group I ($t = 2,57$, $p < .05$) and in the group IV ($t = 2,21$, p. < 05) between pre-test and post-test (2 Blocks together). No change occurs between pre-test and post-test in the others groups. So it appears that the first and fourth groups coaches have been more effective than the others coaches.

3.2 Interventions of coaches
3.2.1 Engaged time
Considered as a very important determinant of the student's achievement, the active learning time between "effective" groups (I, IV) and "ineffective" groups (II, III) shows no difference.

3.2.2 Feed-back
Results collapsed across interventions in feed-back and guidance show differences between group I-IV and group II-III ($\chi^2 = 12,84$, $p < .001$). Number of all feed-backs does not differ (4,1/min./group I-IV versus 4,01/min./ group II-III). Yet the internal distribution of feed-back is different ($\chi^2 = 27,65$, $p < .001$) : the "effective" coaches reacting less by praising and more by informating than the "ineffective" coaches. Another important difference occurs about guidance interventions ($\chi^2 = 136.7$, $p < .001$) : "effective" coaches give more informations about timing and analysis of the ball trajectory (1.1/min.) and few informations about accuracy and control of the movement (0.6/min.). Opposite, "ineffective" coaches give more informations about standards of performance (2.28/min.) than about lecture of the ball trajectory (0.34/min.).

Table 2   NUMBER OF COACHES INTERVENTIONS/SESSION/GROUP

===

	G.I	G.II	G.III	G.IV
Evaluative Feed-Back	89	38	188	67
Prescriptive Feed-Back	92	24	55	42
Guidance				
Control of movement	31	103	122	29
Ball trajectory analysis	54	1	32	58

===

3.2.3 Learning tasks
In groups II and III, the coaches used principally learning tasks with reduction of the required precision of
the response (e.g. using sticks with a doubled striking
area, balls with larger diameter...) and the training in
the criterion task is very short (2 min./group II ; 3
min./group III). Opposite, the coaches of groups I and IV
made use of learning tasks focused on the ball trajectory
analysis (e.g. analysis of the timing during the bounce),
with decreasing the criterion-task's complexity at the
stage of stimulus identification. Before the right
post-test, they trained the students in the criterion
task.

4. Discussion

The results show that only group I and group IV progress
for absolute error. These groups have received more
prescriptive feed-back than evaluative feed-back in the
learning session. They confirm that the content of the
feed-back, depending largely of the coaches' skill to
identify errors and to applicate a remedy, has to provide
instructions for the future performance in the motor
skill and not only to provide an appraisal of the skill.
In the same way, group I and group IV have received
accurate informations of guidance about the analysis of
the ball trajectory. These results confirm that in a
coincidence-anticipation task, the learning session must
consist in decreasing the task's complexity. Yet all the
simplifications are not avalaible. The coaching effectiveness depends both in the internal consistensy of the
session between the sequencing of learning tasks and the
criterion task, and in the consistensy between the task's
requirements and the coaches' prescriptions in order to
allow the students to construct adapted strategies.
These results must be extended and generalized : we must
now replicate this experiment with a larger sample of
coaches, from varied sports and with other kinds of

criterion-tasks to accurately describe the spectrum of strategies used by coaches in sport skills learning.

References

BLOOM, B. (1979) Caractéristiques individuelles et apprentissages scolaires. Bruxelles. Ed. Labor.

DURAND, M., FAMOSE, J.P., BERTSCH, J. (1985) Caractéristiques spatio-temporelles des tâches et performance motrice. Paper delivered at the Congress "Body, Space and Time" : MARLY LE ROI.

HOFFMAN, S.J., (1983) Clinical diagnosis as a pedagogical skill in. TEMPLIN, T., OLSON, J. Teaching in Physical Education. Champaign : Human kinetic publishers, 35-45.

JENSEN, M. (1980) Teaching : an open skill, implications for teacher training. QUEST, 32, 11, 60-70.

PIERON, M. (1983). Le retour d'informations dans l'enseignement des activités physiques. Motricité Humaine, 1, 12-17.

SIEDENTOP, D., BIRDWELL, D., METZLER, M. (1979). A process approach to measuring teaching effectiveness in physical education. Paper delivered at the AAHPERD Symposium. New Orleans.

COACH EDUCATION IN THE U.K. - THE CONTRIBUTIONS OF HIGHER EDUCATION

J.S. CALVERT
Centre for Physical Education and Sport, University of Newcastle
upon Tyne.

Abstract
Institutions of Higher Education in the United Kingdom play a significant part in the Coach Education programmes of the National
Coaching Foundation and the national Governing Bodies of Sport
(Sports Associations). Recognition of the importance of co-operation between education and community sport prompts a range of activities affecting different levels of performance and coaching, and a
positive policy towards access to facilities and sports related research. Enquiries were directed to Universities, Polytechnics,
Colleges and Institutes of Higher Education inviting an indication
of particular examples of partnerships and new initiatives, and
similarly to Directors of Coaching in the English Sports Associations. A selection of the replies is presented in this paper which
identifies specific areas of expertise and resource availability
essential to the development of Coach Education programmes. Against
a background of resource reduction and continuing reorganisation in
Higher Education, the enquiry confirms an optimistic prediction for
future co-operation between the institutions and the associations
at national and local levels.
Key words: Higher Education, Awards, NCF, Facilities, Courses,
Research.

1. Introduction

John Lyle's paradigm paper (1985) refers specifically to Coach Education in Higher Education in the United Kingdom confirming that
Universities, Polytechnics, Colleges and Institutes play a much less
central role than elsewhere in the world in those areas of professional development beyond the Sports Association Coaching Award stage.
However, the enthusiasm with which the institutions welcomed the
initiatives of the National Coaching Foundation, both in relation
to the preparation of the series of Introductory Study Packs (1984)
and in the presentation of Coach Development Courses in each of the
nine English Regions, is evidence of the importance attached to co-
operation with the various Sports Associations.
    Participation in Coach Education is but one element in a positive
policy whereby individual institutions seek to extend their contacts
with community agencies at regional and local levels. This paper

reports on those areas in which the institutions have made significant contributions, and observes on particular projects which represent good practice in an essential partnership.

Following Calvert's study (1985) enquiries were addressed to
different sectors of Higher Education inviting Directors of Physical
Education and/or Heads of Departments to indicate their respective
contributions to various aspects of Coach Education. Additional
information from the Directors of Coaching to the English Sports
Associations, provides examples of collaboration and views on the
direction of future co-operation.

2. Higher Education in the United Kingdom

It is important to consider the various contributions against the
prevailing attitudes and problems which confront the institutions as
they contemplate government policies for the 1990's outlined in the
May 1985 Green Paper. Commonwealth colleagues will recognise the
massive reorganisations which have taken place in recent years, not
least in those institutions where teacher training was the major
activity, and where Physical Education was a specialism. College
closures, institutional mergers, and course and subject diversification have proceeded at a pace not anticipated when this Conference
was last held in Scotland.

The Committee of Vice Chancellors and Principals (CVCP) has
responded to the Secretary of State for Education and Science in "The
Future of the Universities" (1986) and, in the interests of national
economic and social recovery, stresses the need for people "with the
intellectual and personal skills which Higher Education provides".
CVCP Chairman Maurice Shock refers to "disaffected academics, an increasing emigration of the most able and the shadow of financial
difficulty". Significantly in the context of this conference, the
report provides strong support for those areas which "provide for
self-education through the intellectual, sporting, political and recreational activities that complement academic pursuits." This
provides encouragement for the development of sports programmes beyond those encompassed by a particular course of study, and under-
lines the partnership between P.E. and Sports Departments and the
activities of the students' Athletic Unions and Sports Federations.
The report refers to the 'binary system' of Higher Education recommending that we "build upon the particular strengths of each sector..
(and) extend co-operation across the binary line...".

Clearly 'Coach Education' provides an excellent opportunity for
such co-operation with a pooling of staff expertise and facilities
made available to the Sports Associations.

3. Coaching Awards

The introduction of students to the elementary and preliminary levels
of sports coaching, well established in the former Colleges of Education and other teacher training institutions, certainly appears to
be standard practice where B.Ed. and the more broadly based 'Sports
Studies' courses are offered. A degree of accommodation has been

achieved between the requirements of the Bachelor's degree courses
and the P.G.C.E., and the syllabuses of the coaching awards. Indeed
where lecturing staff hold the Senior Coach Awards it is not uncommon
for Sports Association Teachers' Certificates to be awarded coincid-
ental with the course requirements of the institution.

This 1986 study was not sufficiently detailed to establish the
extent to which substantial numbers of students taking courses other
than those involving physical education and sports studies were
introduced to this level of sports coaching. Recognising the outstanding performance talents amongst the student population, and the
prospects of their continuing involvement in their chosen sport,
institutions and sports associations could profitably exploit this
potential market for coaches.

In acknowledging the response from colleagues, it would be ted-
ious to present a catalogue of contributions and, therefore, this
paper refers to examples of good practice and innovation.

The Department of Human Movement, Dance and Recreation Studies at
the College of Ripon and York St. John, (a clear indication of the
effects of reorganisation and diversification) provides extensive
guidance for students on a range of 23 award courses in 10 sports.
With former Olympic gymnast Stan Wild on the staff, this programme
is extended to Advanced Club, County and Area Coach Awards of the
British Amateur Gymnastics Association.

St. Mary's College, Twickenham, offers a series of coaching and
umpire/referee awards on a three year cycle, while Swansea University
opens some of its courses to members of the public. Sheffield University's programme aims chiefly at the P.G.C.E. students but includes
students from all university faculties, and Edinburgh focus particular attention on Outdoor Pursuits courses at their Firbush Point
Field Centre.

These opportunities for students to gain access to the lower
levels of Sports Coaching are a major contribution from the institutions.

4. National Coaching Foundation and liaison with Higher Education

Sports Council Director of Development Services, W.J. Slater (1986)
writes of this liaison: "The Council relies on the NFC to encourage
the development of coach education programmes, as distinct from
governing body coaching award courses, in universities and other
institutions of Higher Education." He refers to the joint inputs of
institutions' staff and experienced coaches to the NCF Study Units
and to the programme of NCF sponsored research projects.

1985 and 1986 NCF Course Programmes demonstrate the roles of
lecturers and sports coaches in the presentation of the units available to coaches on a regional basis. In the East Midlands The
University of Technology at Loughborough acts as the co-ordinator of
course programmes and in addition to Rod Thorpe's work on a video to
support his Unit 1 booklet 'Planning and Practice' (1985), the Department of Physical Education and Sports Science is arranging a residential NCF Level 2 course in conjunction with the Loughborough
Summer School.

The North West Region's 1986 NCF Programme confirms the essential role of the Institutions - 12 units are being offered at four locations, Crewe and Alsager College, Lancaster and Salford Universities, and the C.F. Mott Campus of Liverpool Polytechnic, with substantial lecturing inputs from institution staff.

The National Coaching Foundation has provided a list of current Research Projects involving the strongest liaisons between academic research workers and practicing sports coaches and performers. The following examples illustrate the best features of this liaision:

Bath and Birmingham Universities have combined the interests of Engineering students, and the expertise of Canoe Coach John Handyside and World Slalom Champion Richard Fox, to design, construct and test a canoeing ergometer to carry out physiological testing of canoeists.

Sheffied Polytechnic is currently developing a coaches' guide to micro computing with particular reference to match analysis and performance information, and a second related project especially for Women's Lacrosse.

Despite the response from the National Cricket Association (1986) "...Higher Education does little for cricket and cricket does little for Higher Education..." the Fast Bowling Research Proposal at the Carnegie School of Physical Education and Human Movement Studies at Leeds Polytechnic will bring together NCF, NCA and Carnegie to carry out a 'scientific investigation of the fast bowler and the fast bowling action'.

5. Access to campus facilities

It is singularly unfortunate in 1986 to hear continuing calls from the world of sport, from the Minister and the Sports Council at national level to the Sports Associations and the Clubs locally, for greater access to facilities provided in the education sector. Those of us in Higher Education who identified years ago with the principles of Joint Provision and Dual Use can only suggest to our reluctant colleagues that there is as much to be gained by the institution, be it school or college, as by the local community and by sport, from the development of partnerships and joint initiatives.

This study confirms the essential part which campus facilities play in the various aspects of Sports Coaching Programmes. The combination of residential accommodation, playing facilities, laboratory and study spaces, and the teaching resources both human and technical, provide the ideal location for annual coaching courses, centres of excellences, squad training sessions and study conferences.

It is to the credit of many Sports Associations that they have developed specially designated centres - the Football Association at the National Recreation Centre at Lilleshall, Sailing at Cowes in the Isle of Wight, and other water sports at the Sports Council's Holme Pierrepoint in Nottingham - but clearly the Higher Education campus is regarded by many Sports Associations as an essential feature of Coach Education.

Royal Yachting Association (1986) "College campus facilities are ideal for courses... a race management course for coaches, or our annual Trainer's Conference under the National Windsurfing Proficiency Scheme".

British Orienteering Federation (1986) "We use college facilities for
conferences and courses and would welcome using physical testing
facilities where these are available. Some universities, like Keele,
East Anglia and Essex have maps of the college which make them particularly suitable for coaches' courses." Kevin Hickey, Amateur Box-
ing Association National Coach (1986) confirms the importance of
H.E. campus facilities for courses and conferences at national,
regional and local levels and for squad training "thus creating a
workshop where boxer, coach, physiologist, etc. get to know what
'each is about'! - I would add that squad training is as important
in coach education as it is in relation to the personal performance
development of individual boxers."

Fortunately this is not a paper which requires a high response
rate to the information request to validate the observations, but a
less than 30% return from the Sports Associations was disappointing.

6. Courses in Sports Coaching

Others at this Conference are best placed to speak about the details
of the United Kingdom's two full-time courses leading to Diplomas
in Sports Coaching at Carnegie School, Leeds, and at Dunfermline
College of Physical Education in Scotland.

J. Lyle (1985) referred to "the conservative nature of Higher
Education in Britain" and the extent to which the diversification
from Physical Education courses to Sports Science and Sports Studies
fell short of specific Degree or Diploma courses in Sports Coaching.
Lyle (1986) has observed that, "DCPE in the late 1970's decided to
orientate a proportion of its resources specifically to coach education and services. The specific results were the establishing of
the Diploma in Sports Coaching and a Coaching Resource Centre."
With the present contraints on student recruitment and financial
recources it is difficult to envisage major advances in this field
in the immediate future.

There are optimistic signs, however, in an area as yet not fully
exploited by Sports Coaches. Liverpool University's School of
Physical Education and Recreation indicate a positive encouragement
for Higher Degree studies in areas of Sports Coaching. The
University of Glasgow offers a Higher Ordinary Sports Science course
and opportunity for suitably qualified coaches to register for the
M.Ed. degree in Physical Education and Sports Studies. Notwithstanding the earlier reference to 'conservatism' and recognising the developments in Continuing Education, the Sheffield University Advanced
Professional Diploma Course (1986) offered in consultation with the
Institute of Leisure and Amenity Management, may offer a model for
advanced level courses in Sports Coaching, since the entry requirements include "a technical speciality in and experience of work in
an appropriate leisure environment over a five year period, and the
attainment of a role at least involving managerial experience."
While this qualification is a University Diploma it is offered by
the 'Sheffield Consortium for Leisure Management' representing the
University, the Polytechnic and the Colleges who "now collaborate
closely to deploy their resources on a consortium basis to meet the
needs of the leisure profession."

7. Specific partnerships, projects and research programmes

A number of particular contributions to Coach Education lie outside
the categories already outlined, and again there are those present
more qualified to speak of the details.

The Northern Ireland Institute of Coaching (1985) is a unique
partnership between the Sports Council for Northern Ireland, the
Northern Ireland Council of Physical Recreation, and the University
of Ulster (formed in 1985 by the merger of the New University of
Ulster and the Ulster Polytechnic). "It was the first venture of
its kind in the United Kingdom and seeks to utilise existing physical and human resources for the further improvement of sports
coaching in the province. " As at 31st July 1985 the Institute had
32 organisations, chiefly Sports Associations, in Full Membership,
4 Statutory and 7 Voluntary Bodies in Corporate Membership, and 165
Individual and Associate Members. Study of the range of this membership indicates the breadth of 'human resources' which will
contribute to Northern Ireland's Sports Coaching programmes.

The Institutions' academic activity in recent years, both in
teaching and research has resulted in the development of Physical
Performance Laboratories with associated lecturer expertise in
specialised areas of sports performance. Queen's University, Belfast
staff are present at this Conference and will expand on their major
fitness testing programme being used to develop computer-based field
test batteries for use by sports clubs. The Royal Yachting Association partnership with G. Barrel and J. MacFadyen at Southampton
University involves the development of a fitness training programme
for the British Sailing Team.

The Martial Arts Commission, in referring to future developments
identify the sports scientist and the exercise physiologist as partners in research and comment on Loughborough's assistance with training requirements.

The Orienteering Association identified Jordanhill College's work
in the production of coaching films and the development of curriculum
units in schools.

8. Conclusion

The Institutions have cause for considerable satisfaction in any
assessment of their contributions to Coach Education. It is essential, however, to note those observations from the Sports Associations which indicate the nature of future partnerships. D. Rutherford
(1986) accepts that in the context of general education the
Institutions "have an important part in educating all those who are
interested in improving their sporting knowledge." Along with his
coaching colleagues in Women's Hockey, who probably have more direct
contact with the institutions than most sports associations, he
emphasises the need for coaching knowledge specific to the sport.

The BAAB's Director of Coach Education Carl Johnson (1982)
indicates the role of the Institutions:

"We believe that within our educational establishments

lies a wealth of resources in specialist areas of physiology, psychology, biomechanics and many other sports related sciences, which if drawn into the Coaches' Education programme, could bring immense benefit to the further development of the sport as a whole."

References

British Orienteering Federation (P.Palmer) Correspondence Feb. 1986.
Calvert J.S. Training of Coaches and Trainers Nippon College of P.E. Sept. 1985.
C.V.C.P. The Future of the Universities Jan. 1986.
Hickey K. (ABA) Correspondence) Feb. 1986.
Johnson C. The role of Colleges in the new U.K. Coaching Strategy Athletics Weekly. Mar. 1982.
Lyle J. Coach Education - Preparation for a profession Glasgow '86. July 1985.
Lyle J. Correspondence Feb. 1986.
National Cricket Association (K.Andrew) Correspondence Feb.1986.
National Coaching Foundation Introductory Study Packs 1985.
Northern Ireland Institute of Coaching Annual Report 1985.
Royal Yachting Association (V.Over) Correspondence Feb.1986.
Rutherford D. (RFU) Correspondence Feb.1986.
Sheffield University Advanced Professional Diploma Course Brochure 1986.
Shock M. Letter to Secretary of State Jan.1986.
Slater W.J. Correspondence Feb.1986.
Thorpe R. Planning and Practice NCF 1985.

TOP LEVEL PROVISION FOR EXPERIENCED COACHES

SUE CAMPBELL
The National Coaching Foundation

Abstract
This workshop will allow countries to 'trade experiences' about
their present provision for top level coaches and to investigate
the possibility of future joint developments. The NCF presentation
will focus on the various opportunities it is providing in the
United Kingdom. Firstly, the special provision grants for experienced coaches which are awarded to assist them to undertake periods
of investigation and study in specific areas related to coaching,
to obtain access to facilities and expertise to assist with specific
coaching problems, or to establish links with coaching-related
organisations overseas for the exchange of knowledge and expertise.
Secondly, the research programme where projects from the following
areas are considered - training methodologies and monitoring of
training, training and competition environments, motor learning
and skill development in high-performance athletes, competition
strategy and tactics, programme planning for high-performance
athletes, social aspects of high-performance sport, coaching theories, comparative high-performance sport systems, sport safety,
and sport psychology, sport physiology and sport biomechanics.
Other initiatives by the NCF include a register of expertise,
resource bases for coaches and information database.
Key words: Provision, Experienced, Coaches, Grants, Research,
Expertise, Resource, Database.

1. Introduction

The National Coaching Foundation has been established to provide
a service to coaching at national and local levels. It provides
training programmes, information services, and technical data
from home and overseas.

We at the Foundation recognise the need to provide top level
coaches with the best possible service and a range of opportunities
is being developed through our programmes. The purpose of this
workshop is to share with other providers and experienced coaches
our thoughts on the kind of provision necessary for top level
coaches and to discuss possible ways forward.

2. Background

I will begin the debate by describing in detail our present situation and the dilemmas we face. First of all, the situation in the United Kingdom at this level is a very complex one. Each National Governing Body of Sport operates independently and some employ a full-time Director of Coaching or National Coach. There is, however, no standard job role and they can find themselves acting as office-bound administrators; technical directors; coach educators; personnel managers; financial advisers or all 5 at once - a supremo of sport.

It should be noted at this point that there is no career structure for coaches in the United Kingdom and few full-time professional training opportunities. Beneath Directors of Coaching/National Coaches there may be other full-time professional coaching staff, for example in athletics and gymnastics. In contrast other sports have only the one full-timer who is supported by an enormous amateur infra-structure. The vast majority of coaches in Britain work in a voluntary part-time capacity and may receive little or no payment for their services. In recent years local authorities have begun to employ more coaches on their staff but there is still no overall strategy to which everyone is working. This has not prevented many excellent 'amateurs' reaching the top of the ladder and there is no doubt that for years they have been the 'unsung heroes' of British sport.

The British Association of National Coaches was formed in 1964 in an attempt to provide a support service for professional coaches throughout Britain. BANC organises conferences, congresses, seminars and workshops that provide practical knowledge for both its members and others who are interested in coaching. It was established to improve the status of the profession of coaching and is open to qualified coaches from all sports and activities.

Against this rather complex backcloth the National Coaching Foundation was established in 1983. Following discussions with BANC and numerous individual interviews with Directors of Coaching, an initial plan of action was implemented.

3. Research Programme (4 main categories)

3.1 Supported and Joint Research
Research projects may be proposed which benefit coaching in general, or a sport in particular. Under such circumstances this research may be supported in whole or in part by the National Coaching Foundation, or a joint sponsoring venture may be undertaken with other research funding bodies.

3.2 Commissioned Research
The National Coaching Foundation may commission research into specified areas. The main requirement of this research will be the generation of applied knowledge specifically related to coaching.

In the first instance, commissioned research projects will be aimed at supporting the coach development programme of the National Coaching Foundation.

3.3 Co-ordination of Student Research

Undergraduate or postgraduate sport-related research projects essentially provide an academic training in applying research techniques to sport. The National Coaching Foundation will encourage such students to work in areas of value to coaches by making known coaches' needs, collating research ideas, and making these available to institutions undertaking research projects in the United Kingdom. This will be done in the first place through the network institutions.

3.4 Research by Coaches

The National Coaching Foundation will assist experienced coaches to undertake investigations which will aid them in solving particular coaching problems. The National Coaching Foundation will liaise with the appropriate national governing body of sport.

3.5 Conditions

All research must be designed to provide information which can be readily applied. The transmission of research results to practitioners is an important component of this programme. Possible research areas include:-

    training methodologies and monitoring of training
    training and competition environments
    motor learning and skill development in high-performance athletes
    competition strategy and tactics
    programme planning for high-performance athletes
    social aspects of high-performance sport
    coaching theories
    comparative high-performance sport systems
    sport safety
    sport psychology, sport physiology and sport biomechanics

Applications for a grant may be submitted to the National Coaching Foundation by individuals, groups or institutions - for example, experienced coaches, researchers, national governing bodies of sport and institutions of higher learning. Financial support is not provided for student research.

3.6 Present Position

To date 16 projects have been assisted and the toal allocation of money is: £1983/84 - £15,100; 1984/85 - £14,892.

4. Grant Aid for Experienced Coaches

The National Coaching Foundation considers applications from experienced coaches for grants under a number of categories:-

    To undertake periods of investigation and study in specific areas related to coaching.
    To obtain access to facilities and expertise to assist with specific coaching problems.

To establish links with coaching-related organisations overseas for the exchange of knowledge and expertise.
Other approved projects which the National Coaching Foundation deems of value to coaching.

The transmission of the information obtained to other United Kingdom coaches is an important component of this programme.
Applications for a grant may be submitted to the National Coaching Foundation by experienced coaches. Financial support is not provided for student research. To date we have assisted 17 coaches from 8 sports and a total of £6,940 has been allocated. Each applicant has to prepare a full report on their return to the United Kingdom which is circulated by the National Coaching Foundation to all other interested parties.

5. Register of Experts

As a consequence of our 'courses for coaches' programme we are gradually establishing a register of 'experts'. These are individuals who may not necessarily be coaches but who have performance-related knowledge and who are willing to provide coaches with technical support. This register is being used by coaches to help them to identify people who can assist them with specific problems often requiring detailed scientific analysis. The difficulty of drawing up a register of this kind is the assessment of the level of 'expertise'. There is no doubt that sports scientists have access to much of the theoretical knowledge that underpins practical coaching but it is the 'translation' of this information which is so vital. This translation is only possible through close liaison between coach and scientist and not all scientists are suited to this task.

6. Resource Bases for Coaches

In conjunction with a number of institutes of higher education, the National Coaching Foundation is hoping to establish a network of resource centres for coaches throughout the United Kingdom. The National Coaching Foundation headquarters will form the nucleus of the network and be responsible for policy, finance and administration. This structure will have a crucial part to play in the implementation of the Foundation's strategy. As well as playing an important role in the coach education programmes, the centres will also provide a range of opportunities for experienced coaches. This will include consultancy, access to laboratories, libraries, audio-visual aids and facilities previously reserved for students. By establishing these centres we hope to give the vast number of dedicated amateur coaches opportunities to learn in their own time and at their own pace. There will be distance learning modules available at the centres supported by individual tutorial systems. This will extend the chances that coaches have to gain access to materials and expertise which might otherwise have been unobtainable.

Each resource centre will eventually be linked by computer to the National Coaching Foundation, thus creating an information network for coaches. Local coaches will be able to go to their nearest centre to gain access to the National Coaching Foundation database and a range of software packages covering a wide range of topics. The networking of these centres will allow a 2-way communication system which we hope will eventually spread to every coach's home!

7. Information - Database

We are at the moment establishing an information service for coaches. This is obviously available to all coaches but we are particularly anxious to provide our top-level coaches with assistance. We have already launched a magazine 'Coaching Focus' which takes an in-depth look at specific problems. Edition 1 was on 'Drugs and Sport'; edition 2 looked at 'Competitive Sport and Young Children'; edition 3 'Coaching as a Profession'. As well as this we will shortly be launching a current awareness bulletin to keep coaches well informed of topical research and ideas.

8. Discussion

It is difficult to assess the impact these various services are having or will have on coaches at this present time. However, we recognise the need to provide an individually 'tailored' service for experienced coaches rather than a general education programme. This does, of course, require greater resources and more detailed liaison work but we are endeavouring to make these available.

The workshop discussions will focus on the type of provision being offered to experienced coaches throughout the Commonwealth and the possibility of developing international links between the various programmes.

A JOINT APPROACH TO COACH EDUCATION IN GLASGOW

FJ CLEMENT, Department of Parks and Recreation,
City of Glasgow District Council
AG COWIESON, Community Education Service,
Strathclyde Regional Council

INTRODUCTION

1 Coaching, can be described as the guidance, development, preparation and motivation of sports people. It is one of the essential elements of Sports Development. Governing Bodies of Sport certainly recognise this and many of them have developed and actively promote coach education programmes. Despite their efforts however, there are generally insufficient coaches in most sports.

With the growth of the Leisure and Recreation Industry it has become clear that suitably trained leaders and coaches are required in many sports at all categories of participation from Initiatory to Representative levels. (See Table 1).

TABLE 1
CATEGORIES OF PARTICIPATION IN SPORT

Category	Description
1 Initiation	Sampling, trying, introduction to participation, coaching required
2 Informal Participation	Casual, irregular participation minimal forward planning, some may progress no further, coaching required
3 Interest Development	Member of club, frequent participation, coaching required, training/practice
4 Committed	Member of club, regular training/practice, involved in competitive events (local), coaching required
5 Representative	Member of club, regular competition, regular serious training/practice, high level coaching required

Increasingly local authority departments are promoting development schemes aimed at increasing participation and at improving standards of performance where well qualified coaching personnel are essential ingredients to the overall success of the schemes.

2 In Glasgow the Parks and Recreation Department, Community Education Service and local Sports Council have also recognised the need to create a fund of well qualified coaches and these agencies, together with the governing bodies and the Scottish Sports Council have joined forces in one common objective, namely TO PROVIDE A FUND OF WELL QUALIFIED COACHES IN GLASGOW.

3 This paper describes the Coach Education Programme currently in operation in Glasgow and indicates the plans for future development.

HISTORY

4 Traditionally governing bodies of sport have been the main agencies responsible for the promotion of courses for sports coaches. In Scotland the majority of sports are organised on a voluntary basis with limited funding provided by the Scottish Sports Council. The sheer scarcity of governing bodies' resources and the need to apportion these resources over a wide area of operation results in insufficient courses in Glasgow to meet the demands of the sports.

5 Until the late 1970's the development of sport and recreation in Glasgow had occurred largely under the auspices of the Regional Council where school facilities are made available at night to organised groups. In addition to school facilities the Regional Council operates a range of facilities where sport takes place. These include football pitches, athletic tracks, tennis courts and community centres. The resultant demand for suitably qualified leaders prompted the Regional Council to organise a leadership training course programme and for several years this scheme ensured that a steady stream of leaders was maintained. As the pressure was put on the Local Authorities to reduce expenditure the Regional Council were forced to withdraw from the programme leaving a gap to be filled.

6 At District Council level, the third tier of Government in Scotland, steps were being taken to reorganise the old Parks and Baths Departments (in 1980) and the new Parks and Recreation Department was created with an emphasis on Leisure and Recreation. Under the auspices of the District Council new sports facilities have been constructed and significant steps taken to increase the usage at existing facilities which comprise mainly swimming pools, a few sports centres and very many outdoor recreational activities.

6/ Additionally reorganisation within the Regional Council saw the creation of a "Sport and Recreation" post and it was not long before both these agencies were working together for the benefit of Sport & Recreation in the City. This joint approach now covers many inter-related areas including Joint Use of Recreational Facilities, Sport for the Disabled, Children's Play, Organisation of Events and of course Coaches Education. It is clear that there are considerable benefits to be gained from this approach not least of which is that the considerbale resources of the respective agencies can be used to mutual advantage.

COACH EDUCATION

7 Studies have shown that participation rates in sport and recreation are increasing steadily. In Scotland participation in indoor sporting activity has gone from 9% in 1973 to 22% in 1977 to 25.5% in 1981. At the top level it is also clear that standards of performance are improving as new world records appear in many sports on an annual basis. If these statistics are to continue to improve then greater emphasis must be placed on the creation of necessary development packages aimed at supporting the participants at all levels of participation within the various sports.

8 The development of sport and recreation is dependant on a complete range of factors but there are several which can be singled out as essential "elements of sports development". Chief amongst these are:-
Competition - the seeking or striving for success in opposition to others.
The provision for adequate facilities although still far short of the desired provision significant improvements have been made recently.
Coaching - Taken together these elements comprise the "support package" to which I referred earlier. My brief does not include "competition" and "facilities" but my purpose in referring to them is to make it clear that "coaching" cannot be considered in isolation but as an integral component within the "Sports Development Process".

THE NEED
9 In simple terms we have identified that insufficient well qualified coaches exist to cater for existing and future requirements. We have also identified that the development of suitable coach education programmes is the prerogative of national sports governing bodies who possess the necessary technical expertise to design the syllabus for these courses but who, because of insufficient resources, are unable adequately to mount sufficient courses throughout the country. And we have shown that the local authority departments of leisure and recreation of both Regional and District level have a major role to play to ensure that well qualified coaches are appointed for projects and schemes for which they have responsibility.

10 In the long term the coaching profession must develop along fully professional lines as have other professional disciplines eg, medicine, engineering, law, etc. Signs of this happening are becoming apparent with degrees and diplomas in sports science and coaching now featuring in several courses offered by universities and colleges.

11 In the meantime we must work within the existing structures. Many governing body courses are well designed and structured. Others are less so. Quite deliberately we have not attempted to influence the standard of these courses. Rather, we have accepted them at face value as being the best currently available.

12 The need then is to improve the numbers of coaches in the City of Glasgow and we have tackled this by using the resources of all those agencies involved in the leisure and recreation field thus maximising the effectiveness and avoiding duplication of effort.

THE AGENCIES

13 The project involves five main agencies all of whom have a commitment to the training of coaches. Each of these agencies has distinct aims and objectives and under different circumstances and with different personalities involved it could have proved impossible to create meaningful development. However, a true spirit of co-operation has been created within the project team and as a result it has been possible to implement a sound programme aimed simply at training coaches for the benefit of the general community at large.

14 The Agencies involved are

14.1 The Scottish Sports Council - the national agency responsible for the development of sport and recreation in Scotland. They have provided advice and assistance together with welcome revenue support.

14.2 The National Governing Bodies - they have endorsed the programme and supplied the technical expertise in the form of tutors.

14.3 The Sports Council for Glasgow - a local voluntary organisation representing the local sports club interests. They have provided financial support as well as a valuable organisational input.

14.4 Strathclyde Regional Council (Community Education Service) (SRC(CES)) - they have provided financial as well as organisation input together with suitable facilities and equipment.

14.5 Glasgow District Council (Department of Parks and Recreation) (GDC(P&RD)) - like SRC(CES) they have provided financial assistance, organisational input and access to suitable equipment and facilities.

THE PLANS

15 Some 18 months ago when representatives of SRC(CES) and GDC(P&RD) met to discuss joining forces in the preparation of a major sports development programme in the City it became clear that such a scheme could only be progressed in reasonably simple stages. In order to determine whether the joint approach could work and because "coaches education" forms an integral component of the sports development process it was agreed to select this element as a trial project. The original objective was and still is to prepare a comprehensive sports development programme for specific target sports and progress on this front is being made currently in respect of gymnastics and table-tennis - two of the sports contained within the Coaches Education Programme.

16 The organising group was then enlarged to include representatives of the Scottish Sports Council and the Sports Council for Glasgow and Phase I of the scheme was planned, designed and launched within the space of six months.

17 A leaflet was prepared advertising all the courses and circulated throughout the entire City; Libraries, Sports Centres, Swimming Pools, Sports Clubs and Community Centres.

18 Costs to individual candidates were kept as low as possible in order to encourage applications. For those successful candidates, ie those who gained a certificate and coached or planned to coach in Glasgow grant aid was made available from the District Council. A maximum of 50% of the total costs was available.

THE RESULTS

19 In Phase I seven sports were offered, namely; volleyball, gymnastics, table tennis, badminton, swimming, trampolining and basketball. The courses were designed primarily for those who wished to coach at an elementary level. The courses were all mounted between April and May and 90 candidates were successful and gained a governing body certificate.

20   The costs of the programme are detailed in Appendix I and the number of coaches in each sport are given in Appendix II.

21   The selection of sports was a reasonably simple matter. Although there are over 60 sports on offer in Scotland only have recognised coaching structures.   This, taken with the demand which was known to exist in the City and the ability of the governing body to respond to our initiative meant that these seven were prime candidates.

22   Phase II was launched in January 1986 and netball was added to the list.   49* candidates gained certificates on completion of these courses and the relevant statistics are given in Appendix II.

23   A list of qualified coaches has been prepared and this has been circulated throughout the Community Education Service and the Department of Parks and Recreation.   Each Governing Body retains a list of its own successful candidates and all these individuals are kept informed of possible coaching appointments within the City.

24   The Future

Although the "Coaches Education" Programme has been developed as one component of the more comprehensive "Sports Development Scheme" it is clear that it is able to stand on its own right as a worthwhile venture.   Applications for inclusion in the next stage have been received from several new sports including hockey, judo, athletics, weight-lifting, tennis and short tennis and it is planned to incorporate these sports in the September 1986 programme.

25   As more sports are included the overall costs will increase unless some changes are made to the present financial plan. Currently the governing bodies make a charge for the services of their tutor. One possible saving would be for the governing bodies to waive these charges since they do receive funding from the Scottish Sports Council for this purpose.   Another approach is to make the courses self-supporting by increasing the course fee paid by the candidates.   Although a 50% grant can be obtained this may have the effect of reducing the number of candidates.   If the programme is to expand in the long term then it is desirable for the courses to operate on a self-funding basis and a revue of the financial arrangements will be necessary.

*Some courses were still in operation at the time of writing the report.

26 At this stage most of the courses are geared at the elementary (or basic) levels. Experience has shown that few basic level coaches progress to the next stage. Consequently it is necessary to organise several basic courses in order to obtain sufficient candidates for a more advanced course. For the successful implementation of the "sports development plan" it will be necessary to have a solid cadre of committed coaches many of whom will be qualified to the second tier level (ie one level above the basic).

27 Consequently, with the exception of those sports where coaches already exist within the City it is not yet appropriate to launch the sports development scheme proper. By early 1987 however it should be possible to implement the initial stages, namely the creation of teaching centres in specific sports which will feed into existing clubs giving those talented sports persons the opportunity to develop their potential. Thereafter, through the creation of Advanced Training Centres, budding Internationalists will be given the opportunity to train under the best possible conditions. Suitable facilities will be made available together with advanced coaching and high quality equipment.

28 Until recently Glasgow has been devoid of good quality sports facilities. Over the past few years however the City has invested considerable sums of money into facility based projects and now we can boast of four new sports centres, (three of which are joint use ventures with the Regional Council), one new leisure pool, one new outdoor track constructed to international specifications and of course our jewel in the crown, the Kelvin Hall which will house five basketball courts, one indoor running track (200 metres) and spectator provision for 5,000 together with conditioning and fitness areas, ancillary changing and showering. This complex will be regarded as the National Sports Centre for several sports and will be the major resource for our Sports Development Scheme.

29 The Coaches Education Programme, in itself, is not a unique project. Courses are being run all over the country, all over the world. The important feature of this scheme is, not so much the content as the way in which the programme has been planned and implemented, as a joint venture between all those agencies who have a vested interest in Coach Education. It is my firm belief that, due to the relatively low priority given to leisure and recreation in the eyes of National and Local Government, only through joint projects of this nature will the development of leisure and recreation be able to progress at a rapid enough pace to meet the demands placed upon it.

COACHES EDUCATION PROGRAMME

SUMMARY

EXPENDITURE		INCOME				
		Course Fees	Grants	Strathclyde Regional Council	Glasgow District Council	Total
Activities	£2912.04 55.0%					
Advertising	£ 776.26 14.6%					
Application Forms	£ 700.00 13.2%					
Meals	£ 560.00 10.5%					
Catering	£315.60 5.96%		SSC* £550	£1233.95	£1233.95	
Sundries	£ 30.00 0.56%		SCG** £500			
		£1776.00				
	£5293.00	£1776.00 (33.5%)	£1050 (20%)	£1233.95 (23.3%)	£1233.95 (23.3%)	£5293.90

*SSC – Scottish Sports Council
**SCG – Sports Council for Glasgow

APPENDIX II

A JOINT APPROACH TO COACH EDUCATION IN GLASGOW
PHASE I & PHASE II - SUCCESSFUL CANDIDATES

SPORT	AWARD	SUCCESSFUL CANDIDATES	
		PHASE I April '85	PHASE II Jan '86
VOLLEYBALL	SVA INTRODUCTORY AWARD	17	14
GYMNASTICS	BAGA TEACHERS INTRODUCTORY AWARD	15	12
TABLE TENNIS	INSTRUCTORS/ COACHING AWARD	9	
BADMINTON	INSTRUCTORS AWARD	15	15
SWIMMING	AS A TEACHERS CERTIFICATE	8	N.A.
	SASA PRELIMINARY TEACHERS CERTIFICATE	N.A.	RESULTS AVAILABLE 27 MARCH 1986
TRAMPOLINE	GRADE E AWARD	13	?
BASKETBALL	ELEMENTARY AWARD	13	7 + 1 INTRODUCTORY AWARD
NETBALL	GRADE 1/2 COACHING AWARD/UMPIRING AWARD	N.A.	RESULTS AVAILABLE IN JUNE 1986
TOTAL		90	49

COACHING: A BEHAVIOURAL SCIENCE APPROACH

J.H. DUTHIE, Ph.D.
Faculty of Human Kinetics, University of Windsor

Abstract
Individuals still confuse the role of a sport psychologist with
the functions of a psychiatrist: the psychological dimensions
of athletic contest remain opaque. As a result of a lack of
focus on the process of coaching (and undue emphasis on the
personal qualities of the coach) the functions of a coach in
competitive sport are viewed as mysterious not only to the man-
in-the-street but also by athletes themselves. These athletes,
however, continue to operate in emotionally highcharged,
achievement-delineated sport situations where individual and
group performance is compared in absolute units of height,
distance, speed, time or in such specific productivity indicators
such as goals or runs scored. Successful transactions between
coach and athlete are haphazard and attributed far too frequently
to personality factors.
    When coaching as a process is studied analytically coaches
are seen to be either change agents (teachers) or evaluative
feedback providers who monitor and evaluate the quality, rate
and level of work output. The trap of motivating by means of
extrinsic satisfiers where motivation may become manipulative
and repressive, teaches athletes to evaluate performance in
materialistic terms with a consequent deterioration in overall
performance.
    Athletic success, resting as it does on the improvement and
maintenance of event specific behaviours, depends largely on
the extent to which coaches are able to plan and apply those
reinforcement contingencies which control sport specific skills.
Once this view is accepted, confusion as to long and short term
objectives diminishes and the role of the coach is clear. Job
specifications and procedures involved in preparing coaches
become precise while the involvement of coaches in policy making
is made obvious.
Key Words: Coaching, Process, Evaluation, Productivity,
Reinforcement, Contingencies.

In professional efforts to penetrate, categorize and then eluci-
date coaching behaviour it is helpful to seek out systematic
and useful distinctions before proceeding to generalization
and eventual definition. These papers in the Coaching Section
of the VIIth Commonwealth Conference would not be necessary
if the set of operational definitions or carefully articulated
key concepts needed to typify coaching behaviour were already
available. This Section itself is a recognition of the necessity
to investigate and clarify coaching as a process once its essential characteristics have been enumerated.

These remain obsure for several reasons. The first is that
few of us perceive the full range of performance change in the
individuals we coach. What most coaches see are limited
increments in a narrow cross-section cutting through the continuum
from novice to high-achieving, elite performer. Coaches work
in a delimited range of human performance. Some teacher/coaches
are mainly engaged in those fundamental, low level skills common
to all humans while others deal only with highly specific,
superior level performances in elite athletes. In efforts to
clarify the coaching process we are adjured to omit the former
and focus on more highly structured, competition-focused coaching.
It is to be noted that beginners are frequently reinforced for
a reasonably complete set of movements (rather than high quality
performance in a narrow, specific response) by those other than
a coach, while in the elite or superior older athlete, extremely
fine increments in very carefully prescribed responses may require
instrumentation or computation before being registered and
evaluated by highly trained experts. Coaches at these two levels
may not occupy the same cognitive or social domain, function
in similar ways or even find communication easy. There is thus
a great diversity in the operations within coaching itself arising
from the widely different coaching needs of individuals. John
Lyle, in his paradigmatic 'Coach Education: Preparation for
a Profession,' thus urged us (p. 1) to "to seek to identify
the characteristics which are universal to coaching," while
(p. 2) recognizing that the coaching process is created "not
by the qualities of the coach but by the needs of the athletes
concerned and the circumstances within which the relationship
will take place."

If we agree that the principal function of a coach is to
assist athletes or teams to improve performance in a given sport,
we then may see ways to achieve conceptual and hence material
control over such a process. To acquire this we must consider
the common sense, man-in-the-street view of the process, for
common sense uniquely provides the ultimate field of application
as well as controlling examples of coaching practice where we
may try out new ideas and against which we test theory. Theory
in this model evolves as a supplement to the common sense view

of coaching. This procedure will fix the field of application while supplying from the widest range of athlete behaviour, everyday ways of regarding and thinking about coaching.

The interface between common sense and theory this model creates will inevitably provide new insights for then we are forced to consider how and what theories may be applied. Common sense in coaching (and elsewhere) arises from an amphorous body of mostly inherited but always faltering set of presumptions. These are constantly being applied in our everyday interactions with novices and elite athletes or indeed our interpersonal relations with one another. As teacher/coaches and individuals we rely on these because of 'conceptual miserlieness' - we like shortcuts. In deciding how to respond we rarely use a rational checklist. To evaluate sport behaviour - just as more widely the behaviour of others - we frequently make assumptions. When these fail to check out (with continued application in more and more situations this is inevitable) we become aware of their shortcomings and the need for theory. Coaching involves not only individuals and objects in purposive interaction but also supplies coaches with examples of ways that theory can be usefully applied. Examples of individuals moving and responding are in fact intimate ways of applying theory. It is essential in any analysis of coaching to keep examples of athlete behaviour and responding before us to check if they can easily and usefully be viewed as theory recommends or suggests. Coaches are today equipped to transform inputs from athletes and achievement-sport situations into new performance, better professional practice and more theoretical insight. This process is not new for it is precisely what Francis Bacon advocated over 300 years ago:

> Those who have handled sciences have been either men of experiment or men of dogmas. The men of experiment are like the ant; they only collect and use; the reasoners resemble spiders who make cobwebs out of their own substance. But the bee takes the middle course; it gathers its material from the flowers of the garden and of the fields but transforms and digests it by a power of its own.
>
> Francis Bacon, The New Organon
and Related Writings

For too long coaches behaved as mere ants collecting ideas for immediate use while over time journals bulge with the dross from over-zealous, professional word spiders and spinners. Educating the worker coaches of tomorrow to seek out and apply theory will involve them in learning to scrutinize their own methods and procedures in systematic ways as they continue to evaluate the quality, rate and level of athlete/team output. Once coaches begin the process of accepting or rejecting generalizations based on data while applying their own calculus of efficiency they are beginning to play the science game. They have discovered that the unique strength of theory - to be disprovable at the point of application and evaluation means that no theory is worthy of its salt if it cannot be disproved by example or

evidence. Technical usages and applications occurring at this
level will require to be explained, exemplified and, if useful,
retained. Now coaches will find use for the mass of scientific
evidence for theory generated by others. This can be examined
in the areas of study of sport psychology constructed in the
U.S.S.R. where the efforts and products of many academic special-
ties may be made available to the coach who is in contact with
these.

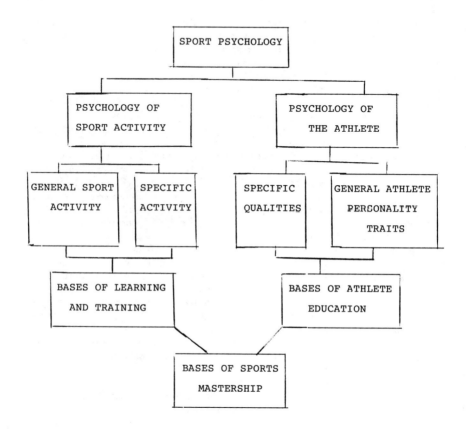

The Role of the Coach

While coaches commonly function as a leader as far as the team
or athlete is concerned, they must also function as the recipient
or consumer of the outputs of the disparate scientific areas
which surround sport and physical activity. The coach mediates
their output in pursuit of ever greater athlete efficiency.
Being equipped to do this is an important part of modern coach
training. This schematic generated from the psychological aspects
of coaching in the U.S.S.R. indicates just how many highly skilled
researchers and scientists may provide input into the coaching
process once channels of communication have been established.

If a payment-by-results system of reward is implemented, this will be regarded as appropriate and applicable at this level provided the rewards are suitable, for high level coaches will have been continuously reinforced for their ability to monitor and evaluate the quality of work output of others in sport specific situations. Here individual and group performance will have been compared in absolute units of time, distance, height, speed and other productivity indicators such as runs or goals scored. Payment-by-results may be difficult if the athlete is involved in a lengthy new skill acquisition process or old skill modifying situation. Coaches must recognize and accept a different reciprocal reinforcement situation along with the athlete performer and both must learn to accept long delays in reinforcement. Reinforcement intimacy is essential in coaches of athletes where quality of performance (judged by expert others) is paramount as in figure skating, gymnastics or high/spring board diving. Here we find that contingent reinforcers become by necessity much more subtle and pervasive. As the athlete is encouraged to experiment with novel ways to achieve objectives so the coach is reinforced in allowing athlete experimentation for there is frequently no definable set of responses which can be recognized and reinforced. Both coach and athletes rely on 'feel,' reacting to subtleties of timing and space relationships, waiting for the creative flash or insight, unsure of what specifically is being attempted. The proof of this strategy lies in the extent of the eventual reinforcement provided or withheld by judges. This is, however, coaching at the outermost orbits of aesthetic and artistic achievement: behaviour modification at this point becomes almost an art form in itself. Coaching such high level athletes as Torvill and Dean or Daly Thompson involves an interpretation of creativity and fulfilling experience: a challenge that only a few coaches need face.

The rare (and thus atypical) athlete who displayed the skills needed to perform with relative ease difficult motor tasks combining agility, speed, strength and endurance was viewed as a 'natural.' Even in these individuals there are limits to achievement without guidance, stimulation and expert assistance. Because of a rapidly expanding knowledge base and the need to draw from and contribute to this, 'naturals' as coaches will be regarded as even more anomalous in tomorrow's world.

Reference

Bacon, Francis. The New Organon and Related Writings. The Liberal Arts Press, New York, 1960, p. 93.

COACH—ATHLETE RELATIONSHIP in HUNGARIAN TOP SPORT

TAMÁSNÉ FÖLDESI
Hungarian University of Physical Education

Abstract
This work aims to study what part coaches have had in
their sportsmen's success or failure and what the coach-
-athlete relationship has been in the Hungarian top
sport like from 1945 up to now. Whom competitors consider to be a good coach and what is a good competitor
like in the coaches' opinion. The study is based on a
survey. The sample consists of former and present top
athletes and coaches. /N=1619/ The method of collecting
data were questionnaries, in-depth interviews and deba-
tes in groups. The results show that the coach - athlete
relationship has changed a lot in the last 40 years in
Hungary. It had been more human a few decades ago, now-
days it can be characterized as rather official. The
reasons for this are the antimuman and alienating ten-
dencies in competitive sport in the first place the
fact that victory is no more one of the values, it has
become the only value. Human relations have not changed
only in sports. Certain fields of Hungarian social life
certain social strata, groups and consequently the human
relations have become more closer. The pushing of human
aspects into the background, the performance-centric
attitude becoming more or less exclusive had disfunctional consequences.
Key words: Coach, Top athletes, Competive sport, Olympic, Human Relations, Social, Sociology, Survay.

1. Approaching the problem

Depending on branches of sport and the competitors coaches have an important role in their athletes' success
and failure. The effectiveness of a coach's work is only
partly based upon his professional knowledge. The common
results also depend on the way how coaches impart their
knowledge to their pupils and how these competitors
accept them. Even coaches of outstanding knowledge failed because they were unable to make their athletes

accept their experience, and coaches of less knowledge attained outstanding results because their pupils identified themselves with it.

This problem has been analysed mainly from pedagogical and psychological aspects, so far. Sociological researches have only referred to it while examining coaches' social status /Theberge 1983, Masiah 1984/, recruitment /Hill and Lowe 1974, Jackson and Lowe 1979/, social mobility /Sage 1975, Hill and Vander Velden 1984/, creativity /Loy, 1976/ and their personality-characteristics /Sage 1972/. Socialogical approaches put a stress on the study of the coach's role in the coach--athlete relationship. They examined for example how the coach's personality characteristics influence the coach-athlete relationship. /Snyder 1975/.

The aim of this study is to introduce coach-athlete relationship <u>from the point of view of the athlete,</u> too and to contribute to the clarification of how social changes effect the relationship between coaches and athletes.

2. Aims, methods

At the beginning of the eighties a survey was conducted in Hungary on the social status and role of top-athletes after World War II. The coach-competitor relationship was also analysed during the research. In connection with this subtheme the aim was to throw light on the following problems:

What has the coach-competitor relationship been in Hungary like, from 1945 up to our days? Is coach-competitor relationship different in the case of male and female athletes in the different sports and in the different periods of time?

What are the personality characteristics of a good trainer in the athletes' opinion and those of a good competitor according to coaches?

How did the changes in society and in the social sub--system of sport influence the formation of coach-competitor relationship, in the past 40 years?

The olympic movement in Hungary is very popular, sport policy is olympic-centric. The main objective of the competitors is to get through to the Olympic Games. Therefore as the <u>sample</u> of the examination we chose the members of the Hungarian olympic teams between 1948 and 1976. /N = 1369 males 1112, females = 257/

The number of athletes in the olympic teams by periods was the following: 128 in 1948, 189 in 1952, 111 in 1956, 180 in 1960, 182 in 1964, 167 in 1968, 232 in 1972 and 232 in 1976. 3.2 % of the competitors in the olympic teams died and 9 % defected the country. The ratio of male athletes refusing to answer was 1.2 % and 0.5 % with females. In spite of the higher ratio of the deceased and defected in the period of 1948 to 1956, the sample may be considered as representative.

The other sample consists of coaches. There was no way to find the coaches of all athletes many of them are not even alive, some 250 /90 % male/ coaches were drawn into the examination.

The methods of collecting data in case of athletes, were the following: autobiography, in-depth interview and questionnaire consisted of multiple-choice, evaluative and open-ended questions and carried out during personal interviews. In the case of coaches data collection was done with the help of in-depth interviews.

3. Result and Discussion

3.1. Coach-athlete relationship

Coach-competitor relationship is a very particular one in top-sport. There is much more at stake here, conflicts are more frequent. Master-pupil relationship has a more important role. As a result of the sometimes one-sided-like but in reality mutual dependency, the coach--competitor relationship may determinate the career of both the coach and the competitor; it can effect the level of competitive sport.

Former participants at the Olympic Games worked together with several coaches during their sport career. There were two types of coaches with competitors: club--coaches and coaches of the national teams. Selection of the first ones depended on athletes that of the latter one, not so much. Hungarian participants at the Olympic Games between 1948- and 1976 changed coaches about six times during their sport career. "Consumption of coaches" was the highest in football /12/, water-polo /9/, volley-ball, fencing, gymnastics /8-8/, swimming track and field /7/. The reasons of coach-changing are complex. It was partly caused by the structure of competitive sport and partly by psychological, sociological factors, financial interest or lack of cooperation between coaches and competitors. In our research "COACH" meant master number one, with whom the given athlete had been working in the national team for the longest period of time. In case of athletes who participated at two or more Olympics this was true for two-three coaches.

Former olympians evaluated their relationship with their coach on a scale of five levels. They denoted what their relationship was like during their participation at the Games. Number one marked the worst, while number five meant the best. 73.8 % of sportsmen considered their relationship as good, 13.1 % as medium and 10.5 %

as bad. 66.7 % of sportswomen found their relationship during the Olympic period good, 22.5 % medium and 9.4 % thought it was bad.

The opinion of male and female athletes shows a significant difference /Table 1/

Table 1: Opinion of athletes about their relationship with their coach

What the relationship was like?	Male	Female
Good	663	130
Neither good, nor bad	118	44
Bad	94	18
No opinion	23	3
Total	899	195

$x^2 = 11.67$ $P < 1 \%$
$df = 3$

There was no significant correlation between the athletes' performance and opinion. Even successful competitors had a negative opinion about their coach and inversaly. Sportsmen classified the most important qualities of a coach as follows: responsability, empathy, cooperation, professional knowledge, clear judgement, humanity, creativity, intelligence, sociability, sense of humour, originality and justness. Male athletes appreciated professional knowledge, creativity and sense of humour more, while females preferred empathy, cooperation, intelligence and professional knowledge. They considered the following qualities in a coach, as the worst ones: dogmatism, conservatism, agressivity, subjectivism, injustice, authoritarianism and performance-centric mindedness at the expense of the athlete's health.

Most of sportsmen rejected dogmatism and conservatism. Sportswomen rejected subjecivism and injustice. Extreme performance-centricness was among the worst personality characteristic of a coach in the opinion of male and female athletes of the past decade. Competitors explained it with the fact that while there had been more part-time coaches previously, coaching has become a full-time job in top-sport nowadays. Thus successfulness of the pupil has become a question of existance for the coach. Consequently the interests of the coach and his pupils do not always coincide: today's success is more important for the coach, the athlete looks forward to a longer period of time.

In coaches' opinion top-athletes' mentality has changed since top-sport has become a full-time profession: many of them are more agressive, unfair and money-grubbing. Success for the athlete is a question of living. Coaches consider athletes who achieved the highest performances, as their best pupils and remember them as obedient, hard-working persevering and reliable ones. Few coaches appreciated creativity, intelligence or fair play. And even very few of the team-sport coaches range cooperation or sociability to the first place

There are significant differences of opinion different sports /Table 2/

Table 2. Opinion of athletes in different sports on their relationship with their coach.

Sports	Average of scores given by the athletes from 1 to 5	
	Male	Female
Basketball	4.2	—
Boxing	3.8	—
Cycling	3.6	—
Fencing	4.6	4.2
Gymnastics	3.7	3.7
Handball	3.6	3.7
Jachting	4.2	—
Judo	3.5	—
Kayak-Canoe	3.9	3.5
Modern pentathlon	3.8	—
Riding	3.6	—
Rowing	4.0	3.7
Shooting	3.9	—
Soccer	3.9	—
Swimming-diving	3.9	4.4
Track and field	4.0	3.9
Volley-ball	4.2	3.6
Water-polo	3.9	—
Weight-lifting	4.7	—
Wrestling	3.8	—
Total	3.8	3.7
	N = 899	N = 195

Men took a more extreme standpoint here. Weight-lifters estimated coach-competitor relationship 2.13-higher than yahtsmen. There is only 0.86 difference in the average of scores given by the two extremes i.e. female swimmers and kayakers. More male athletes have either a very good or a very bad opinion about their coach, than female athletes do.

According to the athletes' opinion the most harmonious coach-competitor relationship existed in the case of males in weight lifting, fencing, volley-ball, basketball, rowing and in track and field. In the case of

females it was so in fencing, swimming and track and field but men gave "excellent" or "good" scores more often
In the case of males the yachtsmen and judoists had the most unfavourable opinion about their former "masters". In case of females the kayakers and volley-ball players did so, but men gave more "bad" or "medium" marks. There are individual and team sports on both poles. The <u>character</u> of the branch of sport then did not effect decisively the coach-athlete relationship. This is supported by the data according to which the relationship of male and female athletes with their master was quite different even in the same sports. Male volley-ball players and kayakers for example judged this relationship more positively whilst female players in volley-ball and kayakers did so more negatively.

According to special literature, changes of coaches, conflicts and extreme emotions are more frequent with women, in competitive sport. Therefore we found it quite surprising that sports-women remembered more harmonic master-pupil relationships. It may be explained by the fact that they characterized their relationship to coaches with whom they had cooperated during their preparation for the Olympic Games. And these coaches had been chosen by female athletes after several changes of coaches and on the basis of principles that were very different from those of the male athletes. In the case of males first principle at choosing their master was professional knowledge. If they thought that their professional development was ensured with the help of the given coach, they cared less about emotional background. A male competitor of the sixties said about this problem:
"... We got along well with may former coach but unfortunately my results did not improve after a while. So I went over to Mr X the coach of international fame, whom I had not even liked. But at the third training he told me what to change in my technics, and within a year I won a medal..."

Female competitors did not often work together with a coach with whom they were unable to form good human relations. They required mutual sympathy even if at the expense of the coach's professional knowledge.
One of the female competitors of the fifties wrote in her autobiography:

"...In my opinion a good coach is fond of his/her pupils and believes in them. Belief and love can make more miracles than any of today's scholastic priggery..."
For male competitors sympathy or antipathy to their coaches were not without interest either but they got a special stress only when lack of sympathy jeopardized their results.

It is very propable that male competitors do talk
about their former coaches extremely because they either
had a close relationship or many of them tackled contradictory or even bad human relations with their masters, for the sake of the improvement of their performance. When coach-competitor relationship worsened women
preferred to look for a new coach. They had a harmonic
cooperation with coaches whom they stayed with in the
end but they seldom had a real close relationship. This
was partly due to the relative shortness of their relationship and partly to the fact that the majority of
sportswomen had male coaches. And in competitive sports
friendship between men and women is less likely than
between people of the same sex.

Finally we must also admit that much more male athletes declared they had a life-long friendship relating
them to their coaches. Female athletes had long-term
friendship rather with their male coaches, and this was
more a love-relation than a friendly one. Only one or
two sportswomen said they made good friends with their
female coaches.

3.2. Changing world - changing relations

The olympic participants in different periods look at
their relationship with their coaches, differently. Considering the main parts of the development of Hungarian
physical culture, we compared the opinions of athletes
competing before and after the Olympic Games in Mexico.

The average of scores given by male olympians /from
1948 to 1964/, concerning coach-competitor relationship
was 4.10. It was 3.89 given by females. In case of
athletes at the 1968-76 Olympics the average was lower
with both sexes: 3.81 with males and 3.73 with females.

The number of athletes who remembered a bad coach-
athlete relationship, became doubled. At the same time
"excellent" rating was less.

The ratio of those estimating master-pupil relation
positively, diminished especially in case of men.

Accoording to x^2 - calculations the differences of
opinions between the completitors of the two periods
is significant /Table 3, see the next page./

In the case of female competitors of the above two
periods the differences of opinions were not significant
on the basis of calculations /x^2 = 5.32, df = 4/ We do
not give the contingence-table containing the nonsigni-
ficant results.

Men have a worse opinion about coach-competitor relationship by olympic years, as we l /Table 4, see the
next page./

Table 3. Male athletes' opinion about their relation
with their coaches, by periods.

What the relation was like?	Top-athletes from 1948 to 1964	Top-athletes from 1968 to 1976
Very good	197	126
Good	164	173
Neither good nor bad	60	58
Bad	36	60
No opinion	15	10
Total	472	427

$\chi^2 = 20.68$
$df = 4$
$p < 0.1 \%$

Táble 4. Opinion of male athletes about their relationship with their coaches, by olympic years.

Olympic year	Good	Rather good	Medium	Rather bad	Bad	No data	Total
1948	49.2	33.8	7.7	3.1	3.1	3.1	100.0 n=65
1952	44.0	32.0	12.0	2.0	5.0	5.0	100.0 n=100
1956	40.4	40.4	11.5	5.8	0.0	1.9	100.0 n=52
1960	41.7	33.9	18.3	1.7	2.6	1.8	100.0 n=115
1964	38.6	36.6	11.0	6.2	5.5	2.1	100.0 n=145
1968	29.5	43.4	16.3	3.9	4.7	2.2	100.0 n=129
1972	29.0	36.9	13.6	9.7	7.4	3.4	100.0 n=176
1976	29.6	43.2	11.2	10.4	4.8	0.8	100.0 n=125

The trend is unambiguous: the ratio of competitors
pleased with master-pupil relationship decreased gradually and the number of those who were not pleased,
increased. Among the competitors of the seventies there
were less who considered their relationship excellent
and were more who thought it was unfavourable.

The question raises: does not time lend enchantment
to the view? Do not memories seem to be much nicer from
a certain distance? Do problems not seem to be less important? It is very likely that "embellishing distance"

also has its role in the answers but on the basis of the interviews and athletes' autobiographies it seems that coach-competitor relationship used to be really different. Competitors of previous Olympic Games mostly said that coaches in their active period cared not only with success but with the athlete, too. Athletes of the post--Tokyo period admit that their coaches did care for their human problems but, according to the majority, only when and to what extent those problems jeopardized their performance. Otherwise they concentrated on the results and tried to promote it first of all with the help of financial means. In many athletes' opinion, money is very important but it alone, is not enough to promote performances. In former athletes' opinion the greatest problem is that top-sport activity got mechanized, performance is more important that the athlete himself, fair play or humanistic values. Athletes can also see that these changes do not mean that coaches are less committed. The change came about because today's structure of sports and the different relations of interest prevailing in sports demand an other type of coach-attitude than two or three decades before. Today a coach who does not accept that performance must be achieved at any price and does not agree with the devaluation of human values, is not able to work effectively in most sports. Many former competitors said that they did not choose to work as coaches because they realized this contradiction.

Former sportsmen who work today as coaches see collision of values even more clearly. A coach who had participated at the Olympic Games in Rome, said the following when he tried to find the reasons for this change:

"In former times the career of a coach had been a vocation, in our time it is a job. In former times a coach used to be everything: professional authority, power, fatherly friend and an ally. Today the coach must be a clerk otherwise he will not stand all official demands. And there are only a few coaches who can afford marking themselves out from the crowd..."

Another coach, former participant at the Olympic Games in Munich, drafted dramatically:

"... Yesterday's results are not even worth enough to get a long credit for them the next day. A coach today has always got to mind today's results. And this is like a well that has no bottom. You cannot be an intimate friend of your competitor, there is not enough time for it anyway; because in that case you should notice that his foot hurt because of his recrudescent injury; you should also see that his heart is breaking for his girlfriend was unfaithful; or he has a head-ache because secondary-school is too difficult for him, even at correspondence course. But if you want success you are not supposed to notice or see anything because you cannot give long credits to anyone either..."

4. Conlusions

Former top-athletes' and coaches' opinions are not exempt from a certain subjectivism but nevertheless they signal a unambiguous tendency: the growth of performance-orientation and the loss of importance of human aspects. Throughout our research it became evident that coach-athlete relationship had been more human a few decades before and that it had been better and more convenient for both sides. The change in this relationship was not the partners' will, it is a symptom of the changes of values in competitive sport. Victory is no more one of the values, it became the only value; thus the value of human relations has been devaluated. In spite of the common task the coach-competitor's clash of interests grew and is growing by the fact that both the coach's and competitor's activity has become a full-time occupation. Coaches and competitors both have become more defenceless.

The data of the research warn us that overdone performance-orientation might lead to disfunctional consequences: it may alienate many people from the aims of top--sport. Human relations in competitive sport should be humanized because only in a human-centric sport organization that cares for the athletes' and coaches' individual interests one can answer the ever-growing requirements or identify himself with the aims of top-sport.

When analyzing coach-competitor relationship one must also take into consideration that human relations have not changed only in the world of sports. In the past decades, connected to the economical-social changes, sometimes contradicting them; other fields of the Hungarian social life, certain social strata or groups and consequently human relations have in a way become mor and alienated.

References

Hill, P. and Lowe,B. /1974/ The Inevitable Metathesis of the Retiring Athletes. International Review of Sport Sociology. 3-4. 5-32.
Hill, K. and Vander Velden, L. /1984/ Social rigins and areer Mobility Patterns of Coaches of Woman's Intercollegiate basketball. Olympic Scientific Congress. In: Sport Philosophy-Sport Sociology scentific program abstract. P. 106.

Jackson, J. and Lowe, B. /1979/ Sport as a Career. Pub-
    lished by the University of Calgary. CAHPER Sociology
    of Sport Monagraph Series. p.88.
Loy, J.W. /1976/ Sozialpsychologische Faktoren der Inno-
    vation bei Trainern. Die Soziologie des sports. /ed
    G. Luschen, and K. Weis/, Luchterhand Verlag, Darms-
    tadt pp 246-251.
Masiah, A. /1984/ Social Characteristics of Coaches in
    Israel. Olympic Scientific Congress. In: Sport Philo-
    sopy - Sport Sociology scientitific program abstract
    pp. 133-134.
Sage, G.H. /1972/ Value Orientation of American College
    Coaches Compared to Male College Students and Busi-
    nessmen. In 75th Annual Proceedings of the National
    College Physical Education Association for Men pp.
    174-186.
Sage, G.H. /1975/ An Occupational Analysis of the Colle-
    ge coach. In Sport and Social Orders: Contributions
    to the Sociology of Sport./ed D.W. Ball, and J.W. Loy
    Reading, Mass: Addison Wesley pp. 39-455.
Theberg, N. /1983/ The Status of Women in Coaching in
    Canada. Some Preliminary Observation. In Sport et
    société contemporaines. Société Francais de Sociolo-
    gie du sport. Paris, 1983 p. 164-186.

RIGHTS, RESPONSIBILITIES AND AUTONOMY TOWARD COACHING IN THE YEAR 2000

P.J. GALASSO, Ph.D.
Faculty of Human Kinetics, University of Windsor

Abstract

Rights and responsibilities need to be elaborated upon as fundamental concepts within any coaching preparation unit. Such a
unit would include an analysis of coaching in order to identify
the various knowledge and ability levels contained within this
very broad term ranging from dealing with elite international
athletes to the knowledge base required for understanding young
children. Applied ethical theories should also be incorporated,
but only to provide insights into understanding the bases for
decision making through ethics. The above factors need to be
related to the objectives at the various levels of competition
to provide an understanding of the coach/athlete relationship.
At the international level, ethically, the developmental
base is quite fundamental, in that the objective is to win.
If the objective is the development of citizership and the attainment of a society that is cherished by the majority of people
within the framework of education in general, then the development
of autonomous citizens through respect for their right to self
determination and right to knowledge requires explanation.
Can the autonomous person emerge as a winner, or will the mal-
leable robot emerge triumphant in either of the two scenarios
prescribed as a base for coaching development programs?
Key words: Rights, Responsibilities, Autonomy, Ethics, Coaching,
Curriculum, Independent, Knowledge.

As the complexity of the coaching environment increases,
so do the moral questions associated with the education of
coaches. The complexities which have arisen due to greater
internal and external pressures must be taken fully into account
in projecting curricular components. Some of the complexities
with moral overtones which should be considered in this planning
process are taken in a Canadian context. It seems appropriate
to take this tack, in that Canada is somewhat in a midway position
between the highly competitive hothouse approach in the United
States, based on the Darwinian theory of survival of the fittest,
and what currently exists in Britain as outlined by Mr. John
Lyle in his paper on coach education. It should also be pointed
out that the federal government takes a much more active role

in coaching development in Canada, with its certification program, than is the case in the United States and Britain. Associated with this has been the development of centres of excellence in a number of universities with programs sponsored by the federal government through the Fitness and Amateur Sport Department.

Another factor is the existence cf highly organized and developed minor sport organizations which also present a major challenge to the Coaching Association of Canada in developing a sound certification curriculum for these volunteers. This level of coaching will not be discussed in light of the focus on coaching as put forward by Mr. Lyle; however, it will be alluded to in light of its place on the spectrum.

Coaching itself has undergone a revolution in the past decade. Professionalism and certification are the trend causing more changes than had occurred in the previous fifty years. Largely, this change has taken place through the initiative cf the federal government with the cooperation of the provincial governments and a number of universities.

In addressing coaching environment complexities as a base for interpreting the needs of coach education, hopefully, it will become evident that there is a need for a major segment of the coaching education curriculum being devoted to an ethical dimension. This is not to say that it has been totally neglected, but rather that it has been a peripheral consideration.

The following problem areas and complexities warrant discussion and interpretation:

All forms of ergogenic aids and drug use have raised moral questions which need to be dealt with. Electrial stimulation to build strength, blocd doping and the use cf illegal drugs cannot be ignored as a focal point within an ethical curricular segment of study.

Athletes are placing greater pressure on national sport organizations to select national coaches who respect their rights as individuals, and who are supportive rather than directive. The Canadian Athletes' Advisory Committee is an example of athletes providing input into the administrative and legislative process at the highest level.

The constant negative influence cf professional league coaching behaviours on volunteers and young professional coaches must be dealt with much more effectively.

Confrontations between coach and athlete are increasing in the areas of training methods, strategy, discipline, appeal systems and clarification of objectives and how to attain them.

The coach as God, that is the United States model, also has a carryover influence cn the Canadian scene, particularly in the large cities that are located on the border between the United States and Canada. The ever-present influence cf the media adds to this problem with respect to coaching styles and philosophy.

A lack of clarification as to a hierarchy of values as a base for coaching development programs must be faced up to. Who is more important - the coach or the athlete? This is a question not only for the coach and athlete, but also for those developing the curriculum and the government officials involved.

Fiscal restraint at the university level and reliance on more vigorous recruiting have led universities down the path to being influenced by government and its efforts to produce international gold medals, as well as appeasing alumni groups. As universities become fiscally starved by governments, they appear to be relying upon the intercollegiate athletic programs as a means to an end, which places great pressure on the coach to be more than a coach, but in addition, to be well versed in marketing and sales. An advertisement for a head coach of the men's varsity hockey team, that is ice hockey, in the Toronto Globe and Mail on Saturday, February 22, 1986 required the following: 'The head coach is expected to develop a working relationship with the Thunderbird Hockey Alumni Society.' And thus, public relations is added to the role cf the coach, which increases its complexity and raises more moral questions associated with recruitment and subsidizing of athletes.

The arrival on the scene of experts in biomechanics, exercise physiology, relaxation and stress management, sport management and sport psychology has intruded upon the stereotypic image of the all-in-one coach who epitomized the expert generalist.

The existence cf data banks on strategy, weaknesses and strengths of opponents, along with refined electronic scouting systems, also puts pressure on the coach to maintain a proper ethical decorum, while at the same time having more and more information on which to base decisions.

One of the problems that arises with the creation of the centres of excellence, at a select few universities, is its attractiveness to the best athletes, and thus artificially destroys the usual balance of competitiveness that has existed for decades amongst the universities. In addition, there is resentment by the coaches in that sport at the other universities in light of the migration of athletes toward the centres of excellence. This is escalating athletic recruitment.

Personal information is being gathered on Canadian athletes through psychological, physiological and biomechanical testing. The utilization of this information by coaches raises ethical issues, to say nothing cf the ownership of the information in the first place. The whole question of who the client is the athlete or the organization paying for these services is a vital question.

The increased use of quality circles and Theory Z as a basis for decision making places a responsibility on those designing coaching certification programs to incorporate these sound principles as a basis for coaching development. Many of the problems that currently arise between individual athletes and their coaches have emerged from theories of the 1930's with piecework and obedience being the pillars of interpersonal relations.

At the university level, coaching is included as part of overall workload, and coaching performance applies to promotion and salary increases. Thus, there is a far greater opportunity to develop coaching competence at these institutions. It is for this reason that the majority of international coaches come from universities.

In the private sector, many clubs have hired coaches on a full time basis to maximize the development of athletes in their geographic area and those who wish to travel and reside in that same location. The human relations problems that arise in this particular segment of the coaching profession focus on working with volunteers as parents and club officials.

These complex issues and problems must be taken into account, along with athletes' needs, in determining the coaching development process.

Historically, while looking back a few years, the late Geoff Dyson of Great Britain, with whom I worked as a member of his staff at the Royal Canadian Legion Coaching Clinic in Guelph, Ontario, epitomized the ultimate development of the total coach. He embodied the knowledge of biomechanics, physiology, skill development, motivation and organizational expertise. He also had highly developed communication skills. However, with the current burst of knowledge, accompanied by an increasing development of specific experts in the various areas of coaching, it would appear that a different role model is needed as a basis for coach education.

In designing this curriculum, the concept of coaching itself must be analyzed in order to understand the various parts and how they relate to each other in performing the task at hand. This, fundamentally, means that the coach must know how to work with athletes and the other experts in an effort to assist athletes to improve their performance and to operate maximally as often as required.

Coaches are also looked upon as the embodiment of suitable values. This must be addressed in laying down a code of ethics.

Coaching certification programs have evolved as a linear progression from beginning coach to international coach. The introductory or basic program, which should be used to prepare coaches for local sport organizations, should be divorced from the preparation of professional coaches. The philosophies are quite divergent. The needs of the athletes are also significantly different, and to indicate that there is a linear relationship from step one to the ultimate plateau is to create a false image or goal for beginning coaches.

Coaching must be both sport and athlete specific. One needs to recognize that there are differences in coaching demands in the way of training and preparation when observing the needs of athletes in track and field, swimming, field hockey, equestrian, ice hockey, soccer, and so on. Tactical and technical sports would be another way of categorizing the basis for developing coach education programs.

The coach-athlete relationship, as it used to exist, can no longer carry the day, in light of the fact that we have other specialists who should be directly involved with the athlete in the form of exercise physiologists, biomechanics experts and sport psychologists. These new relationships must be worked out in order to enhance the relationships so that their impact is additive. In order to coordinate the expert input from various other individuals, the coach must be educated to appreciate and understand the information being transmitted to the athlete to enable the athlete to make his or her best decision with the assistance of the coach. In this respect, the basic philosophy behind such coaching development schemes should be within the framework of support rather than direction.

In team sports, the coach must be a manager not only of strategy, but must also have a working knowledge of the other areas of expertise. A parallel could quite readily be drawn here with major corporations with experts serving it from different departments. It should be understood that the coach must not be a filter, funnel or broker between the other experts and the team. Direct access to knowledge is essential for autonomy to evolve.

An exemplification of the relationship of success to autonomy was expressed by the Canadian downhill skier, Laurie Graham, in a Toronto newspaper. She stated, "We get along very well (with their coach, Currie Chapman), but he has a lot of other responsibilities now, such as working the the coaches' committee. He can do that now because we have become more independent."

The right to knowledge and other rights are foundational to the development of the athlete as an autonomous individual. It is the contention of this paper that the most successful athletes and citizens will be those who meet the challenges of competition and life through their own personalized responses. The concept of the coach as the font of knowledge and motivation will be a thing of the past. Those operating at this level will find limited success.

The concept of the say-do gap should also be incorporated within the program. This will train coaches to achieve congruency between what is said and what is done to effect a consistent coaching style. Mutual expectations and perceptions can be drastically altered by the existence of a wide gap between what is said and what is done.

Basically, the coach needs to be educated to think ethically. Through the use of case studies and the Harvard Business School approach to this, coaches will be assisted in the process of logical decision making. Without this ethical base, we will do nothing but continue the current state of ad hocery in coaching styles, as currently witnessed, with its flagrant violations of rights and codes of behaviour. The areas of discipline, team selection, motivation, and testing of athletes are loaded with potential traps which in turn devastate the coach-athlete relationship. The call in this paper for a program based on the needs of the athlete to maintain the right to self determination as a basis for coaching development overrides the science of performance and its transmission.

As an outgrowth of this perspective, another person who must be added to the team of experts working with the coaches and athletes is the applied sport ethician. This individual could serve as a consultant on many contentious issues surrounding team selection, curfews, discipline, and confidentiality. Two other roles for this applied sport ethician could be as an arbitrator or ombudsman in dealing with contentious issues.

As to who is responsible for the development of coach education programs, it would appear that the government has taken the lead with the cooperation of university personnel. The coaching programs in universities do not have sufficient scope and depth largely to produce top flight coaches. The professional coaches operating at the high school level have found these university coaching programs to be deficient. Thus, the responsibility for developing professional coaches now rests with government.

Bibliography

Fisher, M., Skiers Praise Coach's Work as Developer. The Globe and Mail, Saturday, March 8, 1986. p. A12. Toronto, Canada.

Galasso, P.J. Ministry of Tourism and Recreation. The Rights of Children in Organized Sport. 1984.

Interview with Dr. Geoff Gowan, President, Coaches' Association of Canada.

Interview with Dr. Dan Smith, Manager, Coaching Development Program, Sport Canada.

Interview with Mr. Ole Sorensen, Senior Sport Consultant, Sport Canada.

Kidd, B. and Eberts, M. Ministry of Tourism and Recreation. Athletes' Rights in Canada. Available from Ontario Government Bockstore, 880 Bay Street, Toronto, Canada. 1984.

Men's Varsity Hockey Coach, advertisement, Globe and Mail, Saturday, February 22, 1986, Toronto, Canada.

OPEN LEARNING AND ITS POTENTIAL ROLE WITHIN COACH EDUCATION

P. EDWARDS   Department of Sport and Recreation Studies,
                    Liverpool Polytechnic
K. WOOTTON   Amateur Rowing Association

Abstract
It is accepted that coach education is necessary at two levels;
(1) sport specific education, i.e. work directly related to the
coach's specific sport and/or event; (ii) discipline based
knowledge, i.e. the acquisition of relevant information based on
the results of research in sport science and sport medicine. Coach
education programmes approached via traditional learning methods
are meeting increasing customer resistance in terms of limited
financial and temporal resources on the part of the coach; and the
selection of material appropriate in level and content on the part
of the educators.
    A strategy for overcoming these shortcomings lies in the
adoption of a learner centred approach, which can be facilitated by
the use of open learning processes. The use of a multi-media
approach including television; radio; audio and video cassettes
plus expert systems and the new and powerful tool of interactive
video allows the student to exert greater control of his/her
learning and assessment strategies.
    The National Coaching Foundation (NCF) is developing this
approach with respect to their different levels of coach
education. This paper examines progress to date, and postulates a
strategy for the future development of coach education programmes,
where Information Technology (IT) plays a vital role.
Key words: Open learning, Videotex, Audioconferencing, Telewriting,
Telesoftware, Telehomework, Interactive video, Expert sytems.

Introduction

The objectives of this paper are to discuss the concept of coach
education in relationship to open learning using the National
Coaching Foundation (NCF) as a pardigm; to consider the technology
currently and potentially available for the implementation of such
systems; and given best and worst case senarios propose an open
learning strategy for the NCF in the 1990's and beyond.
    State of the art in Information Technology (IT) is strictly
short term, and much 'hype' has and will continue to exist
regarding the power and applicability of both hard and software

systems. The reality is that technology alone is not the sole
limiting factor, financial constraints and human limitations are
equally important. Work pioneered by the Open University and
British Telecom in the '70's and '80's will be used as evidence of
what has worked, is working and should be technologically possible
by the turn of the century.

Coach Education

...The conceptual base for coach education permeates the system:
content is dictated by custom and with few exceptions is very much
sport specific... Education implies more than formal training...
Coach education ...ought therefore to imply conferences, seminars,
literature and exhibitions...
                              Lyle 1985
    Lyles description clearly pinpoints the two facets of coach
education:

1. Sport specific education, i.e. that which is related to the
    coach's specific sport/event and is the type of work
    traditionally carried out by the independent and autonomous
    Governing Bodies of Sport (GBS).

2. Discipline based knowledge, i.e. the acquisition of
    information based on the results of research in sport science
    and sport medicine.

    As there is no statutory certification or accreditation system
operating within UK coaching both these aspects of coach education
are largely undertaken as a matter of personal choice, sometimes
guided or demanded by the G.B.S.
    The first aspect of coach education i.e. related to coaching
award schemes has been progressing favourably, with GBS experience
increases in the number of individuals successfully following their
coaching award schemes. This is illustrated in Table 1.

TABLE 1. Increases in Basketball Coaching Awards 1980-85 inclusive

	1980-81	1981-82	1982-83	1983-84	1984-85
SENIOR COACH	–	1	–	1	–
COACH 1	8	15	16	13	10
COACH 2	437	547	456	308	366
PRELIM-COACH	188	383	612	847	693
LEADERS AWARD	–	–	–	46	149
TOTAL	666	946	1084	1215	1218

However, at level 2 progress has not been so smooth, and problems have arisen which could be summarised as:

(1)   Coach education courses were organised by totally independent bodies, and rarely was there any cohesion.

(2)   While courses were held in different regions of the country a very high proportion were held either in the London area, or based on centres of sporting excellence such as Loughborough, thus limiting the number of prospective candidates.

(3)   The course content was of differing standards from the banal to the abstruse.

The results of this strategy (if such it can be called) have been that

(1)   Unless a coach was "in the know" he/she frequently missed courses. In other words no system existed for the efficient dissemination of information.

(2)   The cost in terms of time and money created problems for professional and amateur coach alike.

(3)   The matching of course content to level of coach was frequently inappropriate, resulting in a great deal of dissatisfaction on the part of coaches linked to a growing distrust of sport scientists.

This latter was exacerbated by the coach perceiving himself and his athletes as "data fodder", being used as subjects in experiments which produced information which appeared to be totally in the domain of the academic. The gulf between scientist and coach was fast becoming a chasm, with a disasterous loss of information vital to the development of elite athletes.

The National Coaching Foundation (NCF)

In 1983 the National Sports Council stepped in and attempted to rectify the problem by the establishment of the National Coaching Foundation whose brief was to provide a service for coaches. In order to achieve this remit the Foundation has adopted a two pronged attack:-

(1)   the provision of a comprehensive information service
(2)   a coach development service which is based on a heirarchical programme of coach education.

In the organisation, administration and operation of both these services the NCF has utilized Information Technology (IT), plus current educational methodology to ensure that some of the problems experienced in previous coach education programmes were eradicated or at least attenuated.

The objective of both these services is to "bridge the gap" between research scientist and practising coach, and to disseminate knowledge and informaion as quickly and efficiently as possible.

The U.K. is currently passing through an anomalous period with regard to financial provision for education. Money is very scarce for some aspects of sport and education, i.e. travel; course fees; traditional learning material. However, in other areas i.e. technology, money is readily available. For example the Department of Trade and Industry is putting £1,000,000 into the production and provision of interactive videos for schools, and £1.5 million to ensuring that every school is provided with the necessary modem equipment to link them into National viewdata and teletext systems.

The NCF has been quick to see the possibility to gain the government money available for the provision of the new technology, and inorder to fully utilize these systems and turn disadvantage into advantage the NCF has adopted an Open Learning Approach to coach education.

Open Learning

This approach was pioneered by the Open University, founded by Royal Charter in 1969, with the aim of providing

...educational opportunities for adults who wish to study in their own homes at their own time...

Open University Guide (1985)

Open learning affords students the opportunity to exert greater control over his/her programme of study in terms of:-

(1)   the organisation of material
(2)   learning methods
(3)   curriculum objectives
(4)   assessment
(5)   location of study

Open learning has various facets:-

(1)   Flexistudy - generally taken as students studying at home using prepared material.
(2)   Modular Based Courses - where the student has control over the composition or elements of the programme of study.
(3)   Distance Learning - where students are in touch with a study centre or tutor by telephone, corespondence or computer link.
(4)   Resource based learning - where students use available resources of finance and equipment to devise their own learning strategies to attain specific objectives.

Within these different forms of learning strategy specific technologies and methodologies have and are being used. The following examples are based mainly on work undertaken by the Open University as research and/or services supplied by British Telecom.

Open learning methods utilize a multi-media approach, with perhaps the best advertised and well known methods being the use of television and radio broadcasts. In the O.U. system these are linked by programmed work texts which provide the opportunity for concurrent feedback with regard to personal performance by way of PAQ's (Personal Assessment Questions). Added to these are the traditional textbooks and recommended texts to support and develop the students breadth and depth of understanding. Later additions to this system have been audio and video cassettes and computer software.

These flexistudy techniques are supported by distance learning packages of tutorials at local study centres, and taught courses held in the form of Summer Schools.

Running concurrently with these relatively traditional and well publicised methods have been other formats. Lack of knowledge of their existence is understandable as many of them have taken the form of research projects or pilot schemes. However, it is felt that a brief description of such will serve to give a comprehensive picture of the potential which exists for open learning in coach education.

1.   VIDEOTEX

Bacsich (1985) (Page 4) describes such systems very succinctly as:

...inexpensive informatin systems using terminals based on consumer televisions linked ... by telephone lines to remote databases...

Perhaps the best known example of such as system is the British Telecom Prestel system. However, this is by no means the only system in existence and many private systems exist, one of which is the OU's Optel.

The generic term Videotex covers two very different types of system:
(1)   the Prestel type
(2)   a message relay service, e.g. Telecom Gold.
These two are differentiated both in their transmission characteristics and in the titles used to describe them. The former is known as viewdata and the latter as teletype. These two titles give a slight clue as to the primary purpose of each.

Viewdata is an eyecatching colour service capable of producing graphics, inverse video and flashing characters. It makes use of the normal domestic TV and operates in 40 column page mode. It is a good medium for advertising, catching the attention of a potential audience or market.

Teletype is not in colour with limited graphics facility and while it will work on a TV such hardware is not recommended due to lack of resolution. It can operate in 80 column page mode, but does not have the same database tree structure as viewdata, i.e. it is excellent for the representation of written material, but not for searching for information stored on a data base. This is an appropriate medium for the transmission of large amounts of information e.g. letters, papers, journal articles, lecture notes, etc. Two examples of the use of videotex in education are two systems operated by the OU.

(1) OCTEL - a database providing University and course information; guidance on course selection; limited computer assisted learning packages plus a directory of the phone numbers of essential personnel within the system.

(2) ECCTIS (Educational Counselling and Credit Information Scheme) run by the OU for the Department of Education and Science. The data base of this system provided wide ranging information of institutions, courses, entry qualifications, plus succeeding courses which would accept a successful candidate for further studies. The objective of ECCTIS was to cut down on wastage by fitting round pegs into round holes from the outset.

These systems can be used for course selection, enrolment and in some cases credit transfer as payment. It also allows prospective students to book and pay for courses from their own home via the TV thus simplifying administration.

2.   AUDIOCONFERENCING

Within the OU the telephone has been used in the tutoring of students since 1977. Unfortunately this system only operates at regional level. A national system similar to the American Wisconsin System has not been implemented due to technical problems with regard to available hardware, e.g. poor line quality and high speech variability have limited the use of the phone for such a national system. The use of audioconferencing in education hinges not only on technology but also on cost and human factors.

In terms of cost the trade-off in telephone vs face to face can be clearly seen by comparing off peak local telephone changes with the cost of travel on the part of student and tutor to study centres.

However, educationally speaking there is another limitation and that is in terms of the way in which humans respond to the system, plus the public perception of the role of the telephone within education. Both tutors and students require to be educated in the correct use of this medium. N.B. One of the biggest problems in the harnessing of new technology to education is that there is a tendency to attempt to use it to run courses designed for traditional methods, a format doomed to failue. The NCF starting from scratch has the opportunity to implement this educational process correctly.

3.   AUDIO GRAPHIC CONFERENCING (TELEWRITING)

Since 1975 the OU has been experimenting with telewriting, i.e. the transmission of handwritten text and simple diagrams over the phone lines.

Early in 1981 a pre production telewriting terminal called Cyclops was made available in limited quantities. Part of the hardware to run the system was a graphic tablet and light pen which allowed for the transmission of graphic information over the phone.

In twenty study centres in the East Midlands a two year pilot project was mounted to test this as a suitable medium for the tutoring of students at a distance. At the end of the study 81% of all lecturers involved indicated a positive attitude to its value in this role. However, financial cuts have taken their toll and the service was terminated in 1983. Nevertheless the interest shown in the project by other parts of the educational community give hope that it may be re-established at some future date.

4.   TELESOFTWARE   PRESTEL

Britain has been a pioneer in the use of Telesoftware both in education and in the home.

Telesoftware is the distribution of microcomputer software down the telephone lines. In 1981 the Council for Educatinal Technology (CET) established a proocol for transmission which ensures uniformity in the process. In 1982 the Prestel Micronet Service was launched. Micronet 800 not only allows members to download selected programs for specific micros; but also to buy pages on which to put up their own software for other members to access. In December 1985 Micronet announced a new and potentially valuable service concerned with the investigation and discussion of Aritifical Intelligence (AI). The concept of AI as exemplified in Expert Systems is one which has considerable potential for distance learning schemes and will be discussed later.

The use of telesoftware is not without its limitations. There is a misguided notion that the downloading of software in this way will solve all the problems of making packages available to interested users. In the field of education, and particularly in the area of CAL some programs are very large, and to download a 30 kbyte program at the rate of 200 bits/sec would take approximately 5 minutes, and in the learning situation this is a definite disadvantage.

5.   TELEHOMEWORKING   PRESTEL

This is the somewhat inelegant but litral title of a service run under Prestel whereby students studying for O level and CSE examinations can work interactively with the system in the form of a tutorial or homework session. Students with problems can be guided towards correct or acceptable answers. The system has developed to such an extent that following public examinations the correct answers are available in the home almost immediately following the exam itself. The same system provides hints on how to revise plus techniques for answering exam papers.

Used in conjunction with tutorial guidance and taught courses this could be modified for different levels of student.

The last two systems which I wish to discuss are only just making an impact in education, although both are currently widely used in the field of training particularly in North America. However, they are two systems which operated either singly or in conjunction with each other are I feel sure destined to have an important role in open learning.

Interactive Video (I-V)

Interactive video is an all embracing medium for many applications, from complex training tasks to information delivery. It is powerful because of its ability to challenge the viewer to become actively involved in his own learning. It is all embracing because, by means of one television screen, it can present a wide variety of message systems.

Griffiths M (1984)

I-V systems vary in their level of sophistication, a hierarchical category known as the Nebraska Scale indicates the degree of interaction of which the system is capable. The highest level currently in operation is Level 3. This comprises:
    a videodisc player,
    an external computer linked to the disc player
    by a standard computer port.
By using the dynamic image presented on the screen, and linking this to specially prepared or authored software it is possible to control the information presented in such a way that the individual operating the system is forced to actively participate in the learning process. The flexibility of the system allows individual learning strategies to operate, for example the path taken through the material may be self determined by the user electing to view certain segments of the information. Or it may be determined for them as a result of their responses to questions asked during the programme.
    The hardware is also condusive to the promotion of learning in that a variety of information can be presented on disc (a 30 minute disc contains approximately 55,000 still frames). The use of disc gives random access and a search time usually no longer than 4 seconds, thus providing speed of response to the learner. While the use of a branching program can lead the respondent who made an incorrect response into a remedial sequence, or direct a correct respondent into a new section of material.

The Domesday Project will hopefully introduce the concept of I-V into schools in the UK, and from there it can only be a matter of time before all branches of education appreciate the value and importance of this medium.

Expert Systems

The linking together of I-V with Expert Systems will be the next great leap forward in education, for while I-V is a powerful tool it lacks the intelligence of the human teacher or coach. The Expert System, a branch of Artificial Intelligence (AI) is a means of partially rectifying this shortcoming. The current developments in the fields of AI and the search for the Fifth Generation Computer have spawned the production of a number of Expert System shells onto which the knowledge of the human expert can be grafted. When a human makes an expert judgement his or her decision is based on fact, ie. well tested and proven theory plus heuristics i.e. the rules of good guessing or good judgement. The Expert System is a program written to make judgements based on the input of knowledge harvested from the human decision making processes. The program is governed by a number of rules, and given certain variables the most likely decision is made.

The sale of Expert System shells onto which it is possible to graft the knowledge of an expert are currently becoming more readily available. The example we have is one developed using the Expertech Xi Expert System shell and is used to teach scoring in Basketball. This was selected because:
(1) It is a relatively complex scoring system
(2) It is essential knowledge to all Basketball Officials
(3) It is rule governed and therefore an ideal project to use in this way.

If this were now linked to an I-V it is easy to see that by adding a dynamic image which can be slowed down, stopped, replayed etc., to the knowledge of the expert as contained as the program the student would have an ideal knowledge delivery system. In no way is it suggested that either I-V or Expert Systems could replace the human teacher, far from it. Their role is to support and supplement the teacher and to allow them to input their experience and knowledge into areas where their presence is necessary e.g. in areas of potential danger or complex skill situations where there is no single correct response.

The Future

The important factor about using new technology in education is not to be seduced by the gadgets and gimmicks but rather to assess their value and possiblity of application. However, it would be unfair to put forward the suggestion that the immediate implementation on a mass scale is possible.

In purely technological terms by 1992 all schools and institutes of higher education should be on the ISDN system, a digital phone connection offering speech plus 64000 bits/sec data. Some more complex two way video systems will be operating via satellite and some domestic users will have cable systems some of which will be interactive. The increased speed of transmission and interactivity will facilitate computer conferencing and the delivery of full-text documents with diagramatic graphics and telewriting. This will mean that distance learning systems will be able to offer good tele-conferencing with high-grade audio-conferencing and slow scan, plus computer conferencing with effective pictorial support.

By the year 2000 it is projected that all telephone users will be connected to ISDN with the possibility of video telephony to business users plus certain domestic users prepared to pay extra for the system. Most institutes of higher education should have full motion video conferencing using the 1000,000 bits/sec rate. Document delivery will be available to every home and "printed" distance learning material will be sent down the phone line.

The NCF in the 1990's and beyond

The NCF's current strategy for coach education i.e. a balance between distance and fact to face learning is an excellent one on which to develop into the 1990's. The balance between these two will, I feel, depend on three prime factors
(1) the speed of technological change
(2) the financial limitations
(3) human factors i.e. will coaches accept this form of teaching.
All things being equal the following recommendations are proposed:
(1) Respond to the market.
    Coaches at all levels are suffering from a lack of time to pursue coach education programmes. Personal disposable income is limited and priorities have to be set.
    Organisational income is equally limited. Therefore the use of the flexibility of time and cost afforded by open learning is one which should overcome market resistance to coach education programmes.
(2) Technology is there to help, use it. All the systems discussed have a role to play in open learning. The question will be of selecting the appropriate medium for a given level of coach education programme and also of deciding which will be centre based and which home based, for undoubtedly by the year 2000 many of the services currently available in institutions will be available to ordinary domestic users.
(3) The NCF's planned development of National and Regional Network centres is one which will lend itself ideally to the harnassing of technological innovation, and should be developed. For example by the use of teleconferencing techniques all students will be able to receive teaching from "the experts" i.e. the top people in the field. This will afford uniformity of coverage and alleviate some of the

problems which have occurred with regard to quality of teaching acorss the centres used.
(4) Obviously there are still going to be many problems and limitations; one of which will be that the NCF may be forced to make a choice between:-
   4.1 To wait for almost universal development of the technological services i.e. into almost every home. (There is always the outside chance that if a Governing Body considered it sufficiently important they might pay the extra to have the system installed in the coach's home).
   4.2 To target in on centres rather than homes i.e. most institutions which will make multi-use of the equipment, therefore making its installation a cost effective propostion.

The latter would appear the most realistic senario, nor does there have to be too wide a network. The technology will link the National Centres to Regional Centres with few problems. The major problem might appear to be, will there need to be a great number of Regional Centres to make it relatively easy for prospective students to reach them? Again work done by the OU appears to disprove this contention. Bacsich (1985) maintains that

...the main problem is due to ... the "armchair syndrome". This states that if a student is sitting in his armchair at home considering whether to go to a tutorial, the main decision he makes is whether to go out of the house - once he is outside, it is not important how far he has to drive...

Therefore by judicious selection of centres the NCF could satisfy market demand nationwide.
   In conclusion it is hoped that a persuasive case has been made that the future of coach education lies not solely in the realm of traditional methodology but rather in the application of open learning techniques; and that the potential exists to harness Information Technology to make such a system operate with maximum efficiency. The final word must however be that IT alone will not achieve success in coach education. Coaching is about people and people interacting with people. For this reason the NCF must balance the new with the old and continue to allow coaches to meet and exchange ideas for its is often this process of cross fertilization which brings about innovation and change.

References

Bacsich, P.D. (1981) The Open University Viewdata system. Proceedings of Viewdata 81, London.
Bacsich, P.D. (1982) Optel and Cyclops: a status report. Optel Report 13, Open University.

Bacsich, P.D. (1982) Audio-videotex teleconferencing. Proceedings of Viewdata 82, London.

Bacsich, P.D. (1984) Videotex in Education: the British Situation. Proceedings of Videotex 1984, Sao Paulo.

Bacsich, P.D. (1985) Teleconferencing for Distance Education and Training: Is The Open University Experience Typical? Optel Report 16, Open University.

Bates, A.W. et al. (1984) The Role of Technology in Distance Education, Croom Helm.

Bosco, J.J. (1984) Interactive Video: Educational Tool or Toy. Educational Technology, April '84.

Cohen, V.B. (1984) Interactive Features in the Design of Videodisc Material. Educational Technology, January '84.

Copeland, P. (1981) The Educational Significance of Electronic Media. Aspects of Educational Technology XV, Distance Learning and Evaluation, Kogan Page, London.

Council for Educational Technology (CET), Information Sheet No. 5. Open Learning, January 1985.

Council for Natial Academic Awards (CNAA) Consultative Document, Open Learning, 1a/33 September 1981.

Cross, T.B. (1985) Computer Conferencing: new electronic management. Oxford Surveys in Information Technnology 1, 215-243.

Griffiths, M. (1984) Media in Education and Development. Jnl. of the British Council, 17, Dec. '84.

Elliott, K. (1983) Interactive Video, The Authoring Approach. Training Officer, August '83.

Laurillard, D. (1984) Interactive Video and the Control of Learning. Educational Technology June '84, 7-15.

National Coaching Foundation (1984). Information Sheet No. 1., May '84.

Robinson, J. (1983) Opportunities for lifelong learning in the 1990s: an optimistic view of information technology. Association for Recurrent Education - occassional papers 1.

Spencer, D.C. (1980) Thinking About Open Learning Systems, CET.

Zorkoczy, P.I. et al (1984) Opportunities for Information Technology-based advanced educational technologies, IFT-TF, European Commission.

SELECTION IN SPORT: HOW TO COPE

SARAH GILROY
School of Human Movement Studies, Bedford College of Higher Education

Abstract
Poor management of the selection process can lead to: 1) discontent
amongst athletes; 2) athletes dropping-out; 3) a decrease in the
satisfaction that coaches and selectors get from involvement with
the sport. Despite these and other problems there is little available to help coaches and selectors manage the situation. Findings
from a study conducted by the author in Canada combined with information gathered about sports in Britain, reveal common problems.
These problems were mainly concerned with a lack of communication.
From the analysis of these problems the following recommendations
are made. Close communication should be maintained between the
coach/selectors and the athletes. Athletes should be informed
about the nature of the selection process and the criteria for
selection. Coaches should be prepared to counsel athletes after
selection. The selection process, if managed carefully can be
a useful learning experience. This is essential if athletes and
officials are going to continue to benefit from and contribute
to sport. Strategies for coaches/selectors to adopt are discussed.
Key words: Communication, Counselling, Cutting, Drop-outs, Failure,
Identity, Selection, Status-passage.

1. Introduction

1.1 Is there a problem?
Despite the increase in literature on coaching there is little
to guide the coach through the process of selecting athletes.
Many coaches are involved in selecting athletes for team competition
and although the nature of the problems therein may vary according
to the level of competition, it is nonetheless a problematic process.

People coaching at high-school level generally have to become
all things (selector, coach, manager, driver) to all the players.
The higher the level the greater the role differentiation, so
that national teams may well have coach, assistant coach, manager
and physio and a representative of the selectors and/or of the
governing body. Problems created by the selection process however
do not disappear as role differentiation increases; differences
of opinion can develop between the coach and selectors over not

only who should be in the team, but also who should compete in
any particular event. Although it could be argued that selecting
athletes is commonsense and that certainly by the time coaches
and selectors have reached national level they have developed
a successful and nonproblematic formula, evidence shall be presented
which suggests that this is not the case.

But the importance of this issue lies not solely in easing
the problems encountered by coaches, selectors and athletes but
also in promoting an image of sport which represents participation.
The title of an article written by Scott back in 1974 refers to
the product of competitive sport: "Competitive sport outcomes
- self fulfillment and participation or self destruction and elimination?" In the article Scott identifies the benefits of competitive
sport involvement but also highlights elements of the experience
(in particular the try-out process) by which, according to Orlick,
(1980) we are cutting our own sporting throats. The problem is
not only a short term one as Orlick points out. Elimination from
sport is also perceived to be a long term process insofar as negative
feelings about sport may develop which will curtail the future
support (both emotional and financial) of sport. So for the interests
of all those involved in selection processes, and for the future
of sport, more information and guidance is needed to avoid mismanagement.

2. What's the nature of the problem?

The lack of literature on selection processes can indicate several
things. Firstly, some might argue that the area is a non-issue
because the processes are not problematic. Others might argue
that although in some instances there may be some problems, in
general they are not that serious. Finally, it could be suggested
that there is some reticence on the part of sports officials to
engage in a debate on the philosophies and methods involved.
Whatever the reasons, the following accounts suggest that there
is indeed a problem that all of us involved in competitive sport
have to confront.

2.1 Disruption
Anyone who has been involved in competitive sport, particularly
a team sport, will no doubt have heard the expressions "Your face
has to fit" or "You have to have blue eyes to get into the team".
Underlying these expressions are sentiments felt by athletes about
the 'fairness' of the selection process. Merit alone is not what
counts but whether you are seen to be the 'right' type of person.
Two notions about selection can be derived from these sentiments;
firstly that merit should be the most important factor, and secondly,
that any other factors should be identified and made clear to
the aspiring athletes. Involvement in a team sport to a high
level has given me an insight into the damaging effects that perceived unfairness can have upon aspiring athletes. Some decide
to put themselves forward for selection in another area or even

another country (where eligibility allows). Others decide that putting themselves forward for selection is no longer worth it and so they settle for a level of involvement where they do not experience similar selection problems. This feeling of a team being a 'closed shop' can only be to the detriment of the players, the teams and the sport as a whole.

In some cases disquiet over selection procedures has been more manifestly to the detriment of certain sports. Men's soccer, women's hockey and women's cricket have gained media attention over the past few years because of it. In the first two cases Kevin Keegan and Val Robinson were reportedly not informed by officials that they were being dropped and heard of it either through the press or from friends. With a headline claiming "Hey, that's no way to say goodbye" a Sunday Times article continued to deplore "The shabby treatment of Valerie Robinson, for two decades hockey's national heroine". (Sunday Times 1985). What the reporter finds so surprising is not only that she was not officially notified, but that there were three hurdles of county and territorial and finally England selection and that "even the star performer is at the mercy of each closeted selection committee with their fads and fancies". What is particularly relevant here is not so much the internal structure of the sport, but the perception that the criteria for selection are 'fads and fancies'. The English Women's Cricket Association comes under a similar critical eye over its decision in December 1984 not to select Sarah Potter for a tour of Australia. She is quoted as saying that "her exclusion was nothing to do with her cricket". Comments made by her on television led to the WCA President writing to her. Part of the letter was published in the Observer, but the reporter prefaces it by saying that it was "Not to explain, but to castigate her for hollering about it, (her omission from the team) in public" (1984). In a feature article on her eight months later more fuel was added to the selection fire: "The newspapers cast about and decided her fancy hairdo might be responsible – it certainly wasn't her cricket. It's possible that youth and beauty and good connections might stand her in good stead". (Observer 1985).

The rights and wrongs of these cases are not for discussion here, but what is, is the effect that such publicity can have on those particular sports and on sport as a whole. If one sees through the melodramatic language of the media e.g. "Robinson discarded", "Shabby treatment", "Potter's...exclusion", (emphasis mine) it is evident that the misunderstanding surrounding the selection process is related to the lack of communication between officials and players.

2.2 Drop-outs
For some the lack of communication during the selection process has led to them dropping-out of the sport altogether. The following is an interview extract quoted in the Coaching Association of Canada's NCCP Level 2 Theory Manual (it was also one of the few references made in any of their manuals to selection processes).

"Q.2. Why do you think you stopped (your particular sport)?
A.4 "I was on the national team but was moved down to the B team.
    Nobody said why.   I was really hurt, it hurt my pride so
    I just dropped it completely." (1982: 5.10)
Although elite athletes dropping out of sport may cause immediate
concern, it is of no greater a concern than when any other level
of athlete drops out.   Orlick's (1980) work in Canada suggests
that the majority of children who drop out of sport do so because
they are not given an adequate opportunity to play, or they are
not having fun.   A badly managed selection process can lead to
both of these things.

2.3 Disenchantment

Problems that arise during the selection process do not only affect
the players.   For coaches and selectors, selecting a team is a
thankless task; if they are seen to get it wrong criticism (public
and private) is quick to follow.   If they 'get it right' their
work will rarely be appreciated.   As amateur sport relies upon
its volunteers, support needs to be given to help coaches and
selectors to develop procedures for selecting athletes which will
not lessen their enjoyment of involvement.

3. A Case Study

3.1 Background

Relying upon second-hand accounts of the selection process (e.g.
the newspaper reports already referred to) as an accurate source
of material is fraught with problems.   Not only is the reader's
understanding of the situation mediated through the reporter's
interpretation of events but in the two cases considered earlier
only the player's views are fairly represented.   In order to reach
a better level of understanding of the selection process a qualita-
tive study was conducted by the author.   The study focussed on
four high school girl's basketball teams in Canada.   Two teams,
the junior and the senior teams were selected from two schools.
The research was designed to gain insights into the following:
1. How the coaches structure the selection process?; 2. What type(s)
of 'cutting' procedure(s) is (are) used?; 3. How the athletes
who failed to be selected for the team interpret the process?;
4. How the 'cut' athletes adjust to the 'failure'?.   The data
were mainly gathered through depth interviews with the six coaches
involved and the thirteen athletes who were cut.   Semi-participant
observation prior to, during and after selection provided additional
information, as did documents provided by some of the coaches.
    Theoretically work by Goffman and Garfinkel (considered by
Ball (1976) in his analysis of professional sport) was used in
conjunction with the concept of status passage developed by Glaser
and Strauss (1971).   Goffman's work on 'cooling-out' (1952) and
Garfinkel's on 'degradation ceremony' (1956) draw attention to
how people are disengaged from social activity.   'Cooling-out'
is a term adopted from a type of criminal activity whereby a 'mark'
(someone who has been conned) is 'cooled-out' by a 'cooler'.

238

The 'cooler' is someone who practises the art of consolation and helps redefine the mark's 'spoiled identity'. Thus reducing the likelihood of the mark causing trouble. This is a relatively private process which contrasts with Garfinkel's 'degradation ceremony' which involves the individual being publicly denounced and becoming an 'outsider'. A status passage: "may entail movement into a different part of a social structure; or a loss or gain of privilege, influence or power, and a changed identity and sense of self, as well as changed behaviour." (Glaser and Strauss, 1971:2). The relevance of this work for the selection process in sport is that it is concerned with the management of an individual's identity during a process of disengagement. It also suggests that we in sport can learn from other areas of social life e.g. business and retirement from work. The fact that the individuals concerned are involved with sport is largely incidental as the management capabilities of those involved and problems which ensue are very similar.

The use of theoretical concepts helps sharpen the forms of research. In this case the focus became one of how the coaches structured the selection process (a status passage) and subsequently how they managed the identities of those they wanted to cut (disengage).

3.2 Summary of findings.

In summarizing the findings of the research three distinct areas for discussion emerge: the selection procedures adopted; the criteria used; and the method of informing athletes of the outcome. All the coaches informed the athletes of the intended length of the selection process, although for three of the teams this was later altered by the coaches. This change of plan unsettled some of the athletes who suddenly found themselves under scrutiny for three sessions rather than just one. Also not all the athletes were able to attend the pre-selection talk which all the coaches gave. In several instances this led to problems with some athletes being 'left in the dark'. Most of the coaches adopted a drill, scrimmage and game format for the selection which they would run for two to three sessions. One coach however, set up a series of skill stations and based his selection on the cumulative score of each athlete combined with his perception of the athlete's attitude. This coach was the only one not to make any reference to his criteria for selection, but the stress he put on the 'correct' attitude would have been evident to the athletes from a booklet he distributed at the pre-selection meeting. The following is an excerpt from the booklet: "Determine to succeed, practice with all your might, never forgetting the shame of failure.... Do as your coach says, not as you please, for it is his wish to help you mould your clay and achieve your oneness with God." It was clear from some of the unsuccessful athletes in this school that they did not agree with the type of 'attitude' that both the junior and senior coaches thought was desirable. Some also claimed that they did not know that attitude was so important, they had assumed that ability would have been most important. These athletes found it especially hard to adjust to being unsuccess-

ful.   In general, those who were not informed of the criteria,
or were not listening at the time found it harder to cope with
failure than those who had been aware of the criteria.   It is
interesting to note that even the most highly controlled selection
process (the skill stations) did not guarantee that the criteria
would be self-evident.

All the coaches informed the athletes of their success or 'failure'
by posting a list of those who had been selected.   One of the
senior coaches at School A had, in her first two years of coaching,
talked to every player telling them whether they had got into
the team or not.   Although no longer using this technique, in
addition to posting a list, she and the woman she coached with
told the athletes that if they wanted to discuss the selection
with them they could do so the following day.   (This was the only
team to be offered such an opportunity).   In the event, one of
the athletes they 'cut' was so upset that she could not bring
herself to talk to them the next day.   In future these coaches
decided to tell athletes to wait a week before coming to talk
to them.   This is characteristic of 'cooling-out', when the process
is lengthened and the 'mark's' anger becomes dissipate over time.
It was ironic that where the coach thought talking to each individual
would be embarrassing for the athletes, and that posting a list
would be less so, some of the athletes reported that they found
it embarrassing to go and look at the team list which was posted
on a noticeboard in a busy school corridor.   The junior coaches
at School A also intended to tell the athletes that they could
come and talk to them if they wanted, but they forgot.   In School
B the junior coach felt that just to post a list was rather im-
personal, but on the advice of the senior coach that is what she
did.   She felt however, that the following year she would do things
more her own way.   Several of the coaches said that they liked
the more personal approach of talking to each player, but claimed
that time did not permit it.   In general the players were quite
happy about a list being posted but they also wanted the opportunity
to meet with the coach.   In summary, despite complaints from some
of the players about decisions made by the coach, the way in which
they were informed raised few complaints.

4. Strategies

4.1 Introduction
It is clear then that one of the stumbling blocks to effective
management of the selection process was poor communication.   When
athletes were fully aware of the procedures and criteria, and
felt able to talk to the coaches the process was relatively trouble-
free.   When this was not the case, misunderstandings often arose.
Poor communication is a sign of mismanagement and is unlikely
to lead to a healthy sports environment.   So what can those involved
do to avoid mismanagement?

4.2 Coaches and Selectors
Those involved in the selection process must be empathetic, concerned

for the athlete as a person, and concerned for the sport. Whether the selected team wins a major event should not be of sole importance; the experience that athletes get from participation should also figure highly. Again as Orlick (1980) was suggesting long term effects should be considered as well as the short term ones. This may seem elementary, but consider the following comments written by a basketball coach from the University of Utah, on the problem of cutting high school squads. "The real problem lies in how to do it as quickly as possible without making any mistakes that will return to haunt you later. In addition, there is the concern of dealing with a parent who wants to· know why his son was cut from the squad." (Schakel, 1977:14) (emphasis mine). Where is the concern for the athlete here?

Coaches should reflect upon their current practice, when does it fall on a continuum of 'cooling-out' to 'degradation'? How are they managing the status passage athletes are involved in? How are they managing the identity of the athletes who have been unsuccessful? Each individual needs to be considered; athletes at all levels can suffer due to mismanagement of the selection process. Coaches and selectors might consider trying some of the following; inform all players of the length and nature of the selection process (explaining any changes to this pattern as necessary) supply each athlete with details of the criteria for selection; personally inform those who are unsuccessful before a list is posted, and discuss future plans with them: e.g. another team for which they might be eligible; another way in which they can still be involved with the team; ways in which they can improve their performance. Finally, two things which coaches and selectors should think about. Firstly, Frank Rosato (1974) advocates athletes being more involved in decision-making in sport; why not work with athletes to identify the criteria? Secondly, is it always necessary to 'drop' or 'cut' people when selecting a team? Orlick (1980) and Scott (1974) would suggest that athletes, although not selected for the team, should still be able to attend coaching.

4.3 Athletes

Management is a two-way process, and athletes should be prepared to become actively involved. If the criteria are not clear, they should try to find out what they are. Coaches and selectors are involved in sport because they want to pass on their knowledge and experience; if some problem, perhaps over selection, is preventing this from occurring then athletes must feel free to say so. Acting constructively, in this way can only be to the betterment of sport.

5. Conclusion

Competitive sport has much to offer in terms of personal fulfillment and enhancement of life. We need to ensure that this potential is not thwarted at the selection stage. Selection, when it is necessary, should be a positive learning experience for all involved. We must hope that come the next Commonwealth Conference there will be no place for this kind of paper, because the problem no longer exists.

References

Ball, D.W. (1976) Failure in sport. American Sociological Rev., 41, 4, 726–39.
Coaching Theory: Level Two (1982) National Coaching Certificate Program. CAC, Ottawa.
Garfinkel, H. (1956) Conditions of successful degradation ceremonies. American J. of Sociology, 61, 420–24.
Glaser, B.G. and Strauss, A.L. (1971) Status Passage. Aldine, Chicago.
Goffman, E. (1952) Cooling the mark out: some adaptations to failure. Psychiatry: J. for the Study of Interpersonal Processes, 15, 451–63.
Observer (1984) Fury over Potter's Bar. 9th December.
Observer Colour Supplement (1985) Potter's Craft. 4th August.
Orlick, T.D. and Botterill, C. (1980) Every Kid Can Win. Nelson-Hall, Chicago.
Rosato, F. (1974) The Group Process. The Physical Educator, 31, 2, 87–89.
Schakel, D. (1977) Cutting the squad...objectively. Basketball Clinic, Dec.
Scott, H.A. (1974) Competitive sport outcomes – self fulfillment and participation or self destruction and elimination? Katimavik, 1, 1.
The Sunday Times (1985) Hey, that's no way to say goodbye. 3rd February.

GOAL SETTING FOR ATHLETIC EXCELLENCE

B.D. HALE   Department of Physical Education
             The Pennsylvania State University
S.J. DANISH Department of Psychology
             Virginia Commonwealth University

Abstract
Goals are dreams, but dreams being acted upon. However, even when
an athlete is committed and willing to work hard to accomplish a
dream, goals may be difficult to achieve if they are not developed
in a realistic step-by-step manner. Our purpose is to teach athletes and coaches how to identify athletic goals and then develop
procedures to attain them. The first step involves assessment of
one's athletic experience and problem areas in performance. Athletes are then taught to state goals positively, identify specific
behavioral outcomes, and determine whether the goal is under their
control. Next, they explore the importance of the goal and assess
their commitment towards the required effort. Roadblocks from lack
of knowledge, skill, risk taking, or social support are then analyzed. Using this information, each individual plans daily step-by-
step subgoals that allow him/her to attain long-term achievements.
Target behaviors included in each step provide adequate evaluation
opportunities and reinforcement. Finally, athletes learn to deal
with new obstacles and reward improvement and success. This model
is easily generalizable to other life situational goals.
Key words: Goal, Motivation, Achievement, Individual goals, Team
goals, Commitment, Short-term, Long-term.

1. Introduction

Motivation has been separated into two components by Martens (1974).
"Arousal" is described as an energizer for human behavior, while
"direction" refers to behavior that is a function of needs, goals,
and personality. Many coaches and athletes take athletic goals for
granted and assume that all players will be optimally motivated.
But setting and attaining goals is a skill (Danish and Hale, 1983)
like putting a "birdie" or "dropping a goal." Players must be
taught how to set goals properly so they can reach their athletic
potential. As skill level improves, mental preparation often determines ultimate success more than physical talent and skills.
  Goals should not be confused with day dreaming or wishful thinking. In reality, goals are dreams but dreams being acted upon.
However, even when an athlete is committed and willing to work hard
to accomplish a dream, goals may be difficult to achieve if they are

not developed in a realistic step-by-step manner in which they can be attained.

Recent reviews of industrial and sport psychological research have offered several fundamental principles which should be included in goal setting models. Locke and Latham's (1985) industrial studies revealed that:

(1) Specific, hard goals lead to better performance than vague or easy goals;

(2) short-term goals can facilitate the achievement of long-term goals;

(3) goals affect performance by affecting effort, persistence, direction of attention, and by motivating strategy development;

(4) feedback regarding progress is necessary (though not sufficient) for goal setting to work; and

(5) goals must be accepted if they are to affect performance.

In fact, several researchers (McClements and Botterill, 1979; O'Block and Evans, 1985) have attempted to mathematically predict future performance through several goal setting models. To date, very little research has tested the validity of these models in sport.

The supported findings of this research have been adapted in our practitioner's model, which seeks to teach the skills of goal identification and attainment procedures for individual and team achievement. This model has been taught to hundreds of coaches and athletes from adolescent, intramural level to Olympic elite athletes and professional teams. While it is difficult to test this model because of the incomparable goals that each athlete sets, future investigations will collect data concerning the model's usefulness.

2. The Model

2.1 Defining goals

When an athlete is unhappy with the way he/she plays, he/she often identifies the problems he/she is having in performance. Although identifying problems may help pinpoint areas that a person needs to work on, a problem orientation stresses the negative. It is more effective to recast the negative into positively-stated goals. Setting a negative goal almost always ensures a negative outcome.

When the focus is on something the player wants, rather than on something he/she wishes to avoid, the outcome is more likely to be positive. First, each participant must change his/her "I can't..." into "I would like to...". In identifying positive long-term goals, consider the following questions: "What would have to happen for me to play better?" "What skills, capabilities, experiences or information would help?" Such questions may help an athlete develop a clear definition of the goal.

Second, each individual must identify the goal in behavioral terms. Behaviors are concrete, measurable, observable activities. It's not enough to have athletic goals like "being a better player" or "becoming more relaxed." Athletes must be helped to clarify their goals concisely in order for continuous evaluation to be available so quitting and frustration are minimized.

A third important element is focusing on one's own goals, not on those of others. Since each player only has control over his/her own behavior, appropriate goals are ones which represent changes in his/her own behavior, not others'. Setting only goals of victory (end-products) often leads to athlete dissatisfaction because the opponent's behavior is not always under his/her control. Help them to focus on behaviors (skills, achievements -- process oriented) that they control in order for success to be attainable more often.

2.2 Goal importance

Some goals result from the expectation of others. Unless an individual can honestly state, "I would like to...", commitment to the goal may be lacking. Most individuals do what they want, not what they ought to or should. Thus, when the athlete accepts a goal that does not truly match his/her real desire, he/she will not likely work hard to achieve it.

This fact explains why coaches need to set goals in conjunction with athletes and teams, not for them. Helping athletes determine what are realistic and important goals is the key to successful motivation. Getting all athletes on a team to expend the necessary effort to succeed is the hardest part of commitment and teamwork. Letting all athletes have a say in what is an acceptable goal is the simple solution.

2.3. Roadblock analysis

Athletes must learn to explore what is preventing them from achieving their goal so they can pinpoint deficiencies to work on. In knowledge roadblocks, an athlete lacks the necessary information for attainment. A swimmer might not be aware of which proper strength exercises can enhance performance. Skill roadblocks involve a lack in ability; athletes lack the mental and physical skills necessary for proper performance. For example, a gymnast might not know how to move a body part efficiently in part of a routine, or a rugger doesn't know how to relax before attempting a penalty kick. When an athlete knows what to do, but is afraid to do it, lack of risk-taking may be the problem. Cost-benefit analysis (risk = benefits - costs) may be necessary. Finally, some athletes feel that important people in their lives don't understand or help with efforts to reach goals. Lack of social supports can make maintaining new behaviors particularly difficult.

Once athletes can recognize a roadblock (s), then they can begin to plan efforts to overcome this obstacle(s) and obtain long-term goals.

2.4 Goal attainment

Depending on the roadblock(s) involved, the next step is setting up a problem-solving plan to overcome the obstacles. A list of steps in order should result. Each step must include target behaviors-- descriptions that state when, how often, and under what conditions behaviors must occur. For example, if "relaxing during competition" was a step, then the following attainment level could be used: "In the next two weeks (When?), I will take deep breaths and relax my arm each time (How often?) I step to the foul line to shoot a free throw (Under what conditions?)."

Often athletes attempt to learn a new behavior or skill in one giant step trying to out-do Superman or Wonder Woman; or conversely they try to do five things at once. It is essential that athletes learn to break the task into parts and make the first steps small and manageable (little short-term goals) so progress is feasible.

Before work is begun on the steps, help athletes to determine their present level of competence by recalling past attempts at achieving the goal. This process aids in identifying realistic goals. Sometimes if an athlete cannot achieve a certain step because of a roadblock, then coaches can also help them describe ideal and poor examples of the attempted behavior in order to get a clearer picture of the behavior to be achieved. Then the step can be further divided into more manageable steps so success and improvement continue.

The next step is for each person to develop a systematic program of practice for each step. Practice and hard work over time are necessary for achievement. Athletes should be encouraged to monitor their progress and positive reinforcement should be self-administered and/or coach administered when steps are accomplished. For example, in the foul-shooting goal, a sub-goal might be to practice imagery twice a day for ten minutes for two weeks. Practice behavior should be charted and rewarded daily when progress occurs. Self-monitoring can also be a built-in motivator.

2.5 Team goals

This model suggests that individual athletes must be responsible for setting their own goals and maintaining the motivation and commitment necessary for individual successful performance. It is also recognized that many athletes compete within a team framework whether their sport is purely interactive (rugby) or independent (bowling). Special team goals need to be set by the players in conjunction with coaches to allow for optimal group success and teamwork. The proposed model is also directly applicable to team goal setting; the basic thrust for individual responsibility is maintained and several group procedures are just added to the individual process already completed.

The coach must adopt an active role as a facilitator for team goal identification. Problem areas can be suggested, examples provided, questions asked, and "homework" can be given in order to encourage all athletes to participate in the team meetings. Discussion should be encouraged so players agree on compromise about basic team-orientation goals. Team meetings can be held prior to the season to set long-term seasonal goals, and then weekly or regular sessions can follow to allow constant evaluation and reinforcement of the step-by-step progression towards long-range goals. Strategies can also be suggested by players and coaches to provide direction and rewards for achievement behavior. Written records should be kept of long- and short-term goals so continual progress can be charted and concise evaluation made possible. Botterill (1979) has suggested the following five areas of potential sub-goals: technical (skill development), tactical (strategy and understanding), physical (fitness development), mental (attentional and behavioral control), and environmental (social and educational considerations including enjoyment, roles and relationships, school, special interests/activities). To this list, performance (end-product) and risk-taking sub-goals could also be added.

Optimal individual performance is the cornerstone of team success. But individuals that perform together and are evaluated as a unit need to be working together toward common goals. The use of pre-season, seasonal, and post-season goal-setting planning forms and team meetings can enhance the possibility for group success in sport.

3. Conclusions

Using this systematic model as described should enable more athletes to reach their goals, and this success should enhance further athletic participation and performance in all ages and abilities. Feelings of pride and enhanced self-confidence should result from accomplishment. Once the initial goal is attained, then other tougher goals can be tackled. As an end result, the athlete learns to become fully responsible for his/her own athletic motivation and effort, and coaches can be freed to convey technical and performance information. When this skill of goal-setting is mastered, athletes can apply it successfully to other problems in their lives (academic, family, social, career, etc.).

References

Botterill, C. (1979) Goal-setting for athletes, with examples from hockey, in Behavior Modification and Coaching (ed. G.L. Martin and D.H. Hrycaiko), Charles C. Thomas, Springfield, IL., pp.67-85.
Danish, S.J. and Hale, B.D. (1983) Sport psychology: Teaching skills to athletes and coaches. J. Phys. Ed, Health, Recr., and Dance, 54, 11-12, 80-81.
Locke, E.A. and Latham, G.P. (1985) The application of goal setting to sports. J. of Sp. Psy., 7, 205-222.
Martens, R. (1974), Arousal and motor performance. Exercise and Sp. Sci. Revs., 2, 155-188.
McClements, J.D. and Botterill, C.B. (1979) Goal setting on shaping of future performance of athletes, in Coach, Athlete, and the Sport Psychologist (ed. P. Klavora and J.V. Daniel), Human Kinetics, Champaign, IL., pp. 199-210.
O'Block, F.R. and Evans, F. H. (1985) Goal-setting as a motivational technique, in Psychological Foundations of Sport (ed. J.M. Silva and R.S. Weinberg), Human Kinetics, Champaign, IL., pp. 188-196.

SPORT IN ASIA WITH PARTICULAR REFERENCE TO SWIMMING IN HONG KONG

DAVID J. HALLER, Head Swimming Coach, Jubilee Sports Centre (Hong Kong), National Swimming Coach, Hong Kong Amateur Swimming Association.

Abstract

Purpose of Paper

The author would like to give his views on swimming coaching in Asia with particular reference with work done as National Coach in Hong Kong. The author has travelled throughout Asia and has given coaching clinics in China and Australia. He has organised an Olympic Solidarity Coaches Course for 38 coaches from 14 Asian countries. The author would like to explain the Jubilee Sports Centre's role in the development of sports coaching in Hong Kong. The Centre is now internationally recognised and many overseas sportsmen and teams have trained and competed at the Centre since its completion in 1982. He would like to explain his work with his trainees in Hong Kong and to give some idea of the difficulties of coaching in an Asian environment after having been the Great Britain National Coach for 8 years.

Key words: Jubilee Sports Centre, Co-ordinated Competitive Structure.

After the 1980 Moscow Olympic Games, after coaching the Great Britain National Swimming Team for eight years, I decided to change my working environment completely. To this end I joined the Jubilee Sports Centre in Hong Kong in November 1980.

The Jubilee Sports Centre is unique in Asia. It was built jointly by the Royal Hong Kong Jockey Club and the Hong Kong Government at the cost of 15 million pounds and was opened in July 1982. At the present time of writing the operating costs are met by the Jockey Club. The Centre is used for the training of top-class talent, developmental groups, and for the training of coaches. The Centre employs 22 coaches, Chinese and expatriate with the nine sports there being Tennis, Judo, Swimming, Soccer, Squash, Badminton, Table Tennis, Gymnastics and Fencing. The Centre also employs short-term contract coaches, for example, Mr. Chris Perry has been out for Rowing and Angela Smith ranked no. 4 in the world as a ladies squash player, coached the Hong Kong Ladies Squad for one month last year.

The Centre is also being developed as a competitive venue.
Originally the concept was just for training but now the Centre is,
under the new management of Howard Wells, being developed into a
competitive venue as well, because obviously training and competition go hand in hand and should not be divorced. A Sports Science
Unit is being developed at the Centre and a Sports Injury Treatment
Centre has just been completed. There has been a great deal of
interest shown by Asian countries. Many teams come from all over
Asia, from Japan, China, Korea down to Indonesia and India and so on
have come to train and also compete in many different sports. We
have also attracted top-class performers from Europe and Australia.
Peter Evans, an Olympic Gold Medallist in Moscow and winner of 2
Bronze medals in the Los Angeles Olympic Games has trained at the
Jubilee Sports Centre. Adrian Moorhouse, 1983 European Champion
and 1982 Commonwealth Champion, trained in 1985 for two months at
the Centre prior to winning the European Championships. We have
also run Olympic Solidarity Coaching Courses at the Centre for
Swimming, Hockey and Judo involving all the Asian countries. Other
experts who have visited the Centre are Coaches from China - Canoeing, Rhythmic Gymnastics; Chinese Gymnasts, Li Ning and Tong Fei,
etc; Mr. Warwick Forbes (Gymnastics), Mr. Jeff Bond (Psychologist),
Mr. Bill Sweetenham (Swimming), Mr. Douglas Turnity (Psychologist)
from the Australian Institute of Sport; Mr. Jeno Tihanyi (Swimming)
- Canadian Olympic Coach and Mr. Dung Pu Feng, son of Mr. Deng Xiao
Ping.

The Centre could point the way forwards towards further sports
development in the Asian continent. China has sent many experts
to the Jubilee Sports Centre and has made careful studies and
intended to build similar centres, not just for training but also
for coach education. Asian countries tend to rely on importing
coaches, importing expertise from other countries particularly from
Australia, Europe and America, and that is, as we all know, a
stopgap measure. In the Jubilee Sports Centre we all have assistant
coaches who are ethnic Chinese and we are trying to train them.
When the expatriate coaches have finished their term or decide to
leave the Jubilee Sports Centre in Hong Kong the assistant coaches
who have been trained should then be able to take over the
programme. The concept of the Centre originally met with some
resistance. It was felt among sports bodies that the Centre,
because of the financial backing of the Jockey Club, would try to
take over Hong Kong sport but that has not been the case. Its job
is to assist in the development of Hong Kong sport as much as is
possible. The coaches are also involved with disabled athletes
and the FESPIC Games were successfully held at the Jubilee Sports
Centre in 1982. The Jubilee Sports Centre is developing close links
with the Australian Institute of Sport and also with the Beijing
Institute of Physical Education, and in 1987 will see our first
Conference which should be very interesting. The theme is coaching
and coach education because it is realised that coach education is
the prime ingredient for an Asian sporting success.

249

Not long after my arrival in Hong Kong, an English Swimming Coach
working there independently, commented that I was wasting my time
in trying to persuade the Hong Kong Chinese to do any form of
serious training. In fact this has not proved to be the case. My
group of swimmers in Hong Kong at that stage were very young and
inexperienced and very naive to the sporting world. Once I had
established a rapport with the Swimming Association, the club
coaches and the swimmers and parents and an explanation of what was
required to reach high level in sports, then things started to move.
Hong Kong has a population of 5 million and is a high pressured,
bustling, business centre. Survival is the prime concern and thus
sport and all its implications is very secondary in the eyes of Hong
Kong people. However in the past five years things have changed for
the better. The Government and the Sports Associations, under the
guidance of Mr. A. de O. Sales, have been working very hard to
provide the necessary facilities and structure for future sports
development. The last six years has been a tremendous increase, for
example, in the number of squash courts from 52 courts in 1980 to
over 200 in 1986. The number of swimming pools has shown similar
growth, in fact, this growth has outstripped the expertise to use
them.

All the coaches employed at the Jubilee Sports Centre are heavily
involved in Coach Education. The Centre has established a coaching
foundation course which is held in both English and Cantonese. All
the courses have been oversubscribed. Another example of the great
interest shown in Coach Education is in my own sport. For one
six-day course there were 364 applicants for the 30 places available.

One of critical areas affecting the advancement of sport in Asia
in that of the Educational pressures on the athletes. Generally,
throughout Asia, the Educational Authorities, and in particular,
the parents of Athletes, give sport a very low priority. Western
culture places great emphasis on sport and recreation but Asia,
mainly for reasons of economic and partly social, is unable to
reproduce this. The number of youngsters dropping sport above the
ages of 15 or 16 is a serious problem. Most parents and teachers
tend to be overzealous and create tremendous pressures on the
youngsters to succeed academically. There is a need for a balance
to be created between Education and Sport. Gradual change is taking
place but at present those athletes from countries other than China
and Japan, tend to further their sporting and educational careers in
the USA, Canada, Australia and in some cases Europe. This drain of
talent obviously leads to lowering of domestic standards and creates
frustration amongst the coaches. I have first hand experience of
this problem. More than twenty five of my best swimmers have left
Hong Kong for educational reasons during the last three years.
However two of my Commonwealth Games Swimming Team have taken eight
months off from their American Universities in order to train and
they both have full parental support. I must also say that their

250

decision to take time off was not influenced by me in any way.

Factors influencing development of sport in Asia are these:

(1) The sheer size of the population. Half of the world's population resides in Asia and with these huge numbers it is very difficult to create a sort of co-ordinated coaching sporting environment necessary for success.

(2) Economy. The advanced economy of Europe and the history of sporting excellence is a model for sports development for Asia. China is developing very quickly because its use a sport as a means of promoting their country realises the impact that sporting excellence can achieve internationally. Other countries like India, a huge country, have problems with economy, their own society, and the fact that women carry very little part in sport. In fact generally in Asia women are not active in sport.

Japan is the only country in Asia that has a really strong economy. That is one reason why it has been successful, and this, together with a national sense of discipline, access to good facilities and a traditional interest of sport has led to its dominance in Asia. But Japan is quite insular and this will be a problem for its future development. South Korea has done extremely well in selected sports mainly for political reasons.

(3) Physical Characteristics. The physical characteristics of Asian people lend themselves to sports that require a great deal of co-ordination and speed. The Chinese gymnasts and divers are also examples of the Asian's ability to react and to co-ordinate very quickly. In some ways, possibly because of diet and a lack of knowledge of training and coaching, Asian athletes are training for the wrong events. For example, in swimming, most of the countries are trying very hard to produce sprinters but they do not have the physical characteristics to produce a freestyle sprinter. The average height of the Olympic finalists, for example in 100m swimming sprint for men would be around 6'4" to 6'6". A very few people in Asia are 6'4" to 6'6", and if there are then they are probably playing basketball. I think Asian athletes would do better to concentrate on events that require more endurance and skill and events more suited to their light framed physiques.

(4) Asian Diet. The Asian diet which I believe is not generally conducive to sporting excellence. Asian food contains a great deal of fat but not much carbohydrate. I have been analysing the diet of my swimmers in Hong Kong, and they have a poor diet generally. We have tried to supplement their diets by using Sustagen and it seems to work reasonably well, but diet is a problem. They tend to eat the very fat part of meat and the poor cuts of the joints rather than a high carbohydrate diet which is particularly required for endurance events, and protein which is essential for muscular development.

251

(5) Mental Attitude. Having travelled through most of the Asian
countries and having observed and spoken with national coaches, not
just in swimming, the one thing that the Asian people lack is
confidence in ability to succeed in sport. However confidence stems
from the knowledge that the athlete has trained correctly, and has
had the necessary exposure to the right level of competition. It is
in this area that China is making great strides. During the last
four years, Chinese teams from many sports, have been competing
overseas. As we all know overseas travel is a great motivating
factor for athletes. The thrill of competing in world-class events
and the learning experience is an essential ingredient in the
development of an athlete. In this respect China is leading Asian
Sport and will soon become a world force. I attended the 1982
Asian Games, which were held in New Delhi, the swimming standards
were very low. In fact my last Club team in England, Beckenham
Swimming Club, would have dominated the swimming events. The last
four years has shown a tremendous improvement. In 1986, in three
world meets, Chinese swimmers won 7 Gold medals against opposition
from the USA, German Democratic Republic and the rest of Europe.
Even little Hong Kong has won two Bronze medals.

(6) Coaching Standards. This is one area which we are all
interested in and this is also one thing that is holding back the
development of sport in Asia. It is one of the key factors because,
as you all know, you do not need tremendous facilities in order to
succeed. What you do need is professional coaching at the highest
level and this is what Asia generally lacks. Asia sportsmen try
very hard in very difficult circumstances and conditions but they
are not helped by the low coaching standards generally prevalent
among Asian countries.

   Coaches in Asia tend not to push, they seem very relaxed in
comparison with the western world. Japan is different, particularly
in the Martial Arts where the discipline of Japanese society ensures
that they are very successful in those sports that require control.
It is very important that the coaches from Asia get out and about
and three years ago when I was first in China I spent four hours
with Chinese swimming coaches and their officials. I explained to
them that if they wished to develop it was necessary to compete out
of Asia and more particularly in Europe which is, at present the
strongest swimming area now, and that they must improve their
coaching standards by attending international coaching courses. I
have run one Olympic Coaching Solidarity Course in Hong Kong which
attracted 39 coaches from 23 countries. But even then, two countries sent coaches who had very little understanding of English,
so a lot of what was said both by myself and by two very eminent
swimming coaches from Canada and Australia was wasted. China has
been isolated, as we all know, for a very long time from international competition and they have a lot of work to do but I strongly
believe that within ten years they will be one of the major forces
in world's sport because they are learning very very quickly. In
the past itw coaches relied on very old fashioned coaching methods
but recently China is showing a great willingness to learn. Coaches

from nearly every sophisticated sporting nation are working in China either part-time or full-time. Dennis Whitby, who was the Hong Kong Coaching Director of Athletics for two years, has been working in China for the past three years.

(7) Co-ordinated Competitive Structure. Asia desperately needs a co-ordinated competitive structure. For example in swimming the closest country for my swimmers to go to is China but there are very few competitions held in China and the rest of Asia. Hong Kong probably competes only about three or four times a year in Asia. It is a well recognised fact that high training standards must be complemented by competing at a similar standard. In Hong Kong we are trying very hard to establish international training standards but the competitive element is lacking. This is quite a problem particularly concerning motivation of the athletes. At the moment in order to get top-class competition we need to travel either to Australia, United States or to Europe and that requires a great deal of expenses and a great deal of time, and often you do not get the standard of competition that is required. The standard might be too high or it could be in some cases too low.

So Asia lacks a unity of purpose. Asian countries need to link together. I would like to see for example in swimming an Asian Swimming Federation that is very strong. I would like to see every country in Asia meet every year such as the European swimming nations do, and work out their competitive programmes and their coaching programmes and help each other to provide support, guidance and constructive for development of our athletes. Hong Kong is taking a very active part in Sports Development in Asia probably because it is so central but also because excellent facilities and finance are available. The Hong Kong Amateur Swimming Association promotes two international meets a year for the Asian Pacific area. A strong Asia would also help Australia and New Zealand develop their sporting programmes.

The sporting scene in Asia is quite exciting. Rapid development is taking place and all the coaching staff at the Jubilee Sports Centre have found their work both frustrating and stimulating. It is exciting to be part of, and, assist in the development of something new.

WHICH SUPPOSITIONS DETERMINE THE CONDITIONS OF THE TRAINING OF SPORTS COACHES

by AXEL HILGERS, M.Sc.
Director of Sports, International Sports Academy, West-Germany

Abstract

The paper treats various important points which have to be taken into consideration for the training of sport coaches. Mainly concentrating on circumstances of the coach education in ' least developed countries ' the article deals with

- circumstances of growing-up and early experiences in sports

- cultural understanding of sports and physical education in schools and the general acceptance in society

- possibilities of sports studies at colleges or universities and the selection of students

- equipment and facilities for teaching, training, studies of physical education and research in sports

- anthropological and geographical conditions

- job expectation and influence of international competitions.

Training of sport coaches cannot be uniform. It is indeed true that in the end the ' products ' of coaches are expected to participate in competitions under the same rules and circumstances.

Therefore one may say that the training of sport coaches has to be the same. In only one point this statement is correct. The aim of training competitors is to win the competition, to run a good time or to play a successful match. In order to achieve this aim all coaches should learn specific methods of training and techniques of sports. These methods or the different ways of reaching this aim should be transfered in the training of sports coaches. BUT - at this point it has to be considered that the conditions and possibilities of training are different.

By using a picture I would like to explain why this is so ! Taking the society as a circle we have to place a triangle in the middle of the circle:

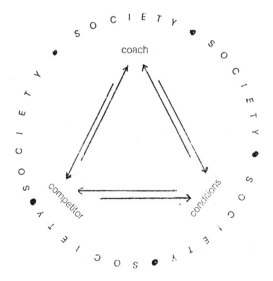

In one corner there is written the term 'coach' while in the second
corner we find the term 'competitor' and in the last corner is the term
'conditions', right? It doesn't matter in which way we turn the circle and
which term is on top - all three factors are equally important or determine
each other. And above all "society" with its values and beliefs creates a
frame which cannot be changed in a short time.

Of course, everything finds its end in movement as long as it stays alive.
Nature demonstrates it quite clearly. The same principles are true for
human beings and society because society is the sum of human beings.
Human spirit and creativity cause movement and this is the reason for
any development inside society and in each of its more specific areas.
Sports is one of these areas and is certainly not one of minor importance.
Attention should therefore be given to the coach. His thinking and
activities take place within the mentioned frame and depend on action
and reaction. We all know the model of interaction based on stimulus and
response. Applied to my picture we have to include arrows pointing from
the coach to the competitor and back or from the coach to the conditions
and back as well as from the competitor to the conditions and, of course,
back. That is up to now a very theoretical view.

There are coaches who work professionally, others voluntarily. Some train
regularly while many do it temporarily depending on their major profession.
According to the acceptance of sports in a certain society the engagement
of coaches may differ. One will understand his job as an idealistic activity
but others are looking for money first. This short explanation already shows
us the dimension of the problem. To make it more concrete let us start
the factor of time. It makes a great difference whether a coach can spend
all his time on training competitors or if he has only a few hours left

a week. His practical experience will necessarily be lower in comparison to his colleague who can continuously stay with his competitor. The relationship between the coach and the competitor is probably quite different and is not as favourable as if the time of knowing each other is reduced. If we call one a professional coach the other one must be looked at as an honorary coach. Deduced from the above we know that we have to take into account that a professional coach needs another job-training than the one who can only train from time to time. The time one is available and the expectancy of what you get out of your job differ. Depending on the type of coach we assume a different degree of performance and dedication. In most countries a professional coach has to complete a specific education in sports, often in only one type of sport. In any case, educational courses will have to offer wide spread contents, including anatomy, physiology, psychology - to name only a few subjects. Furthermore, any training in the particular type of sports chosen by the students must give special attention to practical teaching and theory of training. What about his colleague who trains only on an honour's basis and for a limited span of time? He can make himself available only for a short time because he has to fulfil his duties elsewhere. If we agree that he has less time to be trained we can guess that the contents of training him has to be another. I don't talk about quality of training because it may be that a short training can be more effective than a longer one if the staff is highly qualified and the program well planned etc. The duration of education is not necessarily a sign of qualification but it may contribute a lot. The factor of time, if we see it as the length of any training and as the practical cooperation with the competitor, is an important condition which should not be neglected!

Now, returning to the introductory picture we should remember the arrow toward the term 'conditions'. Do we have qualified staff, modern equipment and facilities for theoretical and practical teaching so that an optimal input can result in a qualified output? Even if the conditions are optimal we can not be sure of a qualified output. Why? That question leads me to another prerequirement for good results. The qualitiy of a coaching course does not only depend on its length, good staff and optimal teaching conditions but good 'material' of students. We will get good students more easily if the job is attractive in both prestige and payment. On the other hand we have to consider the level of general education and whether education is wide spread in the respective country. If the requirements for the entrance of a college are higher under normal circumstances students will leave the coaching course with a higher qualification supposing all the other conditions are in line. Moreover, we can say that the business principle 'demand governs prize' is also a value in the field of the training of coaches. Do we have a great demand for coaches we are forced to lower somehow the requirements and to increase payment and the chances of the job. We did it in Germany about 20 years ago. Probably the quality of training will suffer. At home we try to face the problem by offering refresher courses.

What might be the reason for demand? The elementary stimulus to this may be the interest of society in sports and the extent of public pressure which can push the government to support physical education and sports.

256

One of my favourite ideas is that the level of sports immensely depends on the physical education at schools. If schools give high attention to physical education it is obviously that a lot of pupils want to practise sports outside schools and want to continue after their school time. This, as I said, will be a major stimulus which will correspond with a high number of coaches. Simply expressed, a high number of participants in sports will require a higher number of coaches. In the circle we have to draw another arrow from the term conditions to the terms coach and competitor. There are straight influences from society to the conditions offered because the national acceptance of physical education and sports - including high performance sports - is a major stimulus for any development in sports.

It would be interesting to investigate the motifs for the promotion of sports through the attitude of a society and to see respective answers given by the government in the various countries. But that is another topic.

All the terms in the circle depend on each other. The influence radiate in any direction. The pattern of the circle, however, can give you an idea of the mani-fold influences which determine the training of coaches.

Let us look at 'conditions' again but with a slightly different perspective. Broad physical education at schools will not only motivate pupils to participate and compete in sports but will also increase the number of participants.

Some of them finally will make it their professions. Do they feel stronger interest in sports they might become a coach and if they have gained experiences in active sports it will definitely help them to be a successful coach. Having acquired more practical abilities they can concentrate more on the theory of training. A better scientific understanding will then enable them not only to reproduce theory but also to find ways and forms of creative training. Some will continue to study sports sciences and later contribute as academical staff in the field of training. Most of us here can verify this statement trough their own careers.

Anthropological requirements are also closely connected with what we generally called 'conditions'. Our globe has a lot of different inhabitants or people. Talents and constitutions, characters and mentalities are not equally spread at all. Only GOD knows why! I don't share the theory that in the North of the globe people have more intelligence than in the South, in the West more than in the East. To me these differences depend on the cultural background and on education. However, we cannot neglect the fact that talents and conditions are influenced by biological and biopsychological situations such as climate, living circumstances, nutrition and so forth. Somebody who lives in a region of high altitude will have another blood circulation, vital capacity than a competitor living in a humid area. The first might be more predestined for running long distances while the latter is more qualified for short distances or high jump. In this respect Kenians can give us a good example of proof. Although these natural influences have not been fully examined you know what I try to explain. If it comes to the training of coaches, however, we have to deal with this problem thinking in terms of 'conditions'.

Sports and particular high performance sports need a lot of organisation. The administrative ability of a man depends on his education. There is a difference whether you have learned to organize yourself already as a child or whether others have extremely taken care of you. Organisational talent is partly connected with the tradition of the family structure but it also depends on the development of infrastructure.

Sticking to the problem of infrastructure in developing countries there is no doubt that in some countries we can't phone from one city to another and if we write a letter it sometimes takes weeks to inform somebody. These difficulties in the field of communication for example can be caused by a low technical standard, by bad roads, by insufficiencies in offices and so on. If you want to select or find talents in sports or to bring them together for training or to be in contact with them all the time, practical problems such as long distances can be a serious handicap. Often the family doesn't like to give the child a time off or there is no hostel to stay in or no chance to get in touch with the child from the best school etc. While in Germany it may only take a few days to organize a coaching course, to invite participants, to book full accommodation, to talk to lecturers and to get the funds for payment, it is sometimes difficult to assure these conditions in some least developed countries! There is nothing to complain or to blame anybody - but it must be shown that infrastructure can influence the proper organisation of a coaching course. However, with well-trained administrative staff we then can reduce the problems to a minimum.

It seems clear that organisational problems determinate the quality of a coaching course in both respects
     a) selection of participants
     b) invitation of qualified staff (lecturers)

What is the consequence? Administration as an essential part of a coaching course determines the efficiency of entrance-examination, of instructions offered, the contents of these courses and their final results. Following this line it appears that in an industrialized country with a good general education, an effective infrastructure and maybe with experienced sports organizers the coach can more easily train and can concentrate more on the training with his competitors because he gets more assistance from the organisational side of sports. In a so called 'developing country' the coach has to exercise administrative functions as well to ensure that everything goes smooth, that he can be successful. His work is much more difficult. Therefore, he who develops curricula for a coaching course under these circumstances has to include some lessons about sports management to enable the coach to face these problems. Reality shows that sports sciences and sports administration are not equally developed everywhere. Some countries had to cover 200 years and more time to step forward slowly and to collect the experiences already gained elsewhere. Other countries were given national independence 30 years ago and now they are forced to haste. We have to see these facts if we create a program for the training of coaches. I hope that I have made it clear that 'conditions' as shown in my picture are obstacles which sometimes can seriously inflict with the training of coaches.

Going ahead we should talk about the competitor next. Depending on the intended level of performance of a competitor a coach has to get a different training because it matters whether he is supposed to train beginners or sportsmen on a national level. Therefore it is absolutely necessary to grade the coaching courses. It starts with the entrance examination and ends with the various final examinations. It goes without saying that the contents of each course have to be related to the expected field of training. Mentality, talent, anthropological development, age, participation in school sports, experience in competition, interest in special disciplines of sports and other factors are important elements for the coach to know. Each age-group for example has its own problems - so, if we train coaches, we have to reflect, what is he going to do after his course. If his group are children or youngsters it is quite important for him to know more about physiological changes caused by training. He has to dose the intensity of any training in that way that his participants (pupils or students) will not suffer from an excess of exercises or on the other hand will not practise ineffectively so that an optimal biological adaptation can not take place.

We all know that it is an advantage to start training at an early age. But how can we encourage the pupils to train with us? This question, of course, has to be answered in relation to the situation he lives in: the village, the big town or the bush. Is there any possibility of transport, of staying at a hostel or camp and so on. A coach in Europe e.g. will probably find a different answer than his colleague in South America. We often find some resentiments toward sports in some families, tribes or societies caused by daily requirements, cultural tradition or religious expectations. The coach has to be prepared for all these various differences.

In another paper I used the example of pole vaulting to explain the problems of using modern equipment and facilities. If we do not have money to buy synthetic poles we are forced to train with bamboo sticks. Why not - but you will agree that the technical and methodical approach has to be another one. This shows once more that any coaching course has to consider these varieties!

Working as a coach since years my colleagues and I sometimes argued about the length of coaching courses regarding the types of sports. Some of my colleagues believed a coaching course for coaches of athletics should be longer than the one for football - just name two major kinds of sports. What do you think of it? By considering the manifold techniques in athletics and assuming that an athletics-coach should be able to coach all disciplines of decathlon it seems as if such a course needs more time than a course in football where we have only a few techniques to kick the ball, to stop, to pass and to shoot a goal. In addition to these techniques we have tactics which might take more time than teaching athletics. Here our football fans will probably loudly agree or object. Nobody is free from personal assessment. We may overrate the type of sports we like. I have always been a swimmer and I may therefore answer this question more objectively than a coach for football or one for athletics. But I am surely not enough tolerant if it comes to swimming I reckon.

Anyway, I would say concerning athletics it depends upon the standard of participants themselves. If we have students who have competed in decathlon and who practised all techniques they don't need a longer time than a good football player does for his job. But we have to take into account that the standards of students will never be the same. The length of training will certainly differ from place to place and from course to course or if we want a same duration of each course we can try to limit the disciplines within the type of sports or the extent of practical contents. That could be a solution!

Let me summarize now! The training of sports coaches can never be the same, neither in Germany nor in France, neither in Europe nor in Africa, not in the USA or Russia!

The training of sports coaches depends on:

- circumstances of growing-up and having early experiences in sports

- cultural understanding of sports and physical education in schools and the general acceptance in a society

- possibilities of sports studies at a college or university and selection of students of coaching

- equipment and facilities for teaching, training, studies of P. E. and research in sports

- anthropological and geographical conditions

- job expectation and influence through international competitions

In short, if somebody in Africa, for example, wants to draw curricula for a coaching course he can't just take a program written in the USA or Russia and copy its contents. He has to find out to what extent each of the discussed aspects of training are important for his specific situation and which importance he has to give them. Only then he has a good chance to develop a suitable and successful training for sports coaches!

Having pointed out some aspects and conditions of sports, my paper should be understood as an inspirational help!

COACH EDUCATION - A DELIVERY MODEL

BRUCE L. HOWE
School of Physical Education, University of Victoria, B.C., Canada

Abstract

The paper is a response to the paradigm prepared by John Lyle. It discusses the coaching process, coaching as a profession, the Canadian scene in sport coaching, and a proposal for the delivery of coaching education programmes. The paper argues that those responsible for educating coaches would be best advised to contract the task to universities and colleges who provide the best structure and means of evaluation to operate formal programmes.

Key Words: Coaching Education, Models for Delivery.

1. Introduction

The Coach Education paradigm prepared by John Lyle was properly developed out of his own personal experiences as a coach and teacher of coaches in the United Kingdom. These experiences mould the nature of the paper and are both its strengths and weaknesses. My own reactions and thoughts are from a Canadian perspective and reflect my experience as the Canadian National Rugby coach for four years, co-authorship of the Rugby Coaching Manuals I-III, continuing work as coach of a successful university team, and instructor in the Canadian Coaching Theory programme. Like John Lyle, I have not prepared a research paper and am, therefore, aware that my biases are subject to the same criticism.

2. The Coaching Process

The coaching process for me can be defined within learning theory. Coaching is a highly specialized pedagogical process designed to provide experiences and situations to change the performance of the athlete. Success as a coach should be measured by the positive changes in the athletes. Those other elements that are frequently described as criteria of the successful coach such as the basic knowledge required, coach-athlete relationship, and teaching techniques are useful only as they contribute to the major goal of changing performance. Such a definition is equally appropriate for

261

the different levels of sport and the ages of participants. Just as the early childhood teacher must adapt techniques to provide appropriate experiences for the preschool child who has no academic training, so must the coach of young, experienced athletes provide appropriate non-threatening activities to aid learning. These activities will be different from those of the coach of high school, junior club, or more elite teams. However, all must follow the following general principles:

(1) Learning is best accomplished through active involvement in the process.
(2) Learning will take place more certainly when anxiety is low.
(3) Learning requires adequate practice. This can mean considerable repetition for young players and requires some useful attention to variation if the learning is to occur.
(4) Learning is aided when there is reasonable rapport between the coach and learner.

Lyle's paradigm includes a simple taxonomy of sport practitioners which, in part, considers the variation in commitment but does not recognize that the central purpose of coaching remains constant for all levels. His comments that the recent North American coaching literature has paid more attention to youth sport are true. Representative of such material are the Level I and II Manuals produced by the Canadian Coaching Association. However, there have been good reasons for this emphasis because of long term neglect and the poorly prepared coaches within youth and junior sport. However, it should also be noted that the intent of the programme was also to provide knowledge for the higher level coaches as well. Because of the dual audience, some of the material has not been well received by practising coaches. The critics feel that it was written for beginners dealing with athletes who have no background. My personal experience as a Course Conductor in the Theory and Technical Courses programme, has continually provided me with evidence of the problems in handling the different levels of expertise and being able to challenge the experienced coach.

3. Coaching as a Profession

One of the most important issues to consider is whether coaching can be seen as a viable professional aspiration for young people. Currently, as Lyle pointed out, the evidence is not persuasive in most countries. While a small number of coaches may be employed full time in national organizations, universities, and a few clubs, most are volunteers or poorly paid on a part time basis. Some sports (e.g. rugby) continue to prevent coaches from being paid at any level. Despite this apparent lack of numbers it should be pointed out that a number of high school teachers, who are employed ostensibly as teachers of physical education, are clearly appointed to be coaches in major sports of the school.

Notwithstanding the latter group, the coaching aspirations of young people are most likely to be disappointed. In fact, it is far more likely for a person to succeed as a professional athlete than as a coach and the evidence is clear that this possibility is slight.

What is more difficult for the aspiring high level coach is that he or she must pursue a different career path than their ultimate goal. In today's world, to be chosen as a coach, one needs normally to have been primarily a successful player. This makes it unlikely for any coach to have had adequate preparation in the profession and is a main reason for the high failure rate at the elite levels of coaching.

These points make it difficult to consider a single paradigm that might describe the ideal preparation of the coach. It continues to be necessary to provide a parallel system that considers both the amateur coach interested in pursuing it as a secondary interest to his major career and the coach who wishes to make it his primary career. Perhaps the example that is provided through the Theatre programmes in the typical North American universities offers a useful model. In these situations, students study theatre with either the serious intent to making it a career or to contribute as an interested amateur. They may ultimately use this experience as a professional, teacher, or participant within the amateur setting. The Departments also provide a considerable amount of short term courses for upgrading the experience of individuals outside the formal educational setting.

4. The Canadian Scene in Sport Coaching

For the moment, the structure in Canadian sport is well established for the volunteer coach who wishes to improve his or her expertise. Large numbers of aspiring coaches have gone through the Level I and II programmes in the three areas of Theory (general principles), Technical (sport specific) and Practical (coaching a team). This has been encouraged by the National Sporting bodies who have in turn been pressured by the Federal Sport and Fitness Branch to demonstrate a commitment to the programme. The ability to wield the "big stick" of withholding grants has helped in this regard. Nevertheless, there is no clear evidence that this has improved the coaching in the field. To my knowledge no studies have been carried out to examine the effectiveness of the programme. It is also uncertain how many of those currently coaching in the many sports, hold advanced qualifications as outlined by the system. My own sport of rugby has struggled but without a satisfactory solution to the problem. When provincial coaches have been selected, there has been an effort to select only those with formal qualifications but this has continually been overridden by necessity; either because there have been no qualified coaches willing to apply or the "best" coach has not bothered with formal qualifications. The authorities are caught in the dilemma of choosing between qualified unsuccessful coaches or unqualified successful coaches. It underlies the disquieting belief of many, that coaches cannot be taught but that they are born with the necessary gifts to succeed. It also is complicated by the belief of many coaches that to expose themselves to any instruction is to admit a weakness.

Unfortunately, the courses that are offered do not consider these inherent problems and proceed to require individuals to take all levels of the programme without amendment. The Coaching Association has discouraged use of the so-called "Grandfather" clause which would excuse experienced coaches from beginning levels. It does permit graduates holding physical education degrees to eliminate Level I of the Theory programme. At the very least, there seems to be a need to permit coaches to demonstrate competence by some form of pre-test and be excused from those areas in which knowledge can be demonstrated. This is even more necessary for the Technical levels as the typical Level I and II courses have little relevance for the experienced coach and cause a build up of resentment when they are required to participate. Finally, the practical requirements have also seemed unnecessarily restrictive. It would require very little additional effort to prepare a basic test for practising coaches to demonstrate competence to Level II standards, permitting partial passes where necessary. The great optimism, which was felt when the Canadian Coaching Scheme was launched in the mid 1970's to achieve the two goals of improving the quality of coaching for junior sport and elite athletes, needs to be re-evaluated. It has not come close to meeting either goal although it is true that there is heightened awareness about the concerns for improving coaching within the Canadian sporting society.

One of the major difficulties has been the number of different agencies that are involved and the means of coordinating their efforts. Federal and Provincial Government Agencies, National Sporting bodies, and local organizations are involved and not always effectively. This structure is most handicapping in providing an efficient system for delivery. There is also a very complicated format for record keeping which is difficult for the typical course conductor to administer and creates problems for the centralized Federal Office. For these reasons, the final section of the paper argues that the tertiary institutions provide the best mechanism. It is my contention such a scheme would also be applicable for other countries interested in the field.

5.   The Model for Delivery

It should be noted that this model is operative to some degree in different countries including Canada. Several universities offer Coaching Degrees and along with colleges often provide courses for students and the community under the current Coaching Scheme. The plan here attempts to consolidate this arrangement which would incorporate all phases of coach education and permit greatest flexibility.

Currently, the University of Victoria, under the leadership of the Athletic Department, and with cooperation from the School of Physical Education, has proposed the development of a Coaching Institute for Sport Coaching which incorporates solutions to the problems of preparing coaches. The programme is primarily designed to provide for the development of aspiring elite coaches. It is assumed that the clientele would be suggested by National Sporting bodies and be enrolled as special students at the University. A Diploma would be provided for those who complete the course. It is assumed that the syllabus developed for the course would become the long-awaited Levels IV and V of the Coaching Scheme. It would also require the participants to practise coaching in association with experienced coaches either within the University or the sporting community.

While the initial effort has been to consider the needs of the National Sporting bodies, the course would be made available to other groups such as universities and provincial governments who could sponsor coaches. In addition, it would not prevent individuals from enrolling if space was available. There could be opportunity to gain other academic qualifications through the completion of degrees within the School of Physical Education. This would not however be a primary motivation as many coaches have neither the academic background nor interest to pursue such a programme.

Such a scheme is most effectively tied to a university in that facilities, equipment and personnel are readily available. In addition, there is a system to permit the short term hiring of individuals in a most efficient manner. It also makes the record keeping much more efficient and straightforward. There are clearly costs that may not be appropriate for the University to absorb and the Victoria model has suggested an arrangement by which the Federal Sport and Fitness Officer, B.C. Provincial Sports and Fitness Branch, and the University would share costs. At the time of writing, all partners have indicated a willingness to proceed and it is anticipated that a decision will be made shortly.

However, the Institute as it is envisaged, is only the beginning in meeting the total concerns as expressed in the earlier parts of this paper. It does require more flexibility than is currently proposed. Most importantly, it must accept applicants with varying backgrounds. This might require opportunities for preliminary levels of the current Coaching scheme to be delivered through the Institute (as well as outside). In addition, some opportunity for meeting the standards of the preliminary levels will clearly be required in the initial stages.

Apart from all this, it is inadequate to consider only the elite level of coach education. The Institute, if it is properly developed offers the scope for a large number of courses to be developed for beginning coaches. These would be able to exploit the expertise of leaders in the field who might be involved with the major programme. It could also provide opportunities for the elite coaches-in-training to work with other levels of coaches along with players who might use the facilities for special camps.

The association of such an Institute with an ongoing educational agency provides the consistency and quality control sometimes lacking in the techniques currently being employed. It aids in the consolidation of programmes and the preparation of syllabi under the scheme that makes them readily transportable outside the institution staff. For example, the University of Victoria has an active Extension Office designed to deliver a large number of courses off-campus. It is also hoped that the Institute would prepare further coaching materials for wide distribution. Finally, and very importantly, the mechanisms for researching the effectiveness of the programmes and techniques being suggested can be given high priority.

It can still be argued that this scheme still avoids the concern that there is little opportunity for coaches to pursue their ambitions in the 'real' world. For the elite coach that is probably less important as it is assumed those nominated by Sporting Bodies are, at very least, strong contenders for a future appointment. This would also be true for those sponsored by universities or provincial bodies. In addition, it appears essential that individuals, who because of their ambition or willingness to explore the possibilities, should be given that opportunity as well.

For the majority of coaches, who plan to remain at a casual level, the Institute provides a better structure to consider their needs, by offering make-up opportunities and special programmes. By judicious timing of courses, they could be placed at the time of most convenience for the participants. For example, teachers would be well-served by concentrated summer courses, while others may prefer a series of weekends at appropriate times. It is certain that the coaching of young people will continue to be in the hands of concerned amateurs who maintain their interest as a service to sport and the young athlete. Such generalists have given noble service to sport in the past and with more regularized assistance will do even better in the future. Those individuals who have been involved actively in the Coaching Schemes have claimed that the knowledge gained has been useful in their work. As indicated earlier in the paper, the different levels of interest is a reasonable and healthy approach.

The final advantage of locating such Institutes within a university or college is that a clearly defined administrative structure becomes more readily accountable for its programmes. In Canada, it is difficult to evaluate the success of the current scheme, or in fact decide where problems exist in the delivery of the programmes. The structure as outlined here will not only offer opportunities for the universities or colleges who might be involved but also responsibilities in ensuring that the specific service is provided. Success or failure becomes self-evident which may be threatening for some.

6. Conclusion

The paper of John Lyle is a stimulating discussion of a world wide
concern in sport. Canada has attempted to address this matter by
the establishement of a federal scheme with a centralized structure
but this system has lacked accountability for its delivery and not
maintained sufficient contact with the clientele. To address these
concerns the proposal outlined in this paper suggests that the
Federal Government and Sporting Bodies should contract delivery of
coach preparation to universities or colleges. The current proposal
suggested by the University of Victoria outlines such a scheme with
several adaptations to make it more applicable to the general needs
of coaching, not only in Canada but also in other countries.
   Finally, any scheme should recognize that the improvement in
coaching should be designed to aid the athletes in developing their
interest to the level that they desire. It should not be seen as a
means of manipulating individuals for the glory of the country,
institution, or the coaches themselves. If this becomes the aim,
sport loses its ultimate justification as a unique expression of
human achievement.

PRACTICAL SPORTS PSYCHOLOGY FOR COACHES

K.A. KRUEGER
Practical Sports Psychology Department, Institute of Sports Psychology

Abstract
The importance of mental training as an adjunct to effective coaching
is now well documented. This paper will present a holistic variety
of practices a coach may select for improving performance. The
Practical Sports Psychology system allows anyone to: contravene
psychological barriers; strengthen the body, mind, and spirit; and
reach their potential. Practical Sports Psychology is predicated
on the most recent scientific findings and venerable physio/psycho-
logical, and metaphysical techniques. This paper will offer a succinct intellectual understanding and direct experience of the following topics: The Brain/Mind/Spirit, the blend of these powerful elements for the sports performer; and the following techniques: Concentration, a practice which can bring the mind into focus at will;
Stress Management, eliminates the adverse affects of stress on performance; Nutrition, a balanced diet program for improving strength
and endurance up to 50%; Meditation, a natural, easy and spontaneous
practice for removing psychological barriers, opening energy channels, and developing will power. It brings the state of mind wherein
all ultimate performance occurs; Positive Attitude, achieve what
you conceive; Visualization, enables one to practice without facilities or equipment, it implants a blueprint in the mind for perfect
movement(s). The synergy of Practical Sports Psychology exposes
each person to their full potential through consciously training
the body, mind, and spirit.
Key Words: Brain, Concentration, Meditation, Nutrition, Spirit,
Sports psychology, Synergy, Visualization.

1. Introduction

We have all witnessed spontaneous exhibitions of peak performance
by 'average' people. We have sadly also beheld supremely trained
sportspeople dysfunction or psych-out. This illustrates a need
to approach coaching from an expanded perspective, other than simply
physical training. The modern sportsperson must be satisfactorily
trained in:

   (a) Physical functioning - including skills, conditioning, and

diet;
    (b) Mental control of, anxiety, concentration, etc.;
    (c) Inner-spirit, the source of inspiration, enthusiasm, energy, and more.

"In Olympic competition, a race is won in the mind...winning is 20% physical and 80% mental." One may ask, 'What crazy psychologist said this?...He has read too many books.' The person responsible for this statement is Don Schollander (1971) winner of four gold medals during the 1964 Tokyo Olympics.

The value of psychological training was proven by the Soviets in a study of four equally matched world-class athletes (Garfield, 1984):

Group I - 100 percent physical training
Group II - 75% physical and 25% mental training
Group III - 50% physical and 50% mental training
Group IV - 25% physical and 75% mental training

The significantly greater improvement was exhibited by Group IV then Group III and so on down to the least effectively trained Group I. The chief Soviet sport psychologist, V.A. Romanov, summerizes their feelings on training, "the shaping of psychological readiness is one of the main tasks in preparing athletes for competition." When youngsters get to the national level, they are all just about equal physically. Consequently, we must begin preparing our competitors physically, mentally, and metaphysically.

2. Methods

The material herein presented has been refined from researched material, personally practiced, and taught to sportspeople of all levels around the world. It is presented in a practical, didactic manner; offering a succinct intellectual understanding, and possibilities for personal applications of the techniques.

3. Brain/Mind/Spirit

The brain/mind/spirit is a homogeneous unit. Researchers often seperate them for study because the human organism seems to have more valuable units, like the heart or brain. However, without the endocrine system, or for that matter any other part, these valuable units could not fully function for our total benefit. Without the spirit, the brain or mind would be in a grave situation, and conversely without the brain or mind, the spirit has nowhere to manifest - it would be encased in a 'vegetable' or a mental case. Therefore, the whole person must be trained for one to reach their peak performance.

3.1 Brain

Maclean's (1973) triune theory of the brain illustrates holism very
well. The brain is composed of three parts:

(a) The Reptilian Brain which affects our physical survival
(b) The Old Mammalian, or mid-brain, which affects our mental/-
emotional view of life
(c) The New Brain, divided into hemispheres, which allows for
a logical and intuitively spiritual awareness of life.

It is imperative for these three to be fully developed and bonded
for a person to realize their full potential. The imcompleteness
people feel in life may be the result of the de-emphasis placed
on the spiritual element (Pearce, 1985). We have fortified the
body and reptilian brain with regular physical training; and toned
the mind and mid-brain with various intervention techniques. We
must become whole and complete by tapping the inner spirit and the
New Brain synchronizing its hemispheres. There are now modern technologies to synchronize the brain. This will then facilitate people
to reach their potential.

3.2 Mind

Mental aspects affect the athletes performance in competition –
the body is already trained in strength, endurance, and skills.
Numerous authors have illustrated the importance of mental preparation (Bell, 1983; Cratty, 1984; Gallway, 1974; Garfield, 1984;
Murphy, 1978; Neideffer, 1976). It is only when the mind gets tense
that the body gets tense. The mind then is the source of our success
or failure.

What is the mind? The mind is a psychic instrument. It is the
interface between brain and spirit. The body is the instrument
of the brain. The brain is an instrument of the mind. Simply illustrated – our brain is like a computer and the mind is like the intel-
legent computer programmer.

The Mind has four parts:

(a) the intellect, which discriminates and judges
(b) the subconscious is the active and passive memory
(c) the ego, which claims things as its own
(d) and the 'mind,' which objectively reports the sensory perceptions and also makes images.

The psychic instrument of the mind may function like this: At the
top of a run, a skier looks down the slope before a race's start
– the 'mind' objectively records what the eyes see of the snow conditions and turns; the intellect knowing the weather conditions says
there will be icy spots on the run; the subconscious remembers another time you skied this run under these same conditions – you had
a severe fall, this makes you unconsciously tense-up without you
knowing why; and finally the ego speaks up – 'I may have a hard
time on this run.' All this happens within an instant in your mind.

3.3 Spirit

The Spirit is often called the inner Self or pure Consciousness (Singh, 1979). It is this Self which is aware that we are awake, dreaming, or have had a deep sleep. It is the witness of the mind. The inner Self is the source of our energy, intuition, enthusiasm, inspiration, and more. Sportspeople spontaneously tap into their Spirit when the following five elements combine:

    (a)   relaxation
    (b)   rhythemic activity
    (c)   rhythemic breathing
    (d)   concentration
    (e)   emptying the mind of thought.

Knowledge of the Brain/Mind/Spirit must include methods to enhance them for full melioration. Consciously willed peak performance could then be more readily available for competitors.

4. Concentration

Ledgendary athletes are acknowledged for their powers of concentration. Improving one's concentration will therefore enhance one's performance. Goleman (1977) reports that when the mind gets focused, it reveals its inherent power, which seems to be supernatural for ordinary people, even though it is natural. A clear example is when a small, untrained women picks up an automobile weighing over 1,000 kg. AND removes her child from beneath it. The mother's mind is totally concentrated on one thing - saving her child.

We must begin to control the mind which is as restless as the wind - for unless one concentrates 100% on the task at hand, one is not performing at 100%. We can consciously begin training the mind to concentrate.

4.1 Concentration technique

There are two primary methods to focus the mind - concentrate on the breath OR use a cue word. These physio/psychological techniques have been gleaned from the Zen and Yogic traditions of mind control. One becomes focused faster by combining these methods.

Physiologists note that when the breath calms down, the heartbeat then slows, and the brain-waves consequently reduce their activity. Slow, complete breathing will concentrate the mind while oxygenating the blood. Along with this simple breathing practice, we will also concentrate the mind by paying attention to the sound of the breath. Listen to the sound of your breath coming in and going out. If you cannot hear it, you then mentally repeat the sound of HUM as you breath in and SO as you breath out. This cue word HUM-SO, the sound of the breath, means I Am That in Sanskrit. Practicing HUM-SO also then provides you with a powerful affirmation. HUM-SO is the 'international sound of the breath'. Practice this throughout the day, not just when in need of concentration. It will become like second nature, easy, almost without thinking. This technique is a natural tranquilizer, a gentle antidote for anxiety, a perfect centering device for helping us to operate at peak efficiency (Shiarella, 1982).

In concentrating our mental awareness, we conserve amazing amounts of psychosomatic energy. This preserved and concentrated energy can be used when we choose, giving us greater abilities in our sporting endeavours and daily life.

5. Stress Management

Stress is defined as a factor that induces bodily or mental tensions (Merriam, 1974). Stress can enter our lives at work, within the family, or while participating in sports. All sports have an element of stress. We have all seen or heard of people who do great in local or national competitions, and fail to perform as well in more significant contests. The stress causes them, consciously or unconsciously, to psych-out; the tension overpowers them. Learn to channel or overcome stress. You will have one less obstacle to your potential.

5.1 Somatic Stress
Bodily stress brings tension, not only to the external muscles but to those affecting the digestive, respiratory, and cardio-vascular systems. This stress may manifest in nausea, shortness of breath, and rapid heart-beat prior to competition. The tension of the muscles may be released with two methods - stretching and relaxation/meditation. In essence, stress is brought on by our mental perception of a situation. Without the mental release of stress the physical stretching/release will have only partial value.

A highly beneficial practice for stretching and toning the internal and external muscles, and releasing stress is Hatha Yoga. It can be practiced within an individuals capacity. It can concurrently be used as a warm-up and a cool-down. Pellitier (1979) found that Hatha Yoga both strengthens and lengthens the muscles. These practices also assist in keeping the mind calm and focused before a performance, thus releasing stress while conserving energy.

Hatha Yoga is my preferred method for releasing somatic stress because it is self inflicted. We may also chose the areas of the body to be released, including the internal elements. The physiological release of tensions has a corresponding psychological release. The stretching in Hatha Yoga helps prevent injuries.

Biofeedback and massage are useful for reducing somatic stress (Kauss, 1980). If you are pressed for time, take three complete and deep breaths; or thump your thymus area of the chest a few firm times, this reduces the over production of adrenaline.

5.2 Psychological Stress
Mental anxiety or stress is caused by our perception of the world (Pellitier, 1980). The negative thinking process is a culprit in this concern. Overcome cognative stress by putting the mind-thoughts on something rather than worries and fears. Excellent intervention

techniques for this are described in this paper: Concentration,
meditation, positive attitude, and visualization. When one, or
each prefferably, of these are regularly practiced – psychological
stress becomes like a soft breeze, rather than a gale force wind,
nicely stimulating your senses for improved performance.

6. Nutrition

Nutrients can affect the body, mind, and spirit. Air, liquids,
food, and thoughts are the nourishing forces for humans. The purist
forms of nourishment should be used for peak performance. The best
foods are those that keep the body healthy, elevate the mind, and
free the spirit. The amount of nutrients, when and how they are
injested, can be as important as what is injested.

6.1 The Body and Nutrients
Dramatic examples for the value of proper nutrition are described
by Colgan (1982):
    (a) Improved marathon times of up to 28 minutes, with an average
of over 11 minutes; only about six minutes for the control group;
    (b) Increased strength of up to 50%;
    (c) Intellegence enhanced by an over 20 IQ point difference
for those properly nourished.

What brings about proper nutrition for a person? Generally speaking,
pure, fresh, and whole foods – high in complex-carbohydrates and
low in protein and fats are best. This has been proven by centuries
of use, and recently verified by modern science. Soils may lack
nourishment and the preparation of food may destroy necessary nutrients thus necessitating proper supplimentation. How much and which
vitamins and minerals are needed? This is truly an individual exi-
gency. A qualified nutritionist should be consulted for fine tuning
the body's nutrient needs. Should this not be possible, use applied
kinesiology or a chiropractic doctor.
    The universal nutrient is pure water. It is an imperative.
Hass (1983) and Diamond (1985) explain that, every chemical reaction
in your body, including energy production, takes place in a watery
environment. If your blood, muscles, and organs do not receive
optimal amounts of water, they will not function at peak performance.
The most assimilative form of water comes from fresh fruits and
vegetables then followed by pure spring water.
    What is injested is not the only element for proper nutrition.
It is also important how much you put into the body. It is best
to fill the stomach half full with food, one quarter with liquid
– prefferably pure water. Leave the rest empty for easy digestion.
This formula has been handed done for thousands of years as a way
to stay healthy. This is supported by modern nutritional studies
(Weindruch, 1979).
    Eat right to be fit for life.

6.2 Nutrition and the Mind

Nutrition affects reaction times, strength and endurance. The mind is also dramatically influenced with foods. Learning, moods, and insomnia are just a few mental areas improved with proper injestion of nutrients.

The mood effects of food are real. In a study described by Kagen (1985), neuroendocrinologist and physician, R. Wurtman showed that cmplex-carbohydrates can effect people exactly as anti-depressant drugs. They improve mood, diminish sensitivity to negative stimuli, and ease the way to sleep.

At the University of Sussex, psychologist Angus Craig tested pilots and school children after different kinds of meals. Heavy meals caused significant drop in reaction time and visual perception in the pilots; and made it harder for the children to learn new material (Josephson, 1985).

As food affects your body, it also affects the mind and spirit. A simple example is an athlete who overeats just before a competition in the pole vault. His mind is scattered - preventing concentration; and his energy is directed to digest food in the stomach. He cannot produce a spirited performance.

6.3 Nutrition and the Spirit

The calming influence specific nutrients have on the mind alow the energy/spirit to express itself more freely. Occidental nutritional investigation is devoid of research on foods influence on the Spirit, and vice versa. The Orientals have applied old wisdom and knowledge in the use of foods for uplifting and freeing the spirit, which in turn produces health and well being to the practitioner. One must choose a diet according to individual needs - choosing one which supports the bodies activities, peace in the mind, and stimulates the energy/spirit.

The subtle energy of the spirit can alter the food we injest. Marcel Vogul, director of the Psychic Research Institute, has actually shown that water with the thought form of love transmitted into it, has a different taste and subtle vibration. This may illustrate one of the values in the traditional blessing of food or prayer before eating which is prevelant in most cultures.

There needs to be more research in the area of nutrition and the spirit. The studies should probe areas of the influence the spirit has on nutrition qualities; and investigate how the spirit is affected by foods and qualities thereof (e.g. frozen, canned, fresh, organic, etcetra).

7. Meditation

"Meditation is super concentration. It eliminates psychological barriers, while developing will power. Meditation brings speedy relaxation, manages stress, replenishes energy, and also opens energy channels. It is said to be the state of mind where optimum performance occurs" (Krueger, 1984). Numerous other authors (Gallway,1974; Garfield, 1984; Kabat-Zenn, 1985; Krueger, 1983; Moorehouse, 1977)

have studied the beneficial effects meditation has on sports performance. Kabat-Zenn's (1985) study illustrates meditation's effect
upon rowers.

(a) Enhanced concentration,
(b) improved relaxation before and during races,
(c) improved synchronicity of the stroke cycle, and
(d) reduced the effects of negative thoughts, fatigue and pain
during practices and races.

Meditation has full power to make the impossible, possible; the
unattainable, attainable (Muktananda, 1972). Some examples of this
are:

(a) A Zen master who could sink an arrow into the bull's eye
at sixty paces in a darkened room, and split that arrow with another
(Herrigal, 1953).
(b) Tibetian Buddhist monks raising their external body temperature 19° Fahrenheit, while the internal temperature remained the
same (Benson, 1984).
(c) Yogis walking on hot coals or sleeping on nails.
(d) Yogis and advanced meditators retaining their breath for
extended periods of over 30 minutes, and more...

7.1 Meditation technique
There are many techniques for meditation. Here is one of the effective methods. It begins with concentration. Concentration is focusing the mind on a single point, gathering your thought energies.
Meditation is relaxing your hold on the mind, remaining passive,
detatched, yet alert. You are relaxing conscious thought and opening
to finer energies within your self. Daily practice of 20 minutes
will open you to the witness of the mind, your inner spirit and
true teacher. Meditation opens us to unlimited sources of energy,
knowledge, and potential. It unifies the body, mind, and spirit
in a conscious synchronized bond.

(a) Sit in a straight-backed chair with spine erect, feet flat
on the floor. Fold your hands together in your lap. Eyes may be
opened or closed.
(b) Take three deep breaths, feel yourself relaxing. Imagine
a bright golden white light completely surrounding you, which is
your protection as you open sensitive energy centers.
(c) Gently concentrate on a single idea, picture or word (e.g.
HAM SO) for 10 minutes. Select something that suggests peace, beauty, or a spiritual idea. You may listen to soft, soothing music
(e.g. Barnes & Dexter's Golden Voyage I & III)
(d) If your mind strays from the object of concentration, gently
bring it back to your focal point. (Suprisingly soon, you'll find
your ability to discipline the mind growing much stronger.)
(e) After 10 minutes, seperate your hands and turn your palms
up in your lap. Close your eyes if opened.
(f) Relax your hold on the concentration object, and shift your

mind into neutral. Remain passive yet alert for 10 minutes. Images
and thoughts may cross your mind; placidly observe, and let them
go. You may receive inspiration or nothing at all. It doesn't
matter; just be still, detatched, and flow with whatever you are
experiencing. This is the meditation process.

(g) After 10 minutes, close your palms, open your eyes, and
again imagine that you are surrounded completely by a golden white
light. This is your continued protection. You are totally renewed
in body, mind, and spirit.

This 20 minute practice is not our only meditation practice. We
endeavour to practice the meditation attitude, watching our thoughts
and behaviour, throughout each day. Meditation can help us to be
more fully involved in life because we can watch how we set up our
experiences. Sometimes changes are subtle and sometimes dramatic.

Meditation exposes us to the inherently powerful conscious energy
within - the motivator of all our actions. Meditation is proven
to manage stress, disolve psychological barriers, improve stamina,
bring relaxation, and psychosomatic health. These benefits of meditation are extremely supportive to performers in sport, and daily
life.

8. Visualization

The winning sight is insight. Visualization is this insight, commonly called: mental imagery, mental rehearsal, and/or hypnosis. It
is one of the most generic psychological intervention techniques
to enhance performance. It is simple to learn because we have practiced it at an early age, pretending to be Superwo/man or just mother
or father.

The use of the imagination is an effective tool for developing
a blueprint in the brain for a perfect movement. During the actual
visualization of an action, the body microkinetically goes through
the same motion. The nervous system has no way of telling the difference between a real experience and an imagined experience. Whatever goes on in the mind can show up in the body, and conversely,
whatever does not go on in the mind cannot show up in the body.
Visualization techniques enable a person to:

(a) Practice a skill perfectly without facilities and/or equipment.
(b) Eliminate physical exertion, yet still practice.
(c) Have energy channels open for a perfect movement.
(d) Allow the muscles to subtly know the needful movement prior
to competition.
(e) Refine coordination and proper rhythem.
(f) Possess directness and sureness of movement.

8.1 Visualization Techniques
There are about 112 methods of visualization. I will present two
forms most commonly used by sportspeople. Prior to practicing any

form of visualization, sit and use the concentration technique to calm and focus the mind, then:

(a) <u>Mental</u> <u>Rehearsal</u> - inwardly see yourself at the site of your competition or training. Notice the clothes you wear, the physical conditions (e.g. sounds, temperature, smells, etc.) Feel yourself to be confident and relaxed. Visualize your perfect performance from start to finish, and/or a particular skill or move you wish to perfect. Be conscious of your feelings and emotions during this inner practice. See yourself doing everything perfectly, with finess, power and confidence. Feel the complete experience you visualize as if it were actually happening, use all your inner senses. Picture it so well in your mind as if it were a clear television picture within your mind. Concentrate only on positive images. The more detailed the visualization, the more readily the body will respond. Practice this daily three times in slow motion and about five to seven times at regular speed or faster.

(b) <u>Mental</u> <u>Imagery</u> - Imagine that your body (or part of it) is like a powerful tool or fast animal. Be that which you imagine; feel the strength or speed and fluid movement; e.g. a sprinter imagines her/his legs to be the most powerful spring and the starters signal releases it, then the body moves as a speeding cheetah. Daily before practice and competition see and feel your body to be that tool or animal.

We may practice visualization anytime. It is good to use it as a break in the monotonous physical routine of training. Take about five- two minute visualization sessions per training period. Another very beneficial time is upon awakening or just prior to sleep - at this time, the mind is very open and receptive to the imprinting of positive images.

9. Positive Attitude

You can achieve what you conceive because thought has great kinetic energy. Thought is prior to feeling and action therefore, when we think positive, we can feel positive, and act positive. Thoughts can serve us when we consciously use them - rather than us serving our thoughts. This is the premise of Positive Attitude. Simply put, positive attitude is brought about by reprogramming our biocomputer brain through instilling positive thoughts as affirmations.

It is easy to eliminate negative thoughts that bring you down by supporting positive thoughts that make you feel really good. Nityananda (1985) wrote, "Instead of holding hands with anger, with hatred, with jealousy, misery, pain, unhappiness - why not instead hold hands and make friends with something positive and try to find that source of happiness? Just make this promise to yourself: Everyday I'm going to get up; I will be happy; regardless of the situations that arise in life, I promise to myself that I'll be happy. Then you will see that you can live happily, without having to suffer."

9.1 Creating a Positive Attitude

Once we have a general positive outlook it becomes quite easy to apply it for sports amelioration. Write a strong, positive statement that something is already so – an affirmation. These may be done silently, aloud, sung, or often written down. The application of affirmations for just 10 minutes per day can transform our attitudes and expectations of life and totally change what we create for ourselves.

Create your own affirmation. It can be specific or general. Use it while training or traveling. It is best repeated when the mind is calm and focused (e.g. after meditation or sleep), so the affirmation is solidly imprinted upon the mind. Modern technology is also used to access the brain through synchronation, so as to instil any positive affirmation into the subconscious. Doing effective affirmations will counterbalance years of old mental habits. A few simple affirmations will give you an idea for creating your own:

(a) I am a great sprinter.
(b) I am confident.
(c) I swim a (time) in the (distance/stroke).
(d) Every day in every way, I'm getting better, better and better.

Along with writing the affirmation in the present tense, <u>visualize</u> the results as if it had already arrived. <u>See</u> it vividly in brilliant color. <u>Experience</u> the feelings you will have when it comes to pass. Make it as real as possible. Set your goals high, knowing that life is a mirror of your own beliefs and attitudes. As your beliefs start shifting, you will easily attain things you once thought impossible. The African philosopher, Augustine of Hippo said, "Faith is to believe what you do not perceive, and the reward of that faith is to see what you believe."

10. Conclusion

Researchers may find this holistic approach to peak performance a great project for investigation. Coaches will, of course, find each technique quite beneficial and useful. Maximum results will occur when all the techniques are integrated into the daily training schedule – the synergy effect results.

If anything is excellent...think about such things...apply such things...

References

Bell, K.F. (1983) Championship Thinking. Prentice-Hall, Englewood
   Cliffs, N.J.
Cratty, B.J. (1984) Psychological Preperation and Athletic Excel-
   lence. Movement Publications, Ithica, N.Y.
Diamond, H. & M. (1985) Fit for Life. Warner Books, N.Y.
Gallway, W.T. (1974) The Inner Game of Tennis. Random House, N.Y.
Garfield, C.A. (1984) Peak Performance. J.P. Tarcher, Inc., Los
   Angeles, CA.
Goleman, D. (1977) The Varieties of Meditative Experience. Dutton,
   N.Y.
Hass, R. (1983) Eat to Win. Rawson Associates, N.Y.
Herrigel, E. (1953) Zen in the Art of Archery. Pantheon Books, N.Y.
Josephson, N.F. (1985) The real power lunch. American Health, June,
   N.Y.
Kabat-Zenn, J., Bell, B., Rippe, J., (1985) A Systematic mental
   training program based on mindfulness meditation to optimize
   performance in collegiate and olympic rowers. Paper presented
   at VI World Congress on Sport Psychology, Copenhagen.
Kagen, D. (1985) Mind nutrients. Omni, May, N.Y.
Kauss, D.R. (1980) Peak Performance. Prentice-Hall, Englewood Cliffs,
   N.J.
Krueger, K.A. (1984) Meditation and the ultimate performance in
   sports. Sportsweek, Bombay, Sept 5-11. Presented at the 1984
   Olympic Scientific Congress, Eugene, OR.
Krueger, K.A. (1983) Meditation a new tool in the sports arena.
   Society of the National Institutes of Physical Education and
   Sports Journal. January, Patiala, India.
Maclean, P. (1973) A triune concept of the brain and behavior. ed.
   D. Campbell and T.J. Boag. The Clerence M. Hicks Memorial Lecture
   Series. University of Toronto Press, Toronto.
Merrian, C. & G. (1974) The Merrian-Webster Dictionary. Pocket
   Books, N.Y.
Morehouse, L.E. (1977) Maximum Performance. Simon and Schuster,
   N.Y.
Muktananda, (1972) Mukteshwari. Gurudev Siddha Peeth, Bombay.
Murphy, M., and White, R. (1978) The Psychic Side of Sports. Adison-
   Wesley, Reading, MA.
Neideffer, R. (1976) The Inner Athlete. Thomas Crowell, Co., N.Y.
Nityananda (1985) The great relationship. Siddha Path. January,
   So. Fallsburg, N.Y.
Pearce, J.C. (1981) The Bond of Power. Dutton, N.Y.
Pearce, J.C. (1985) Magical Child Matures. Dutton, N.Y.
Pellitier, K. (1979) Holistic Medicine. Dell Publishers, N.Y.
Pellitier, K. (1980) Mind as Healer Mind as Slayer. Harper & Row,
   N.Y.
Schollander, D. (1971) Deep Water. Crown Publishers, N.Y.
Shiarella, R. (1982) Journey to Joy. Matrika Publications, Ltd.
   N.Y.
Singh, J. (1979) Sivasutras. Motilal Banarsidass, Delhi.
Weindruch, R.H. (1979) Federal Proceedings. Washington, DC. Vol.
   38 page 418.

THE MANAGEMENT AND OPERATION OF COACHING SYSTEMS
A SYSTEMS APPROACH

P.W.J. LEDINGTON Computing Science Group,Royal Military College of
                 Science/Cranfield Institute of Technology
K. WOOTTON   The Amateur Rowing Association.

Abstract
A management study of the coaching system of a national governing
body of sport provided an opportunity to examine the cultural frame
of reference of coaches. A model of Sport as a competitive system
was developed and then used as a basis for the derivation of a
conceptual model of the "Coaching System". This then provided the
basis for an adaptive management problem-solving methodology. The
use of this approach identified three roles associated with the
coaching system and helped to identify role conflict within the
situation.
Key words:Cultural frame of reference, Coaching system, Management,
Problem solving, Conceptual model, Role conflict.

1. Introduction

The paper which sets the theme of this conference, Lyle(1985) brings
to the fore a major issue within the management of sport, that being
"On the basis of what model of coaching should policymaking be
based ?". Lyle goes further and argues that there is no accepted
model of coaching which is available to form the starting point for
the deliberations through which policy is formed. This is a position
with which the authors concur and which forms a contextual starting
point for the work which will be described.

    A parallel situation to that described above arose during a
systems analysis study carried out in conjunction with a U.K.
national governing body of sport. The initial aim of the study was
to try to identify areas within coaching which could be assisted by
new Information Technology. As the study progressed however it
became increasingly clear to the study team that the normal
approaches to such a study were inadequate. Reflection and
discussion of this situation led the team to realise that a useful
analysis could only be achieved once some fundamental
understanding of the "Frame-of-Reference" used by the sports
practitioners in the situation under scrutiny had been captured.

Two concepts form core areas of the F-O-R the concept of Sport and the concept of coaching. A process of iterative interactive modelling of the concepts was used to formalise and make explicit an understanding of each concept. In the following section the basic rationale for such an approach will be discussed, the models themselves will be presented in the second section and issues identified from their use in the third. Finally the work will be related back to the theme of policymaking within sport.

2)."Frames of Reference" and Soft Systems Methodology.

The concept of a "Frame-of-Reference" has become increasingly important to the understanding of policymaking and strategic decisionmaking within organisations (Shrivastava & Schneider 1984). Policymaking depend upon the underlying set of assumptions about the world used by the policymakers to structure and make sense of the information available to them about some issue. However these assumptions are seldom explicitly identified during the policymaking process. Several researchers have shown the importance of surfacing and structuring such assumptions in an explicit form as an aid to such decisionmaking processes (Argyris & Schon,1978; Mason & Mitroff 1981).
The concept of a World-view, or Weltanshauung, helps to explain the way in which human actors interpret and make sense of the world around them and thus act coherently in relation to that world. Particularly in any social organisation the assumptions shared by the actors in the situation is reflected in the development of shared identity, culture, cohesiveness and social stability. It therefore becomes important that any approach adopted in order to tackle "Real-World" problems takes into account the ill-structured nature of the situation with which it is dealing. The approach adopted in the study which forms the background to this paper is termed "Soft Systems Methodology" (Checkland 1981) within which the concept of Weltanschauung plays a crucial role (Checkland & Davies 1986).
Soft Systems Methodology is a process of inquiry aimed at facilitating change within a situation seen as problematic by concerned actors who form part of that situation. The approach is based upon the analysis of purposeful activity through making explicit models of some human activity which is seen as relevant to the problem situation under investigation. A full description of SSM is beyond the scope of this paper but an abbreviated discussion is necessary in order to make meaningful the results described in the sections which follow.
Real-world situations are constructed through the interaction and communication of concerned actors. If therefore change in the situation is to be achieved part of that process can be viewed as facilitating a process of debate amongst the concerned actors. This is achieved through the organised use of systems thinking.

The first stage is to find out about the problem situation after which the analyst and the actors make a first attempt at defining some human activity systems which seem relevant to that situation. These systems are carefully named, the term used for such a name being a "Root Definition". For each root definition a model of the system is then built by assembling and structuring the minimum necessary set of verbs needed to describe the activities of the system named in the root definition. Having created a systems model this is then used in a process of comparison between the model and what is seen to exist in the problem situation. This comparison stage forms the basis for a debate out of which can come possible changes which are both Systemically Desirable (given the root definitions and models used) and Culturally Feasible (for the actors concerned in their historical context). Once this stage has been arrived at the problem then becomes one of implementing the changes in the real-world situation.

In attempting to use this approach a great deal can be learned about the organisation, or purposeful activity, with which the analysis is dealing and it is to the context of this present work that we will now turn.

3).The "Coaching System" in Context.

The original intent of the study team was to consider ways in which computer-based information technology could be applied in order to increase the effectiveness of coaching. The study team attempted to apply a form of SSM, called the Information Systems Methodology (Wilson 1984), to the situation. The first stage of the study was identified as modelling the "Coaching System" so that having done so the model could be used to identify the information requirements of the system and thereby facilitate the design of appropriate information systems.

It was at this first stage that the study team ran into a problem. It proved extraordinarily difficult to identify anything that allowed the formulation of a root definition and conceptual model. The image of coaching was of an athlete - coach interaction system but any idea of coaching as an organised set of activities was simply unavailable and could not be directly articulated. The result of this situation was that the study team concentrated upon using interactive modelling techniques in order to explore various ideas about the concept of "A Coaching System".

What became increasingly clear through discussion was that a very strong definition of "Sport" was used by the coaches concerned. It directed their thinking, what was acceptable and the areas that they felt were of interest or not. The approach adopted was therefore to try to surface in an explicit way the frame-of-reference being used by the coaches. This was far more than an organisational F-O-R but represented a "Cultural Frame-Of-Reference".

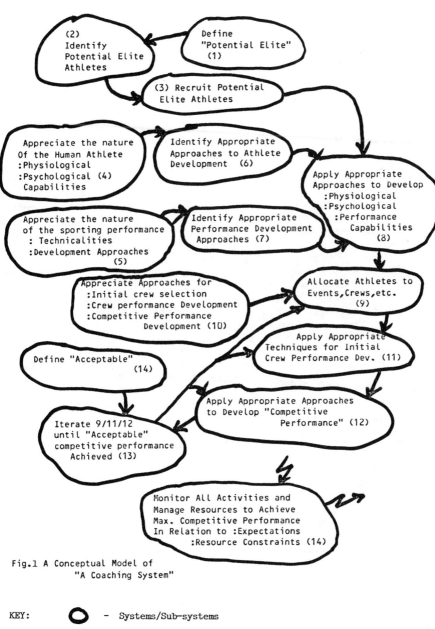

Fig.1 A Conceptual Model of
     "A Coaching System"

KEY: ◯   - Systems/Sub-systems

        ⟶   - Logical Dependencies

        ⟿   - To/From all Activities

Central to the concept of sport as used by the coaches was the idea of "Competitive Performance" which led to the formulation of a model of sport which consists of;

1). A set of PERFORMING SYSTEMS each having components consisting of athletes and equipment.
2). An activity (or PERFORMANCE) carried out by 1).
3). A COMPETITION.
4). An agreed FRAMEWORK which validates the nature of the Performing systems,Competition and defines a valid measure of the notion of "Competitive performance".

This definition is useful in a number of ways in that it separates sporting and non-sporting activities and allows consideration of the formalisation and institutionalisation of each element. Further it changed our view of coaching from a "Competitive performance producing system" to a "Competitive performance developing system". Having set out and tested in conjunction with the coaches concerned this definition it was then used as a basis for the formulation of a Root Definition.

A Coaching System was formally defined as ;

"A system owned by the governing body of sport which operating within available resources converts potential elite athletes into "Performing Systems" having a level of competitive performance appropriate to the nature and level of the competitions within the sport. The system employs appropriate methods for athlete/performance system development and seeks to use the limited resources available in an efficient manner".

This root definition was then modelled in terms of activities and their logical dependencies which is shown in Fig. 1. It must be stressed that these models both of "Sport" and of "The Coaching System" are not descriptions of real-world phenomena, they are logical constructs which can be used as an analytical framework. However they have been tested through both feedback from the coaches concerned in which the models were accepted and through use as an analytical tool in that the issues and problems which they identified were recognised by the coaches as of concern and interest. Explaining the detailed use of these models is beyond the scope of this paper, but in the next section some general findings will be discussed.

3) Some Learning about the Coaching Situation.

The use of the models that have been presented led to many insights about the coaching situation, but the majority of these are situation specific. However two areas have been identified as of general interest. These are the institutionalisation of a sport and an analysis of the role of the coach.

3.1 Institutionalisation.
The model of sport derived was used as a basis for analysing the institutions which controlled the sport. This demonstrated quite clearly that two forms of the sport existed, the first at the national level and the second at the international level. These were different in the forms of the performing system, the form of the performance activity in particular, and also in the ways in which competitions and the framework of rules were controlled. This distinction was so strong that the idea of two cultures within the sport was identified and thus distinct differences in the coaching activities performed. In fact one of the strategic issues within the policymaking about the sport was identified as trying to "Bridge the Gap" between the two cultures.

3.2 The Roles of the Coach.
The activity model generated has a number of distinct forms of activity within it and from these it proved possible to identify three prime roles associated with the coaching system. These are;
    1). The Practitioner.
    2). The Technical Expert.
    3). The System Manager.
with four areas of responsibility associated with each. Thus;

    The Practitioner - 1) Talent spotting and recruitment.
                       2) Athlete development.
                       3) Skill development.
                       4) Performing system development.

    The Technical Expert - Knowledge acquisition and development
    concerned with   1) Athlete development methods
                       2) Skill development methods
                       3) Performing system development methods
                       4) Competition analysis

    The System Manager 1) Resource planning
                       2) Activity monitoring
                       3) Internal management/liaison
                       4) External management/liaison

In the real-world these roles could be carried out by one individual or by specialised actors within a group.
    Using this framework to analyse the work of the coaches we were dealing with identified a strong area of role conflict. It was recognised that the standing of a coach within a sport arose primarily from being associated with successful athletes that is from the "Practitioner" role. The national coaches with whom we worked saw their major contribution as fulfilling the role of "Technical Expert". However they felt strongly that increasingly they were being asked to carry out the activities of "System

manager" activities which they felt were inappropriate to their position and also ones they felt ill-prepared and ill-trained for. This analysis helped to articulate the feelings of unease felt by the coaches and identified a major area of role conflict within their work.

These two areas demonstrate that the learning arising from the use of the models is both useful and potentially generalisable outside of the original situation. Having now demonstrated the nature and results of the study it is now time to relate these findings to the issues raised in the conference theme paper.

4).Discussion.

The work described in this paper is relevant to the issues raised by Lyle in that the failure to find a well articulated model of coaching supports his contention that such a model is unavailable. However this finding does not mean that such a model has no existence merely that it has not been formalised and made explicit. In this paper a method for tackling the process of explication has been demonstrated and the initial results of it's use have been discussed. This paper coupled with that of Lyle suggests that a concern with the nature of coaching as an organised body of activity is growing. The issue that should now be considered is how the process of debate amongst sports practitioners at all levels can be facilitated in a meaningful way and thereby aid the development of coaching both instrumentally and as a worthwhile career.

5). Conclusion.

It has been shown that work arising from a management study of coaching has wider implications. An approach to tackling ill-structured real-world problems has been described. Part of the learning arising from it's use in relation to coaching has been described and models of both "Sport" and "a Coaching system" presented. These have been shown to be useful in identifying problems within the management of sport and there now exists a tentative methodology for sports management analysis. The need now is to apply this methodology in other situations as an aid to the development of coaching and sports management in general.

(The project upon which this work is based was supported by a grant from the National Coaching foundation. The authors also thank the national coaches and members of the national governing body of sport for their participation and to other members of the study team namely
P.Edwards of Liverpool Polytechnic and
L.J. Davies of RMCS/Cranfield for their involvement, help and advice)

References

Arguris, C. and Schon, D.A. (1978) Organizational learning: A theory of action perspective. Addison Wesley, Reading, Massachusetts.

Checkland, P. B. (1981) Systems Thinking, Systems Practice. John Wiley, Chichester

Checkland, P. B. and Davies, L. J. (1986) The Use of the term Weltanschauung in Soft Systems Methodology. Journal of Applied Systems Analysis.

Lyle, J. (1985) Coach Education - preparation for a profession. (conference paper)

Shrivastava, P. and Schneider, S, (1984) Organizational frames of reference. Human Relations, 37(10) pp 795-809.

Wilson, B (1984) Systems: Concepts, Methodologies and Applications. John Wiley, Chichester.

WHY FEMALE COACHES ARE LACKING
IN NIGERIAN SECONDARY SCHOOLS

B.S. MSHELIA   Dept. of Physical & Health
                Education, Borno College of Education,
                Maiduguri, Nigeria.

T.A. ADEDOJA   Dept. of Physical & Health
                Education, University of Maiduguri,
                Maiduguri, Nigeria.

Abstract

Despite some international accomplishments in track
and field and in other sports recorded by some
Nigerian female athletes, sport is still regarded as
man's activity in Nigeria. Discrimination against
womens active participation in competitive sports has
led to insufficient female coaches in Nigerian
Secondary Schools. This shortage has unfavourable
effects on female students and the general administration of school sports programmes. Increased concern
over this issue by sports administrators in Nigeria
has therefore compelled the authors to look closely
into the various factors that account for the negative
attitude of women and shortage of female coaches in
Nigerian Schools.
Key words: Culture, Religion, Society, Sports, women,
Coaches, Physical activity, Nigeria.

One of the major concerns of sports administrators in
Nigeria today is lack of female coaches in Nigerian
Secondary Schools.

Women constitute a special case in the realm of
sporting activities. Unfortunately the Nigerian
community has not given much attention to the cultural
significance of women in sports. As far as women are
concerned assessments of their functions and role as
a consequental force in the world of sports has been
largely a matter of some speculations and chance.

From generation to generation, a widespread belief continues to linger in the mind of people that strenuous sports activity is not only beyond the capacity of women, but it is physically harmful to them. The belief, moreover, hold that even if women can somehow find the physical endurance and emotional resolve for high level sports competition, it is still bad for them. In short, it is unladylike.

This belief for years has confined women to the side-line of sport. In the past it was a silent problem, but today as more and more female schools are being opened across the country, the issue has become a matter of concern. It is the purpose of this paper therefore to examine some of the problems that prevent the Nigerian women from fully participating in competitive sport programs.

Despite some international achievements in track and field recorded by some Nigerian female athletes, sport is still regarded as man's activity.

Going by constitutional provisions in Nigeria every person has the right to education and the right to participate and compete in the various sporting activities of this country (Nigeria). Unfortunately, as it is today, enjoyment of this right has not been encouraging in the case of women, particularly in Sports.

Women, perhaps are victims of ignorance of this right or victims of discrimination which arises from different causes and circumstances. At the moment, discrimination is hard to detect because the laws of Nigeria recognize unreservedly the equality of men and women in every field of human endeavour including competitive sports participation. If the principle of equality is applied in this case, Nigeria can boast of fielding millions of girls in competitive sports and train thousands of female coaches, since last census data shows that there were more women than men.

Research evidence has attributed women's lack of interest in Sports or physical activity to cultural, emotional, physiological, and Social factors, and Nigerian women are no exception to these factors.

There are a number of problems that prevent women from fully participating in the sporting activities of this nation. Problems that are apparent but not discussed. This negligence has led to the continuing lack of sufficient female coaches and physical educators in the Secondary Schools.

Women have been excluded from consideration in most activities taking place outside of the home, especially outside the kitchen and bedroom. Male chauvinism has it that a woman's place is in the home. Our existing culture has been interpreted to mean that a woman must be socialized to believe that once married she is solely responsible for domestic affairs. By and large her duty centers in the house. Leonard's (1980) theory of "Sex role expectations" of females in Society aptly applies to Nigeria.

It is a sociological phenomenon is almost every nation that the child's mother is ordinarily his or her first model and teacher; and the child's earliest ideas of play, patterns of participation, and perhaps ideas of sportsmanship are learned in the home. This suggests that a part of the foundation of the sports life of a nation is built by the mothers of the nation.

In Nigeria, right from childhood a girl is expected to learn how to cook and copy other related household activities from the mother. History tells us that daughters learned from their mothers and other women within the community, how to look after babies, how to cook, and how to handle other domestic affairs like sewing and knitting, while sons learned from their fathers and from other men how to work the land, how to participate in organized hunting, how to wrestle and participate in other related masculine activities.

290

For most girls the problem starts very early, probably at birth. Indeed, by the time girls have reached
age of five or six they have been firmly directed by
their parents, in fact by every influence in their
lives, into a pattern of behaviour associated with being
feminine as opposed to being masculine. The existing
culture expects girls to play separately from boys,
dress differently, behave less boisterously and be less
aggressive in their activities.

The feminine behaviour and comportment is steadily
reinforced and accentuated in schools as years go by
and as various kinds of separate activities for boys
and girls make their appearance. For those at home,
marriage is the answer. In fact, the tradition attach
much importance to early marriage that a lot of school
girls leave school to marry particularly in the
northern part of the country. The fact is, most men
feel that educated girls are hard to control.

Things are beginning to change but the rate of change
has been perceived by many sports administrators to
be distressingly slow. Traditional beliefs about the
physical, sex-role and psycho-social differences
between men and women are deeply rooted in our culture
than most other beliefs. Indeed cultural definitions
of the expectations associated with women's role have
often encouraged them to be passive, gentle, delicate,
and perhaps submissive. As earlier stated, many
parents direct their offspring toward masculine or
feminine behaviour and interests right from childhood.
Many parents may deplore sex-role restrictiveness but
unconsciously set the scene for their own children to
fit into those same stereotypical molds.

One other thing which in modern times perhaps places
the most difficult obstacle is financial assistance
to encourage and enable girls to participate in
sporting activities. In most cases a father of two
(a son and a daughter) is more likely to offer
financial assistance to the sons to purchase sporting
equipment and give every possible encouragement than
he would for the daughter. There is always the
stereotype expectation from the father that the girl
will eventually be married to someone and is expected
to find her fortune there.

Religion is another strong factor that has continued to hinder women's progress in sports. Islam as a religion is a way of life in some parts of Nigeria. Every Moslem is aware that the teaching of Islam frowns heavily at any association between matured men and females. This is a fact of life that everyone in such a community has to contend with. In this kind of environment one will hardly expect any encouragement to women participation in sports. Furthermore, the Islamic religion, a predominant religion in northern Nigeria objects to the mode of dressing for sports women and women coaches on the ground of its being contradictory to the dress code for muslim women. Also some of the movement positions and patterns in Sports and physical activity are seen as falling short of decency for woman folk.

For the lucky few who happen to be in schools they enjoy the sporting facilities provided by the schools. Unfortunately these institutions are far from having enough sports facilities for their girls.

Indeed, the problem of discriminating against girls participating in competitive sports has led to insufficient sports personnel in our schools. Yet it seems that most peopoe find it difficult to consider the issue with any degree of objectivity. There is an urgent need to give a serious thought to this problem if we are concerned with producing potential female athletes in places across the country.

Some may argue that the past few years have seen great changes in women's involvement in sports. This is no doubt true, at least to a degree, but some limited observation would indicate that there has been no radical change. Infact most of the women physical educators, as well as coaches in Nigeria today, fought their way into the profession despite stringent social bonds. By and large, attitudes toward women in sports have been slow to change because of the misunderstanding about women's physiological competence and cultural role definitions. A lot of people still maintain that there is much physiological risk involved in competitive sports for women than mere social consequences.

292

As long as women are kept from physical activities
based on physiological, psychological and moral
"disadvantages" of participation, female coaches will
continue to be lacking in Nigerian Secondary Schools.
Education of women is a panacea to attitude change.

Reference

Adedoja, T.A. (1978) The attitude of University of
    Ife women (non athletes) undergraduates to Sports
    in the University (Unpublished essay, University of
    Ife, Nigeria)

Leonards W.M. (1980) A Sociological perspectives of
    of Sports. Minneapols: Burgess Pub. Co.

Sattler, et al (1978) Theoretical and Operational
    aspects of intramural Sports. New York: Leisure
    Press.

A VISUAL SCREENING PROGRAMME FOR SPORTS

HARVEY RATNER
National Capital Center for Sports Vision
8737 Colesville Road, Suite 850
Silver Spring, Maryland 20910

Abstract
Generally speaking, physical prowess, agility, speed,
co-ordination and strength have been the main criteria
in judging athletic ability. Most athletic training
programmes are designed with those criteria in mind.
The body usually will respond to what we can see.
Despite this fact, little attention has been paid to
vision, which for all intents and purposes is the key
to superior athletic ability. Studies have shown that
superior athletes do have innate, superior vision. It
has been proved now that through proper evaluation,
screening and training of the visual system, an athlete
at any level can improve performance.

1   A Visual Screening Programme for Sports

The human body is a complex, unique machine. We can
listen and sometimes not hear, we can touch and not
feel and very often look and not see or visualise.
The eyes are not perfect; seeing is not automatic and
vision, especially is a learned and developed skill.
Of all of the systems, required in sports, the visual
system is perhaps the last to be achieved successfully
and the most difficult to develop and hold. Once the
visual system is understood, it will be easier for the
coach and the player to achieve success in sports.
Vision requires awareness, concentration, and like
other learned skills, vision can be taught and trained
to improve performance.

Vision is the process of learning and reacting to what
we see. How well one may see is determined by where
one looks. Approximately 80% of actions involves the
process of vision. The other senses, hearing, smell,
touch, and taste complete part of the learning process.
Coaches instructors and trainers put in hours on the
physical development of the body. They train the
muscular system, cardiovascular system, introduce
proper diet, and yet, vision beyond seeing 20/20 is
practically ignored. As a coach becomes more aware of
the visual process and its importance to the athlete,
he (the coach) begins to train a complete and total
athlete.

HOLD THIS CARD IN POSITION
FIGURE 1

Figure 2 is a concept developed by Dr Wayne Martin, OD, wherein, he perceives vision as the hub of the consummate athlete. It is, arguably, a cogent statement, and in reviewing the attributes of the athlete, the coach cannow start to understand why visual skills are of utmost importance.

Figure 2

Due to the fact that presenting a paper on vision is
difficult to do through verbalization alone, I will
very quickly do a demonstration of binocularity, using
a standard piece of equipment known as a physiological
diplopia string.   The purpose of the string is to
check proper alignment and lock on fusion, which is
known as normal double vision (having someone from
audience come up for demonstration of phy-dip string).
(See Figure 3)

BINOCULAR STRINGS EXERCISE

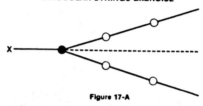

Figure 17-A

In Figure 17-A, X is the tip of your nose. While centered to
this position on the first bead, the second and third bead will be
seen double along the vee lines formed from the first fixation
point.

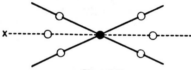

Figure 17-B

When you fixate on the center bead in Figure 17-B,, the first
and third beads will appear double. A double vee or X crossing
will be formed at the center bead.

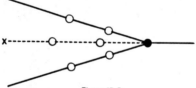

Figure 17-C

In Figure 17-C, when centered on the bead farthest from the
eyes, a vee will be formed coming forward with a doubling of
the second and closest bead.

Figure 3

As a coach, it is absolutely imperative to know if your athlete has the ability to perceive correct double vision and accurately locate in space an object, especially a moving object.

The phy-dip string also allows us to take a look at the athlete's ability to converge or have the eyes turned to an inward position, and also diverge -- going to an outward position.

HYDE[2] Hyde, in a research study of convergence, fixation revealed the following; 1 For short distance, such as hitting the baseball, the eye overshoots, or has a tendency to look behind the target. 2 At a far point, 20 feet or greater, the eye undershoots, or has a tendency to look inside the point of interest. Hyde determined that muscles converging inward react faster than outward divergent muscles. The act to converge is more abrupt and instantaneous than the slower action of divergence. (Do demo of Bullseye Target.)

During the course of a day, you will find that many of your athletes are operating at eye level and below, working in a convergent pattern. If your athlete is spending time in school, this is a normal occurence. Since our eyes are constantly being trained to look down and in, we must now focus on the problem of having our athletes come out and work in a divergent or up and away task. There are exercises that can be done daily to enhance the convergent and divergent muscles, and these should be attended to on a daily basis.

Kinetic Reflexes

The Coach needs to have an awareness and understanding also of the components to maintain control and balance. The two basic components are as follows; Stato-kinetic Reflexes.[3] These reflexes sense angular acceleration of the head and also an awareness of any induced head, eye or body movement. They serve to restore equilibrium - the ability to maintain balance. This is that process in the semi-circular canals -- the ear and hearing. Opto-kinetic Reflexes.[4] These reflexes relate to movement induced by a moving target or moving person. (Demo with J B Stick.)

The head is the chassis which holds the optical system, it holds and maintains an alignment, orientation and balance with the ground. Faulty target and body movement can result in induced opto-kinetic movements, both can result in loss of balance and orientation in space. It is important that the coach stress and know principles of good balance for their athletes.

Hyde[2], Stato-kinetic[3], Opto-kinetic[4], clinical refraction, Borish.

Coach -- Athlete Relationship

A well trained athlete is the result of a well trained and knowledgeable coach. The coach who is constantly striving to improve his knowledge, methods of teaching, communication, and understanding of the athlete's needs, certainly represents the epitome of a coach. In learning to understand an athlete's visual needs, the coach will have to learn various staff members, ie, the trainer, a sports vision, functional optometrist, and perhaps a sports vision company work with the coach and his staff to bring to fruition a programme that will complement the total coaching programme.

Summary

Learning is the result of knowledge. A coach or trainer must obtain knowledge of all of the systems of his or her athletes to produce the optimal athlete. The visual system is perhaps one of the most important systems for the coach to understand in order to maximise performance of his athlete. As the knowledgeable coach looks around his gym, training camp, health centre, he sees a variety of equipment and devices to develop the athlete's body. The coach must now seek and gain knowledge and get the proper materials and equipment to develop the visual system.

PLAYER ANALYSIS BY MICROCOMPUTER

R.H. SHARP
Scottish School of Physical Education, Jordanhill College
of Education

Abstract
The paper describes a research project, sponsored by The
National Coaching Foundation, concerned with the
development of microcomputer software to aid player
analysis. Two software packages are described. One to
examine the footwork patterns of singles, badminton
players and the other to examine the tactical performance
of singles, table tennis players.
Key words: Software, Player analysis, Microcomputers,
Match analysis, Table tennis, Badminton.

1. Introduction

The examination and evaluation of a player's performance
is carried out by a number of people. For example, the
crowd at a soccer match applaud a player's excellence as
they watch him perform on the pitch. A team manager
assesses his players as well as the opponents, in an
attempt to better his team's performance. The coach and
players themselves are also actively involved in
analysing performance to identify faults or weaknesses in
play. (Brackenridge and Alderson, 1985, have recently
presented a review of the aims and methods of match
analysis).

In some sports, reasonably sophisticated technology is
used to assist such evaluations. A manager may
strategically place a number of video cameras to record
play. A coach may record a running commentary on
audiotape. Some sporting organisations employ commercial
firms to computerise details of play as it happens and
produce summaries of team and player performance during
breaks or between games. The use of these methods is
reflected in immediate television replays and stills,
on-screen statistical summaries, as well as the
commentator's ability to recall detailed player profiles

exactly when required.

The impression might be gained that high technology to assist player/match analysis is commonplace. In some sports (e.g., American football, basketball) this is the case but, at grassroots level, the coach has to make do with less sophisticated evaluation methods. Many coaches will of course argue - quite correctly - that straightforward, subjective appraisal is sufficient. There is a call though, for more in-depth, objective analysis, helped by modern computer methods. This has recently been highlighted in some areas of Scottish sport.

2. Background to the project

The Scottish School of Physical Education at Jordanhill College of Education is financed by the Scottish Sports Council to act as a resource centre for Scottish coaches. In this role, the Scottish School loans equipment and provides a consultancy service on all matters ranging from fitness testing and training prescription to methods of player and match analysis. Many coaches are interested in knowing how microcomputers can aid them in their sport and several have shown an interest in using the microcomputer for player analysis. At the time such interest was being shown, it was not possible to help other than say to coaches, yes, your questions can be answered with the aid of a microcomputer. It was impossible to develop the questions raised, because of the absence of computer software. As a result, it was decided early in 1985 to tackle this problem by seeking financial support to write appropriate computer software.

3. Funding

The National Coaching Foundation were approached on the matter and a proposal submitted to finance the development of microcomputer software in a number of sports. The proposal, was supported by the Scottish Sports Council and also the Scottish Microelectronics Development Programme who offered to advise on program writing, etc.. The submission was successful, allowing the employment of a part-time programmer as of November, 1985.

4. Program specification

The National Coaching Foundation advised that work focus on badminton, although the original intention was to work on a number of sports in which coaches had shown interest. It was known at the outset that a number of problems would present themselves. For example, there would be a problem of data capture, particularly with regard to the speed difference between real time action and data entry to the computer. It was also recognised that the software produced would be highly specific to the sport and represent an extensive investment in time and money. A further problem was the need to validate and field test the software - matters which, within the one year time span of the project, might not be wholly dealt with.

At the time of writing, two projects are nearing completion, one in badminton and the other in table tennis. It is planned to develop both projects and also start on a squash player analysis program in the near future. The following section looks at the background of the two projects and describes some of the important features of the software.

4.1 Badminton Project
The last ten years have seen a revolution in Badminton. Changes in racket design have led more to a focus on speed/power, strokes have changed to encourage forearm as opposed to wrist action and fitness levels have changed to put greater stress on leg strength. These changes have led to footwork patterns which are totally different to those coached previously. Campbell (1985) has shown through video analysis that the world's top men and women players tend to adopt particular footwork patterns in ten separate areas of the court. One area, along with the possible movement patterns is given below.

Movement to the forehand net from a central base.

a. Extension of the right leg forward and to the side. A chassis of the left foot to the right then a lunge on to the right foot.

b. Left foot is brought forward in front of the right foot, then a lunge on to the right foot.

c. Right foot is extended in a wide lunge.

The aim of the software is to analyse such footwork patterns with a view to confirmimg their use and building

up an accurate picture of player movement at all levels
of play. In doing this, the software will produce an
objective guide to the manner in which players should be
taught/encouraged to move, and also trained for specific
fitness requirements. The software is designed to take
data from a video recording played at normal speed. It
does not therefore provide immediate feedback to players
or coaches nor is it designed to do so. There seems to
be no reason, however, why the software cannot be used
'on court' - providing suitable accomodation and mains
supply are provided. Data entry is managed via a
'Concept Keyboard', laid out to provide an ergonomic
interface between the operator and the game. At present,
the system has only been tested using a keyboard operator
and a 'caller' who is conversant with the game, but with
a little practice, a coach alone should be able to
combine both operations. The software takes in
information from one player only and records in sequence
for each stroke, the court area into which he moves,
together with the type of footwork pattern adopted. Data
is saved to disc following each rubber and the analysis
lists the frequency of each footwork pattern in each of
the ten defined areas for each rubber, and also totalled
over the game. No attempt has been made to extend the
analysis beyond simple frequency counts but the potential
for more detail is great. For example, it might be
useful to examine sequences of movements or to examine
the success or otherwise of each movement. The latter
would involve noting the outcome of each stroke (winner,
error, etc..) which, at present is not recorded. The
software is written in BBC BASIC and is fully structured
using a set of library procedures and comprehensive
error-trapping routines. The facility to present
analyses on screen between each rubber as well as produce
hard copy on a dot-matrix printer is integral to the
software.

4.2 Table Tennis Project
The Badminton project is concerned with player movement
and makes no attempt at tactical appraisal. In addition,
it is not concerned with real-time analysis. In
contrast, the table tennis project is concerned with
tactical play and intends to provide feedback to player
and coach during the match. In Scottish table tennis,
there are accepted principles by which the game 'should'
be played. Such principles are recognised by the
National Coach and are employed in the coaching of
National Youth Squads. However, the evaluation of these
principles is a problem area. Two difficulties seem to

be the general lack of recognition by the coaching fraternity of their value, and the difficulty in evaluating their effectiveness. The use of video can alleviate the last problem but, because it can only be used after the match, the value of immediate feedback is rendered impossible. It was considered that the use of a computer to record and analyse data would solve both problems, firstly by allowing rapid data capture and secondly, by providing a tool which together with 'friendly' software would encourage more coaches to take on board the value of tactical analysis.

The software is designed around the Concept Keyboard and handles data for one player. Information recorded for each rally includes the following:

whether or not the player serves or receives service.
whether the serve/reception is positive or negative.

whether the player plays the first attacking shot.
the nature of the player's final stroke.
the outcome of this stroke.

The operator is reminded of game and rally number, score and present data item (e.g., SERVICE, POSITIVE) through the screen display. Data is saved to disc and the following analyses are computed between each set, viz..

percentage number of positive serves.
percentage number of negative serves.
percentage number of positive service receptions.
percentage number of negative service receptions.
percentage number of times played the first attacking shot.
percentage number of times received the first attacking shot.
most effective and second most effective shot.
least effective and second least effective shot.

Both screen display and hard copy are available betwen sets and a final hardcopy of all analyses is available at the end of the match. As with the badminton project, the software is structured using BBC BASIC and is fully error-trapped including the facility to 'abort' a rally should a mistake on input be made.

At the time of writing the system presents problems relating to the speed of data capture. A critical factor is the manner in which the concept keyboard is designed. The total number of possible areas does not present a problem but discriminating between them does. At the moment, consideration is being given to the notion of

'texturing' some areas so that the operator can
distinguish them by feel, thus saving time by obviating
the need to look at the keyboard.

5. Field testing and development

The software as defined above is virtually complete but
has yet to undergo thorough field testing. It is
recognised that much work is to be done before the
software can be used with ease and success in the
coaching situation. Much will depend on user feedback to
tailor the software to the coach's requirements.

6. Workshop presentation

The workshop emphasis will be entirely practical. The
object will be to demonstrate to delegates the systems
described above, plus any further software developed in
the interim period. In addition, delegates will be given
the opportunity to observe and examine software presently
used in the Scottish School of Physical Education to
monitor various aspects of perceptual-motor performance
(e.g., maximal oxygen uptake, body fat, reaction time).

References

Brackenridge, C.H. and Alderson, G.J.K. (1985) Match
Analysis. Occasional paper, National Coaching
Foundation, Leeds.

Campbell, A. (1985) (Coaching Director, Scottish
Badminton Union), Personal communication, Feb.

THE ROLE OF THE PHYSICALLY DISABLED IN COACHING

I.STAFFORD
Department of Physical Education and Creative Studies, Sunderland
Polytechnic.

Abstract
The value of sport in the social and functional integration of
physically disabled individuals within the community is now widely
accepted. The central concern of this paper is with one specific
aspect of disabled individuals participating in sport i.e. as
coaches, and primarily, though not totally, as coaches of physically
disabled sportsmen/women. The basic premisses of the paper are that

    a) many physically disabled people lack the motivation,
preparation and opportunity to participate in mainstream community
sport and recreation, and
    b) there is little or no encouragement for physically disabled
individuals to assume coaching and leadership roles in community
sport.

As these issues form an integral part of a Sports Council Demonstration Project, the aims of this project are outlined in the
opening section. The work of related agencies is then examined in
relation to developing a policy of integrating the physically
disabled into the mainstream coaching structure of sport. The
benefits of this exercise are then identified in relation to the
disabled and the able-bodied. Finally recommendations for long and
short term planning are presented which involve the related agencies
in forging strong links to actively encourage this integration.
Key words: Physically disabled, Coaching, Sport, Integration.

Introduction

The valuable role of sport in the social and functional integration
of physically disabled individuals within the community is now
widely accepted, although it may be argued that this acceptance
has not always been developed into workable practice. The central
concern of this paper is with one particular level of participation
in sport which as yet, does not appear to be easily accessible to
the physically disabled i.e. coaching. Primarily, though not totally,
the focus will be on the role of the physically disabled in the
coaching of the physically disabled. The basic premisses of the
paper are that :

a) many physically disabled people lack the motivation, preparation and opportunity to participate in mainstream community sport and recreation, and

b) there is little or no active encouragement for physically disabled individuals to assume coaching, and other leadership roles in community sport.

'Bridging the Gap' - A Sports Council Demonstration Project

The central issues which are to be examined form an integral part of a Demonstration Project proposed to the Sports Council by Sunderland Polytechnic entitled 'Bridging the Gap'. The project's aims are as follows

1. To promote increased participation among physically disabled young people through integration in

a) mainstream physical education, and
b) community sport and recreation.

2. To promote increased involvement of physically disabled young people in coaching, officiating and administrative roles in sport and recreation.

3. To promote collaboration between education, local government, the governing bodies of sport and the wider community in the provision for, and support of, participation and integration in sport with specific reference to swimming, athletics and outdoor activities.

Although the project confines itself to swimming,athletics and outdoor activities and the survey area is limited to parts of the North-East of England it has been designed, and shall be undertaken, in such a way that it should be easily repeatable in other areas and for other sports. 'Bridging the Gap' has been accepted in principle by The Sports Council and is scheduled to begin in the autumn of 1986. By the end of the proposed three year duration of the project the major barriers to integration will have been identified and recommendations submitted as to how these may be overcome. After collating data from initial surveys on e.g. participation, provision and attitudes within both education institutions and community clubs, leadership training courses will be instigated in order to actively encourage participation at all levels.

Role of related agencies

As many, if not most coaches, come into coaching as an extension of their involvement as a performer, the long term development of greater numbers of well-trained, physically disabled coaches is dependent to a large extent on physically disabled sportsmen and women being both actively encouraged and well coached during their involvement as performers and competitors. The greater the base of participants the greater the number of interested and committed people available to involve themselves at all levels within sport. This claim does assume an effective structure exists within sport to promote participation at the various levels required to sustain efficient functioning. Thus, in relation to long term planning, it is of paramount importance that physically disabled performers have not only the equality of opportunity to participate,but also to develop their skills, which is dependent upon expert, committed coaches working with them.

The British Sports Association for the Disabled (B.S.A.D.) in conjunction with the National Coaching Foundation (N.C.F.) are making efforts to encourage this vital first stage in the long term investment. In the N.C.F. courses for coaches a unit of study entitled 'Coaching disabled people' has been prepared by Dr.Bob Price (1985), the Director of B.S.A.D. In the paper which lays the foundation for this unit Dr.Price identifies certain attitudonal barriers to the successful encouragement of coaches becoming involved in working with disabled sportsmen and women. In summarising what should be the rights of all people in sport Dr.Price further identifies the right "to have access to qualified leadership". If this right is denied to the physically disabled then it may well be argued that the right "to have an equal opportunity to strive for excellence", will also have been significantly impaired.

The Central Council of Physical Recreation (C.C.P.R.) has established the Community Sports Leaders Award Scheme. In this scheme it is most encouraging to note that at the outset, in explaining the aim of the course, provision has been made for any prospective candidate who is disabled. By the simple inclusion of an explanatory paragraph and the accompanying undertaking to provide advice and assistance for disabled candidates the C.C.P.R. is stating that

a) disabled individuals are welcomed into the scheme and further that

b) efforts will be made, through the support services offered, to alleviate any attendant problems.

As part of the proposed C.C.P.R. Higher Award in Community Sports Leadership candidates are required to choose two 'Community Groups' to study. One of these options is 'Sport and the Physically Handicapped' which will be undertaken with B.S.A.D. It is to be hoped that two fundamental benefits which will accrue from this scheme are that more quality, able-bodied people will become interested in working with the physically disabled and also that physically disabled people with an interest or active involvement in sport will use this as a valuable vehicle to obtain a recognised qualification in sports leadership. If such a positive approach is adopted by other agencies involved in coach education, such as governing bodies, this would be a valuable investment in the process of integrating physically disabled individuals into mainstream sport.

Problems - not insurmountable

The criticism may well be levelled that although the ideals presented
are extremely laudable, many practical problems do exist which will
hinder the progress of the phyiscally disabled into the coaching
structure. Although it is conceded that certain sports are more
tractable regarding access for disabled coaches, many of the barriers
which cynics may identify are not insurmountable given a positive
approach, specialist knowledge and appropriate support resources.
This sentiment is central to the rationale of the Disabled Living
Foundation (1977) who make the following statement; "The underlying
philosophy continues that if the environment of the disabled is
carefully studied, then ways can be found in subsequent action to
return opportunities in life which have hitherto been lost".

In such a short examination, as it is not possible to explore all
the problems of gaining access to coaching courses and qualifications
in even one specific sport, a practical example may suffice to make
the point. Swimming is perhaps one sport where physically disabled
people have participated in relatively large numbers. It is also
a sport which is accepted as providing many tangible theraputic
benefits for the physically disabled. If the suggestion was proposed
that the disabled should be widely accepted into the coaching structure, however, many fears might be expressed regarding poolside safety.
If the number of qualified swimming teachers and coaches is then
compared to the much larger number of qualified life-savers then
fears for the safety of swimmers, disabled or able-bodied, under
the charge of a disabled coach could be allayed by ensuring that
a suitably qualified life-saver is always in attendance. Again
the criticism may be evident that this is not only wasteful of
staffing but financially and practically limiting. If, however,
certain new proposals regarding the safety of supervision in
swimming pools are accepted, then every swimming teacher or coach
will be required to have a qualified lifeguard in attendance throughout the session. This new safety requirement may well negate much
of the argument against accepting physically disabled coaches into the
mainstream coaching structure in swimming.

The value of the exercise

Implicit in this exposition so far is the assumption that general
acceptance exists regarding the value of integrating able-bodied
and disabled people in sport. Although this may well be the case
it is still a valid exercise to identify the specific benefits which
it is hoped would accrue as a result of recruiting more physically
disabled individuals into coaching. Indeed the argument may be
advanced that it is because of the aforementioned assumption that
the major thrusts of the integration issue have not been put as
forcibly as they might have been. The specific issue to be
addressed here is in relation to the advantages which may be gained
by increasing the numbers of expert and qualified physically disabled

coaches. Perhaps the most obvious advantage is that more qualified coaches will be available to work on improving sportsmen and sportswomen, both disabled and able-bodied. With the physically disabled coaching the physically disabled surely the attitudonal barriers, which have been suggested exist within able-bodied coaches in relation to working with disabled performers, would cease to be a problem. Also, whereas certain physically disabled performers may never be able to compete at a similar level to those who are able-bodied, their disability may have little or no effect on their coaching ability and thus perhaps improve self-esteem while making able-bodied coaches and even performers question any prejudices they harbour concerning disabled individuals. As much of the relevant literature is at pains to point out, disability is not the same as inability and also that any accompanying handicap is likely to be more of a consequence of the erection of certain barriers, mainly by the able-bodied.

If,as in lots of cases,the prime prerequisite of a coach of disabled individuals is a sensitivity to and an awareness of those individuals needs combined with an expert knowledge of the sport, then who is better suited to fulfilling that role than someone who has personal knowledge and experience of the disability, the sport, and how one may effect the other? The improved access into coaching for the physically disabled would extend their involvement in sport in a most valuable manner in that the leadership role and the responsibility such a position entails would perhaps do much to elevate the status of the physically disabled not only in the eyes of the able-bodied but also from their personal viewpoint. As the Disabled Living Foundation (1977) point out

"the disabled have too often been 'written off' as far
as physical recreation is concerned - by themselves and
by the public at large. This attitude has deprived many
of the pleasures and physical and psychological help which
they might have had; further it has helped to build up a
quite unnecessary division between the handicapped and wholly
fit".

Conclusion

Many approaches are in evidence regarding the integration of the physically disabled into sport,from the conceptual approaches reviewed by Craney (1981) in Australia to the practical "Community Recreation Mainstreaming" outlined by Thompson and Zito (1981) in the United States of America. Certainly the development of a wide base of good, qualified, physically disabled coaches will depend to a great extent on the efficiency of the coaching structure to recruit and train those disabled individuals. Thus a commitment is needed from the related agencies such as B.S.A.D., C.C.P.R. and the various governing bodies to actively encourage and take positive steps to cater for the physically disabled in coaching. This commitment not only involves critical introspection in relation to how their own coaching schemes are presently structured but also an obligation to forge links wherever necessary so that the needs of the physically disabled are given precedent over any parochial or protectionist interests which might exist.

In the short term however, and at the most basic level, the belief is stated by Dr.Price (1985) that the "only real need is for 'someone who knows' to come along and show them how". It is to be hoped that by providing a good and qualified service of physically disabled coaches that this not only provides the sympathetic but also the empathetic coaching that physically disabled sportsmen and sportswomen require.

References

Craney, J. (1981) Recreation and disability four conceptual approaches Australian Journal for Health, Physical Education and Recreation Autumn, 21-26.
Disabled Living Foundation (1977) Sport and Physical Recreation for the Disabled. Disabled Living Foundation, London.
Price, R.(1985) Coaching Disabled People. National Coaching Foundation Leeds.
Rehabilitation Research Institute (1983) Fair Play. The George Washington University, Washington D.C.
Scottish Sports Council (1985) Disabled People and Sport. The Scottish Sports COuncil in association with the Scottish Standing Conference of Sport and the Scottish Sports Association for the Disabled, Edinburgh.
Thompson, G. and Zito, A.J. (1981) Community Recreation Mainstreaming University of Missouri-Columbia Extension Division, Columbia.

NATIONAL COACHING FOUNDATION INFORMATION SERVICES

CAROLYNN RANKIN
The National Coaching Foundation

Abstract
The National Coaching Foundation (NCF) information services are being designed and developed to meet the needs of practising coaches, and to support the technical coach education programmes. This paper describes the present NCF services and proposed future developments. The Coaching Focus subscription service encourages direct contact with individual coaches, and the PRESTEL viewdata service is being used to disseminate information to a disparate audience of coaches. Recognising the need to 'bridge the gap' between sports science and the practising coach, the NCF is establishing a bibliographic database using sophisticated information retrieval software. The NCF want coaches to exploit local information services and this will be assisted by the development of the National Network Centres. Many countries have experience and expertise in providing information services of this type, and the NCF will greatly benefit from establishing future channels of communication and co-operation. The National Coaching Foundation coaching database and PRESTEL will be demonstrated during the workshop session.
Key words: National Coaching Foundation, Information services.

1. Introduction

The National Coaching Foundation was established by the Sports Council in 1983 to develop a comprehensive coach education programme throughout the United Kingdom. The main aim was to provide coaches with access to a body of knowledge not necessarily sport specific, but relevant to performance at all levels. An important aspect of the Foundation's role is the provision of information services for coaches. An information officer was appointed in September 1984 to develop appropriate information systems. To help promote this role the phrase 'Providing a service for coaches' is used on the NCF's publicity materials.

The information services are being developed with the following key functions:-

(a) to provide a co-ordinating role for information on all aspects of coaching

(b) to systematically process all relevant material

(c) to evaluate, adapt and 'package' information according to the needs of the particular user group ('bridging the gap' between sports scientists/researchers and coaches)

(d) to disseminate information by a variety of means.

2. Information Technology

To provide an effective service to coaching, the flow of information needs to be organised. The NCF is operating in a United Kingdom capacity, potentially liaising with all governing bodies of sport. In 1985 it was decided that the use of information technology would assist the organisation to carry out its co-operative role. A micro-computer was acquired, enabling the NCF to use database management and information retrieval software as the basis of the system.

3. The User Group

Coaches in the United Kingdom are a disparate group, and will have varying expectations of an information service. The NCF's coach education programme is structured on 4 levels catering from beginner coach to top national coach, and the information services must be flexible enough to cope with differing levels of enquiry. Initially the information services are being developed to support and enhance the NCF's technical programme.

Developing an effective information service is very much a 2-way process. It would be counter-productive to develop services in isolation of the potential users - or a system may be created that no-one finds particularly useful.

4. Awareness

A fundamental problem to overcome is making initial contact with coaches, and then maintaining that contact. The Coaching Focus subscription service for coaches was launched in April 1985, and a year's subscription is £5. To date there are over 1,000 members, and governing bodies are offered a special rate for bulk membership.

Coaching Focus is published twice a year and each issue deals with a topic of concern to the world of coaching. Topics covered so far include 'Drugs in Sport', 'Competitive Sport and Young Children' and 'Coaching as a Profession'. Coaching Focus is not an academic journal, nor is it a chatty newsletter, but a balance of the two. Contributors are invited to present their viewpoints on the subject under discussion. A bibliography is prepared to support each issue, and coaches who wish to research the subject are invited to contact the NCF office for further information.

Subscribers to Coaching Focus regularly receive up-to-date information on courses, new publications and products, and are actively encouraged to make use of the NCF services. Coaching Focus has helped to promote awareness of the NCF to a very wide readership. We hope to maintain contact by providing a relevant and efficient enquiry service.

Contributors are invited to present their viewpoints on the subject under discussion.

5. NCF In-House Databases

5.1 Register of Experts

Governing body national and senior coaches will have considerable expertise in the technical and tactical aspects of their own sport, but may often want to call upon the services of other specialists in tackling particular problems. To provide a service to coaches at this level the NCF is gradually building up a computerised register of sports scientists and coaches with particular expertise who have expressed a willingness to be involved with NCF services. This service is being developed in co-operation with the British Association of National Coaches and the British Association of Sports Sciences. For example, the national archery coach may request advice on acclimatisation and nutrition for competition abroad; the bowls coach may want a sport psychologist to advise on preparation for competition.

This service is still at an early stage of development, but the NCF welcome requests of this nature from governing bodies. The register is also invaluable to NCF staff as it provides information on potential course tutors or possible contributors to our publications!

5.2 NCF Coaching Database

The NCF wish to ensure that coaches have access to the common body of knowledge underlying the fundamentals of good coaching. Coaches attending the courses programme are given suggested further reading, but the aim is to encourage all coaches to search further and make use of the wealth of information available.

The NCF decided that the best way to provide an effective service for coaches was to create a unique bibliographic database. This will provide an on-line catalogue of 'library' records, enabling users to carry out complex subject searches. It was decided that all information added to the NCF coaching database will be evaluated and carefully abstracted. Often coaches will want information in a particular form. They may not want a bibliography listing 50 highly technical research articles, as this tends to produce the 'so what' response. The coach wants information that can be applied to practical situations and will probably find it useful to have an overview of the most recent information written in a language that can be understood.

The decision to create a specialised database was easily taken – the choice of appropriate computer software was more difficult. The

NCF wanted to buy an information retrieval package that was already tested and in operation and which could run on the existing micro-computer (an IBM PC AT). The MICROCAIRS software was eventually selected as it has a good track record and was designed in an information department to carry out the sort of work the NCF wanted – collecting, indexing, retrieval, dissemination and the production of catalogues. MICROCAIRS is also used by the Sports Documentation Centre at the University of Birmingham, and compatible systems are being planned to enable future co-operation.

The NCF system design is almost complete. All recommended texts to support the courses for coaches programme are now on the database. Information on journal articles, research reports, books, and audio-visual productions will be added and it is intended that members of BANC, BASS and BASM will co-operate in the evaluation of material and the production of abstracts. It will take time to build up the coaching database as the policy is to be selective. An important aspect of the system is the indexing, or the adding of key words to enable retrieval. The language problem has to be overcome to enable coaches and sports scientists to make use of each other's terminology. The NCF intends to expand the thesaurus used by the Sports Council to include terminology relevant to coaching. If the indexing language used is carefully controlled from the outset, the database will be a much more effective resource for coaches.

MICROCAIRS is a very powerful package and will enable the NCF to produce technical bulletins and current awareness services for coaches. It can also be used to generate printed indexes so that a 'hard copy' of the computer record can be produced. The intention is that each centre operating NCF courses will have a hard copy of the relevant sections of the NCF coaching database for reference use by coaches. Looking further into the future, the coaching database may eventually be available on-line for access by remote users.

6. Viewdata

Viewdata services offer great potential for reaching the individual coach. The NCF are in the process of setting up a special service specifically for coaches on the British Telecom PRESTEL network. This will initially operate under the umbrella of the Sports Council, who have been Information Providers on the system since 1979. The NCF hope to encourage governing bodies and individual coaches to make use of this service. Most people already have access to a telephone and television – it only needs some additional equipment and they are well on the way to using viewdata!

Information on the system will include details of the NCF publications and course opportunities. The viewdata service can also be used for current awareness, by keeping users up to date with anything that may be of interest to the world of coaching. An electronic mail system enables coaches to send messages to the NCF – so the information pages can be designed in response to requests.

'Closed user groups' are already available on PRESTEL for farmers and the legal and medical professions. The NCF look forward to offering coaches the opportunity to use this technology and hope it will provide a worthwhile service.

7. Future Developments

7.1 Level 3 Course - "How to find out more..."
The NCF coach development programme is being expanded to include a series of courses with an underlying principle of moving towards innovation. It is proposed to offer a course on 'How to find out more - information retrieval and management'. The aim is to allow coaches to:-

(a) gain an understanding of library and information systems
(b) be aware of the range of resources available
(c) make maximum use of information gathered.

This will be offered as a pilot project before being considered for inclusion in a national programme.

7.2 National Coaching Centres
The NCF network of National Coaching Centres based at Institutes of Higher Education will play a vital role in the provision of services for coaches. The availability of a wide range of resources is a necessary part of successful coaching, and this will include access to library facilities. The NCF information centre will support the services offered by the national coaching centres, and will aim to establish co-operative ventures. An important aspect of this work is to encourage coaches to exploit local information resources and this can be facilitated by the Sport and Recreation Information Group.

8. Conclusion

The information services of the National Coaching Foundation are being designed and developed to meet the needs of practising coaches and to support the technical coach education programme. The NCF information services are in their infancy. Many countries have greater experience and expertise in providing these support services, and it is hoped that delegates from abroad would wish to 'trade' experiences and establish future channels of communication.

Through a process of co-operation the National Coaching Foundation would benefit considerably in fulfilling its purpose of providing British coaches with the services they need and deserve.

A STUDY OF PRACTICE RELATED TO THEORY OF THE COACH EDUCATION SYSTEM
FOR TRACK AND FIELD ATHLETICS IN THE U.K.

HAMISH McD. TELFER, D.P.E., B.A.
Centre for Physical Education, University of Lancaster

Abstract
This paper investigates the relationship between theory and practice
at various levels of coaching awards. It identifies the two principle
areas of theoretical constructs and practical application, and research in the form of case studies is undertaken to establish whether
the content of the education programme enhances the ability of the
coach to communicate more effectively and to widen the method of his
or her approach. Specific areas are investigated:

(a) Communication skill and command of the coaching environment
as well as fluency in expression.
(b) Programme Planning and Training Method.
(c) The ability to re-assess and modify sessions and planning
related to training performance.

The paper concludes that experience of the education system of training track and field coaches may assist in the drawing up of other
coaching programmes since it is suggested that the bridge between
theory and practice is not there. The practical case studies
emphasise the need to establish a more student centred than subject
centred approach to coaching; while modular examples of the coaching
process are given, coaching roles discussed, and the art and science
of coaching evaluated, these are of little consequence if communication of theory into practice is neglected.
Key Words: Coaching theory, Communication, Coaching practice, Athlete
preparation, Training methodology, Coach perception.

Coaching Award System

This paper precis Track and Field athletics in the U.K. which has a
three tier system of qualification of Assistant Club Coach, Club
Coach and Senior Coach. At all three levels the coach is involved
in relating theoretical systems and designs of coaching to observation
of practice, and at Club Coach and Senior Coach level a practical
assessment is undertaken. All coaches must enter the system at
Assistant Club Coach level which necessitates some 16 hours of theory
and no compulsory practical coaching component. Courses are normally
of a two day, one weekend nature and no formal assessment of practical

ability is undertaken; the "logged hours" system being adopted for
final qualification.

The author has been involved in the system as an Area Event Coach
for Northern England and as Co-ordinator for all courses in North
West England since the inception of the present system during the
season 1979/1980. Each year over one hundred coaches in the North
West of England move through the system, numbers growing yearly.

During assessments of Club Coaches it became evident to coach
award assessors that although technical knowledge was improving, the
ability to communicate effectively and to coach was showing no significant signs of improvement. Coaches were failing to appreciate
the individuality of their charges, training sessions were not
modified if they showed signs of not achieving the desired result and
the ability to direct athletes attentions and efforts to the task in
hand was generally poor.

Since one of the principle criteria of any coaching education
system should be the ability to communicate and to modify method of
coaching relative to athletic performance, the author set out to
examine the nature and extent of the problem in relation to the first
level coaching award, that of Assistant Club Coach. It was felt that
course design needs to reflect not only the technical training of
coaches but also to improve the practice of coaching by improving
methods of communication and the capacity to modify practical training sessions.

Case Study Method

Subjects were identified on a random basis on application for their
level one award (Assistant Club Coach) and on the basis of various
coaching environments. 20 subjects were selected for review prior to
attending the course, of which three cases are given in this short
extract.

Subjects were contacted on the basis of the facility available
(synthetic track or cinder track; good field event facility or poor;
indoor facilities as well as outdoor etc.) and in relation to their
club as to whether they worked in a large coaching community or small
community. Since applicants at this level are assumed to be coaching
beginners and perhaps in more than one group of events, general points
were identified as being fundamental to the study. They were:

(a) Fundamental technical knowledge
(b) Leadership style
(c) Communication effectiveness
(d) Ability to handle individuals within groups.

This limited range was felt sufficient to establish whether the coach
could deal with athletes in relation to those areas highlighted by
assessors as being poor. This initial empirical study followed the
same format as is laid down for assessors and although the study was
conducted at level one as opposed to the assessed level two (Club
Coach award), the same marking guidelines were used since it was felt
that marking relevance was necessary. It made sense to use the same

criteria in the study as would be used in assessment albeit in more
depth in the specific areas detailed above.

The objective was to review the subject before and after their
attendance at a course and to establish whether any change had occurred in the practice of their coaching as a result of information
received on course.

Case 1 (prior to course)

This course applicant was coaching in a large club with a well established coaching system. He had been team coaching for the previous
three years coming into the sport when his daughter had joined the
club. He was in his middle thirties and was working with a group of
800/1500 metre male athletes between the ages of eleven and fourteen.
The club enjoyed good facilities and a strong committee structure
ensuring good organisation and had the use of cinder and synthetic
tracks.

All three subjects reviewed were aware of my presence but not of my
intentions and proceeded to take charge of the group and conduct the
session.

During the session and using the established criteria set out for
assessing coaching sessions at level two (Club Coach award) the
following notes were made of coaching performance.

Appropriateness of session was deemed satisfactory for all of the
participants although a wide range of ability was evident in the nine
athletes concerned. No attempt was made to modify the session in the
light of the disparity in group ability and all athletes completed
the session but with inevitable differences in training effect.

Those athletes performing at the required level were given almost
exclusive attention while four of the nine received no communication
from the subject at all during the recovery periods and only on three
occasions during the running phase of the session. The remaining
five received almost constant verbal attention and encouragement but
no information of a technical nature was imparted, the communication
being exclusively encouraging and motivational.

The session time was thirty five minutes excluding warm up and warm
down, during which the subject made no contact with the group during
the warm up phase and made no attempt to explain or modify the session
to the athletes. All athletes were given the session and target times
were to be achieved by all athletes. The subject was clearly in
command of the session being visible to the group and audible. In all
the subject communicated to the group or individuals on one hundred
and forty seven occasions, all of which were related to encouragement
and none to elements of technical coaching (relaxing, stride rate,
arm carriage, leg cadence, altering target time in relation to effort,
etc.). The subject did not move from the start and finish line at any
time during the session.

A brief review of the coach in charge revealed a similar pattern of
behaviour. Although performing well in terms of controlling the
session, Case 1 would not have scored well in a formal assessment for
communication to individuals, session relevance to individuals and in
method and style of communication.

318

Case 2

This course applicant was a seventeen year old athlete who had decided
to take up coaching after injury had effectively ended her career as
an athlete.

Working on her own in a small club with a cinder track, she was
coaching a small group of four girls between the ages of twelve and
fourteen, all sprinters. Warm up was led by the subject and she
actively participated in the session up to the main practice. Her
communication consisted almost exclusively of verbal command and
personal demonstration followed by practice, the result being a copy
of the subject's actions, some of them incorrect.

No attempts were made to encourage and technical points were all
limited to effort rather than movement pattern. The subject showed
good control of the session but session quality seemed to be of low
priority in relation to effort. Communication tended to be mono-
syllabic and technical advice was limited to repetition with no focus
on appropriate movement pattern. She was not fluent and found much
difficulty in expressing herself without resorting to demonstration.

Case 3

The subject was a parent of an athlete who showed ability. The
session reviewed was exclusively tailored to his son's needs with
other athletes joining in. He professed to coach the group over the
400 metre event and worked in a poor club structure. Facilities were
poor and the club had no corporate identity with three other coaches
taking their own groups in isolation of each other.

The session reviewed was familiar to all athletes who took part and
the session was conducted in almost complete silence. The subject
made no attempt to communicate while the athletes were working and
during recoveries communicated only on seven occasions; five times to
his son and twice to other athletes. The subject did not move from
the finish line where he shouted times as they passed, and athletes
had to signal their start to him from the other side of the track.
This subject talked exclusively to his son after warm down and made no
attempt to discuss the session with the other athletes.

Conclusions

From the case studies it became apparent that while in some cases
technical knowledge was being gained through trial and error, and
handed down information, communication style and coaching methodology
were consistently lacking. Accepting that a good basic grounding is
necessary with youngsters in all aspects of training and conditioning,
it follows that those coaches involved with youngsters in their formative years should be equipped to deal with these elements and that
their method and style of approach should be conditioned by a sound
coach education structure reflecting this.

All three subjects attended an Assistant Club Coach Course, two
attending the same course and one attending another, but in both cases
the staff of the courses were the same. The course content at the
Assistant Club Coach level covers the following broad areas: Coaching

the Growing Child, Organisation of the Sport, Safety, Skill, Strength and Mobility plus Athletics as part of an Athletes Life, Exercises and their Selection and Planning the Programme. The second day of the course weekend covers the events grouped as Throws, Jumps, Sprints and Endurance events.

While coaching "hints" and "tips" are given, no formal contact with coaching method or communication techniques is undertaken.

A review of each of the three case studies after course attendance revealed similar changes and modifications true to the total sample. Both Cases 1 and 2 showed evidence of more sophisticated planning and training method but on post course observation their method and style of coaching had not significantly altered. Subject 1 communicated considerably more to the whole group perhaps showing a greater aware- ness of group contact and the need for individual attention. Subject 3 showed no evidence of a change in handling his training session. In all three subjects there was no change apparent in vocabulary, in communicating individually to athletes or of realising individuality within group sessions.

As a result of these pilot case studies a further study is in progress based on more objective criteria in analysing case studies with regard to communication style and coaching methodology. Further studies will now attempt to identify specific features in coaching related to the various coaching methodologies adopted by coaches.

Coach Survey

In order to meet the demands of the coaches on course it was necessary to identify certain key areas relevant to a study of theory related to practice. A general survey was undertaken of all course attenders at Assistant Club Coach level during the period 1983/4 and 1984/5 and three hundred and fifty eight questionnaires were sent out one year after completion of the course. The aim of the questionnaire was to establish the experience of the attenders, the extent to which they felt they had been "taught to coach" and whether the course design and content was seen as relevant to their needs. It is worth remembering that a qualification is not compulsory in order to coach in the U.K., course attendance being voluntary.

A return of 37.7% showed that newcomers to coaching formed the larger element; 62.2% compared to 37.7% who professed some experience of coaching prior to course attendance. Of those who had not coached prior to attendance 53.5% believed that the course had taught them "how to coach" while the remaining 41.6% of respondents to this question did not believe that the course had helped in this issue. Of those who had coached prior to the course the ratio was similar with 52.9% believing that the course had taught them "how to coach" while the remaining 43.1% of the respondents did not believe so.

When questioned on communication with their athletes being improved by course attendance, 82.9% believed that course attendance had improved this element and gave reasons primarily relating to technical knowledge rather than communication style of method. Clearly the case studies differ from the coaches perception of their own behaviour. When asked if the course was suitable to their needs the answer proved

similar to that of communication effectiveness with their athletes
(79.2%). Despite this however certain features relating to course
structure need to be reviewed since it would appear that 48.1% of all
attenders felt that the course contained an incorrect balance between
theory and practice, the emphasis being too theoretical. An interesting feature of the questionnaire was the response of 45.9% of all
coaches who believed that prior to course they were good at practical
coaching.

The relationship between the coaches' perception of their own
performance and with regard to the course design and structure appears
to be at variance with the aim of the course and with the changes that
the coaches believe to have occurred after attendance at a course. It
would appear that there exists a poorer relationship between coaching
theory and the effect of the course on attenders than has previously
been thought.

The questionnaire also focused on areas that they would modify as a
result of course attendance, as well as drop out rate and alteration
of approach to coaching.

Conclusion

While this pilot study was set up initially to establish whether
coaches were communicating more effectively as a result of attendance
at course, the lack of evidence of the nature and extent of coaching
prior to attendance was limiting. The use of case study prior to and
following course attendance in addition to questionnaire information
reveals that the system for training track and field coaches in the
U.K. appears on the one hand to be successful at imparting technical
knowledge but poor in teaching ways in which this information is
passed from coach to athlete.

Those who have experience have different perceptions of their
performance than those who are new to the sport. This study in its
formative stages is moving from a general study to specific areas of
the study of communication skills in courses training track and field
coaches and highlights and challenges assumptions made by Governing
Bodies as to the effectiveness of their coaching courses on coach -
athlete communication in training sessions.

BRITISH COACHING: HOW DO WE BEGIN TO MOVE TOWARDS A PROFESSION?

P.J. TREADWELL
Department of Physical Education and Human Movement Studies,
South Glamorgan Institute of Higher Education, Cardiff

Abstract
Coaching goes back many centuries, and it seems, has always had a
pervading influence on sport society. Today in Britain, sport is
clearly a central component of popular culture, and we might assume
that this 'man of exercise' would be held in high esteem. But,
ever since the 1850's when sports became formalised and athleticism
predominated the games player has become deified not the coach.
Indeed the coach in Britain is probably now one of our most
maligned individuals in the occupational structure of work society.
Why is this? What could change this? The paper examines
behavioural aspects of coaching and investigates the whole sub-
cultural world of the coach. It suggests that apsects of
competition and industrial capitalism have externalised coaching
into the simple concern for records, results and money. The irony
is that as we strive for great professionalism of both athlete and
coach we remove any concern for a humanistic element in sport. Also
it suggests that a pragmatic approach to coaching is still
fundamentally important but that a greater degree of sophistication
and certainty is required. In other countries, both socialist and
capitalist, developed and developing, this innovation is being
created via coach education programmes. British coaches should
grasp the nettle of coach education and utilize it to give birth
to a cogent, cohert profession, from which could all prosper.
Key words: Coaching, sub-culture, professionalism.

1. Introduction

If you wander around a display of ancient Greet pottery in the
British Museum, you will see the image of the trainer, rod in hand,
controlling athletes in their pursuit of physical excellence.
Coaching goes back many centuries, and always seems to have had a
strong influence on sport society. Those early 'paidotribes' have
become today's coaches who, as in the past, engage in technical
instruction, training-programme design and scientific assessment.
Sport is their industrial arena, and what results is, without
question, a central component of British popular culture. So we
might assume that this 'man of exercise' would be held in high
esteem. Ever since the 1850s, when games became organised in the
public schools, universities and society we have worshipped sport.
But in those days of Victorian athleticism the games player became
the nation's hero. Some, like W.G. Grace, were born from actual

exploits; others, such as Tom Brown, had their origins in fiction.
Few people would have placed the coach on such a pedestal. To be
seen as a professional, or to be applauded for being 'professional'
in one's approach, were not tolerated or striven for. As Lovesey
(1979) has written, some early athletics trainers made a living
'assisting gentlemen with the breathings' and disclosing the lore of
tactics whilst they massaged young mens bodies with their gruesome
embrocated flesh gloves. But activities were really for men of a
lower class. Coaches were then seen as uneducated, profane and
persons of lower character - truly second-class citizens! I would
suggest that right from those early days the coach at all levels of
British sport has probably been more maligned than any other person
in our occupational structure. But why is this? Surely we should
have paid greater homage to the likes of Sam Mussabini, the
architect of Harold Abraham's success, and seen him as a pioneer
rather than as a dark, deviant character, and also Jack White, the
'Gateshead Clipper' of the 1870s retained as an athletic trainer
by Cambridge University AC.

2. Behavioural aspects of coaching

Coaching is, in essence, about human relationships: those between
coach and athlete, and coach and organisation. Coaches are
significant role models for their charges. They instil such
important values as competitiveness, aggressiveness, hard work,
discipline, subordination of self to the success of the team, and a
striving for excellence. Listen to their dressing-room rhetoric
and, like the embrocation, a heady mix is apparent. Coaches have
a profound influence on athletes, particularly young athletes.
Children, or mini-adults as they have been wrongly dubbed, are
often willing slaves because of the dream of sporting success.   But
what is it that coaches transmit to their athletes? Hopefully, they
are a positive influence, serving as parental substitutes and
providing a high degree of morality, fairness, humaneness and
personal maturity.
    However, sport is a sub-cultural world based on competition and
born of industrial capitalism. Many coaches, I fear, exhibit
negative traits; and the image of a man who is opportunist, scheming
capable of cheating, characterless and thoroughly without principle
is increasingly common! Nobility, generosity and chivalry are now
only infrequently seen at our sporting arenas. The modern sport
hero is often an ill-tempered, selfish champion, due largely to
this craving for elite performance rather than simple participation.
The concern is only for records, results and money. There is the
danger that as we strive for greater professionalism in our approach
to coaching and in our demands for a professional commitment to
training and competition from our athletes, we run the grave risk
of brutalising and demeaning them. Indeed, our exploitation of
young children in some 'youth' sports like gymnastics and swimming
is akin to 19th-century industrial malpractice. Here, coaches'
training demands are often physically humiliating. Sport as a
developer of sound character becomes, in these environments, a

complete falsehood. In reality, the coach simply dehumanises the athlete by autocratic behaviour. Good coaching should build autonomous, self-reliant, self-disciplined individuals. The Olympic motto Citius, Altius, Fortius ('faster, higher, stronger'), should not be attained simply by means of coaching which initiates submission, compliance, dependence and conformity. While seeking professionalism in the promotion of excellence, we must equally have a high regard for moral and ethical principles. We must embody a concern for living as well as for success.

3. The sub-cultural world of coaching

It has been suggested that the inherent pressures and conflicts associated with the role of coach lead to withdrawal from extensive relationships with others. This promotes the existence of a sporting sub-culture where coaches share common values, beliefs and customs. It provides an occupational milieu in which coaches can seek the salvation, support and information needed to cope with everyday problems. In Britain, however, I feel it is ironic that this coaching sub-culture, although providing valuable support for coaches, has tended to be somewhat restrictive and therefore to discourage experimentation and innovation. The world of amateur and professional soccer coaching is an example of this. Perhaps the British athletics coaching system is an example of what is possible. As early as February 1914 they offered Walter Knox, a Scots Canadian the position of salaried Chief Coach in an attempt to improve field events standards. War terminated real development, but the AAA's Achilles connection' of Malcolm Nokes, Sandy Duncan and Roland Harper gave us the idea of the Loughborough Summer School in 1934. Indeed, they it were who appointed Major Geoff Dyson as Chief Coach in 1947 (with a little assistance of £1,500 from the News of the World!).
But few bodies have been as radical as BANC, the British Association of National Coaches. They it was who promulgated the idea of a 'market stall' approach to coach education, which by its very nature demands a sharing of knowledge between sports practitioner and sports theorist. The inference underlying this point is that a change in the definition of the role of the coach, or in the make-up of the coach's role-set, could lead to beneficial changes in coaching behaviour and ultimately to improvement in sport performance. Coaches, I feel, have a responsibility to themselves and to sport in general. Sportspeople should be creative and imaginative as well as just seeking excellence in performance. The profession of coaching can only do this by extending its physical and intellectual boundaries, rather than contracting towards a narrow sub-culture of ex-players with a sweaty 'jock' image.

4. A comparative perspective

The way forward is a clear programme of coach education. Unfortunately, for many years any move towards a sophisticated, institutionalised approach to coaching in Great Britain has been regarded as a threat to the upper-class, amateur-based ethic controlling sport. Geoffrey Dyson had to fight against this right from the start in 1947. As a result, we have become a second-rate sporting nation when compared with others, particularly certain socialist states or the USA. We must learn from their approaches to the profession of coaching.

In the Soviet Union, coaches are the most important figures in sport, with the majority having detailed knowledge of sports science and medicine. Coaches require an official license, and this is only acquired after extensive study through evening classes or correspondence courses (five years), or via full-time diploma/degree courses at any of the 20 'schools' for coaches, 26 physical-culture institutes or 170 physical-education faculties at colleges or universities. Therefore an incredible depth of expert talent exists, able to work with athletes of all ages and ability. Interestingly, when on their courses, the trainee coaches are very much student practitioners - doing 30 weeks' coaching in schools, clubs, factories or pioneer camps. They learn a foreign language in order to study foreign systems and coaching methodology. Theirs is a system and a sub-culture that is highly professional, and recognised as such. In fact, in a recent analysis of the work of coaches at Institutes of physical culture in Moscow, Leningrad and Kiev assesors honed in on the importance of how to 'apply' knowledge. Their present scientific approach to coaching reduces the subjectivism we are prone to. The ultimate accolade is that Soviet coaches can aspire to the Order of Lenin just as do Soviet politicians and eminent cultural figures. Much the same philosophy exists in the German Democratic Republic where arguably the world's finest institutions for athlete and coach exists at Leipzig in the guise of the DHFK, the College of Physical Culture.

It is, admittedly, dangerous to compare like with unlike, because in reality we are dealing with vastly different models of what the coach is in relation to the state. Matters are made explicitly clear in the Eastern bloc: sport reflects political ideology and the development of socialist unity - a consciousness of the body politic, individual welfare and happiness. But it is also fundamentally encapsulates a professionalism and respect for coaching that does not any may never exist in Great Britain. Anybody can coach in our islands; you do not have to seek qualifications in order to practise, neither are you re-assessed bi-annually. It is a chalk-to-cheese comparison which even other Western countries are seeking to alter. The 'Trainerakademie' in the idyllic environment of the Sports University of Cologne offers training for senior coaches over an eighteen-month period, as does the Institut INSEP in Paris. Innovative diploma courses with a high analytical coaching content are rare in Great Britain, with only Dunfermline and Carnegie Colleges existing as prototypes for what could be offered nationwide. Sports 'leaders' awards schemes have recently emerged in England, as has the 'Operation Sport' scheme in Wales, where contact is made with specific target groups for sports participation by untrained, raw coaches. The danger

here in that society sees these people as the neophytes of the
coaching fraternity. By comparison the American Coaching
Effectiveness Program (ACEP) is a far more comprehensive scheme for
educating coaches of young athletes. Founded by Dr. Rainer Martens
at the University of Illinois, training is detailed, innovative,
and forward-looking. These qualities are the hallmarks of a superior
coach and are surely the objectives of any profession. And, it is
in the same light that we must view the work of the Coaching
Association of Canada, founded in 1971, which has quickly laid down
an organization fabric and written rubric for increasing coaching
effectiveness.

5. The way forward

The capacity for any profession or person to innovate depends upon
many skills and attributes, some of which are interrelated. Frank
Dick, arguably one of our most successful athletics coaches, has
talked of the dual provision of creative flair and technical
mastery in coaching. We must move towards a deeper appreciation of
those sciences which, when related to the athlete, will not
eliminate the coaching pragmatism of the past, but merely allow a
greater degree of certainty and sophistication in our work.
    The value of coach education programmes such as those developing
in Australia via their National Coaching Accreditation Scheme is
that they rapidly improve professional confidence and competence.
This will elevate the professional status and acceptability of the
clients who contract into the scheme. In time coaching ought to
become a graduate profession in Britain, in the same way as physical
education has in the last decade, but for reasons of understanding
rather than status. Perhaps the very organisation of British sport
will make this difficult, because ours is a system that does not
have a definitive hierarchical structure. It is too democractic,
decentralised and voluntarily-run. Indeed, it is so de-centralized
that individual Governing Bodies of sport have often made a pseudo-
political point out of going their seperate way. Administrators
and coaches of British sport must establish a stronger bond and
understanding so that we value those accredited coaches who seek an
education which promotes experimentation and exploration. These
new coaches may be our real professionals - individuals who will
see coaching as a practical art, their skills underpinned by a
careful appraisal of all the relevant scientific knowledge. It is,
after all, the coaches who will breathe life into our sports, into
our facilities and into our sporting talent. If we had a real
structure, be it a central institution like a National Technical
Institute as was mooted in 1979 by Alan Wade and Frank Dick, or an
independent agency with which we all affliated then at least we
could have a dialogue with respect to coaching theory or research.
    Braconian conditions of employment will not foster that
innovation either. The exodus of quality coaches like Haller to
Hong Kong, London to Norway and Snellying to Canada emphasises this
point.
    The word 'profession' conjurs up the image of a body of learned

326

men. We have a great opportunity to make that image reality, provided that central government, governing bodies, local authorities and educational institutions all give coaches the support they deserve. Coaches should join together to foster and develop the field of coach education from which a profession will grow, and from which we will all prosper. The National Coaching Foundation, I feel, offers us that control, that opportunity to initiate progress. Its courses, films, interactive video schemes and research generating ability provide us with a planned way forward from which we can once again raise the sporting standards of our nations.

References

Bartlett, R, LE Cooke DW Kellett and S. Wolfson (1982) Proceedings Sport and Science Conference, pp 60 - 90.

Blundell N (1984) Superior Coaching Sports Coach (Australia), Vol 7, No 4, pp 49 - 73.

Coakley J (1982) Sport in Society, Mosby USA.

Central Council of Physical Recreation (1979) Report of the Eighth Annual Conference.

Dick F (1977) Coaching: An Artful Science, Momentum, Vol 2, No 3, pp 1 - 3.

Eitzen DS (1984) Sporting in Contemporary Society, St. Martins Press New York.

Lovesey P (1979) The Official Centenary history of the AAA, Guiness, London.

Pyke FS (1985) Some considerations in the education of sports coaches, New Zealand Journal of PE and Recreation, Vol 17, No 3 pp 3 - 5.

Riordan J (1975) Sport in Soviet Society, Unpublished doctoral dissertation, Faculty of Commerce, University of Birmingham.

Sports Council (1984) Participation taking up the challenge, 15th National Seminar of the Sports Council, pp 96 - 104.

Index

This index is compiled from the 'key words' assigned to papers by their authors. The page numbers refer to the first page of the paper in which the reference is to be found.

329